Practical Machine Learning
with H2O
Powerful, Scalable Techniques
for Deep Learning and AI

Darren Cook

Beijing · Boston · Farnham · Sebastopol · Tokyo

Practical Machine Learning with H2O

by Darren Cook

Published by O'Reilly Media, Inc., 1005 Gravenstein Highway North, Sebastopol, CA 95472.

O'Reilly books may be purchased for educational, business, or sales promotional use. Online editions are also available for most titles (*http://oreilly.com/safari*). For more information, contact our corporate/institutional sales department: 800-998-9938 or *corporate@oreilly.com*.

Editor: Nicole Tache
Production Editor: Colleen Lobner
Copyeditor: Kim Cofer
Proofreader: Charles Roumeliotis

Indexer: WordCo Indexing Services, Inc.
Interior Designer: David Futato
Cover Designer: Karen Montgomery
Illustrator: Rebecca Demarest

December 2016:   First Edition

Revision History for the First Edition
2016-12-01:   First Release
2017-01-06:   Second Release
2018-01-12:   Third Release

See *http://oreilly.com/catalog/errata.csp?isbn=9781491964606* for release details.

978-1-491-96460-6

[LSI]

Table of Contents

Preface

It feels like machine learning has finally come of age. It has been a long childhood, stretching back to the 1950s and the first program to learn from experience (playing checkers), as well as the first neural networks. We've been told so many times by AI researchers that the breakthrough is *"just around the corner"* that we long ago stopped listening. But maybe they were on the right track all along, maybe an idea just needs one more order of magnitude of processing power, or a slight algorithmic tweak, to go from being pathetic and pointless to productive and profitable.

In the early '90s, neural nets were being hailed as the new AI breakthrough. I did some experiments applying them to computer go, but they were truly awful when compared to the (still quite mediocre) results I could get using a mix of domain-specific knowledge engineering, and heavily pruned tree searches. And the ability to scale looked poor, too. When, 20 years later, I heard talk of this new and shiny *deep learning* thing that was giving impressive results in computer go, I was confused how this was different from the neural nets I'd rejected all those years earlier. "Not that much" was the answer; sometimes you just need more processing power (five or six orders of magnitude in this case) for an algorithm to bear fruit.

H2O is software for machine learning and data analysis. Wanting to see what other magic deep learning could perform was what personally led me to H2O (though it does more than that: trees, linear models, unsupervised learning, etc.), and I was immediately impressed. It ticks all the boxes:

- Open source (the liberal Apache license)
- Easy to use
- Scalable to big data
- Well-documented and commercially supported

- On its third version (i.e., a mature architecture)
- Wide range of OS/language support

With the high-quality team that H2O.ai (the company behind H2O) has put together, it is only going to get better. There is the attitude of not just "How do we get this to work?" but "How do we get this to work efficiently at big data scale?" permeating the whole development.

If machine learning has come of age, H2O looks to be not just an economical family car for it, but simultaneously the large load delivery truck for it. Stretching my vehicle analogy a bit further, this book will show you not just what the dashboard controls do, but also the best way to use them to get from A to B. It will be as practical as possible, with only the bare minimum explanation of the maths or theory behind the learning algorithms.

Of course H2O is not perfect; here are a few issues I've noticed people mutter about. There is no GPU support (which could make deep learning, in particular, quicker).[1] The cluster support is *all 'bout that bass* (big data), *no treble* (complex but relatively small data), so for the latter you may be limited to needing a single, fast, machine with lots of cores. Also no high availability (HA) for clusters. H2O compiles to Java; it is well-optimized and the H2O algorithms are known for their speed but, theoretically at least, carefully optimized C++ could be quicker. There is no SVM algorithm. Finally, it tries to support numerous platforms, so each has some rough edges, and development is sometimes slowed by trying to keep them all in sync.

In other words, and wringing the last bit of life out of my car analogy: a Formula 1 car might beat it on the straights, and it isn't yet available in yellow.

Who Uses It and Why?

A number of well-known companies (*http://www.h2o.ai/customers/*) are using H2O for their big data processing, and the website claims that over 5000 organizations currently use it. The company behind it, H2O.ai, has over 80 staff, more than half of which are developers.

But those are stats to impress your boss, not a no-nonsense developer. For R and Python developers, who already feel they have all the machine learning libraries they need, the primary things H2O brings are ease of use and efficient scalability to data sets too large to fit in the memory of your largest machine. For SparkML users, who feel they already have that, H2O algorithms are fewer in number but apparently sig-

---

1 Deep Water is a new H2O project, in development, to allow interaction with other deep learning libraries, and so it will soon support GPUs that way.

nificantly quicker. As a bonus, the intelligent defaults mean your code is very compact and clear to read: you can literally get a well-tuned, state-of-the-art, deep learning model as a one-liner. One of the goals of this book was to show you how to tune the models, but as we will see, sometimes I've just had to give up and say I can't beat the defaults.

About You

To bring this book in at under a thousand pages, I've taken some liberties. I am assuming you know either R or Python. Advanced language features are not used, so competence in any programming language should be enough to follow along, but the examples throughout the book are only in one of those two languages. Python users would benefit from being familiar with pandas, not least because it will make all your data science easier.

I'm also assuming a bit of mental flexibility: to save repeating every example twice, I'm hoping R users can grasp what is going on in a Python example, and Python users can grasp an R example. These slides on Python for R users (*http://bit.ly/ 2gl4GRx*) are a good start (for R users too).

Some experience with manipulating data is assumed, even if just using spreadsheet software or SQL tables. And I assume you have a fair idea of what machine learning and AI are, and how they are being used more and more in the infrastructure that runs our society. Maybe you are reading this book because you want to be part of that and make sure the transformations to come are done ethically and for the good of everyone, whatever their race, sex, nationality, or beliefs. If so, I salute you.

I am also assuming you know a bit of statistics. Nothing too scary—this book takes the "Practical" in the title seriously, and the theory behind the machine-learning algorithms is kept to the minimum needed to know how to tune them (as opposed to being able to implement them from scratch). Use Wikipedia or a search engine for when you crave more. But you should know your mean from your median from your mode, and know what a standard deviation and the normal distribution are.

But more than that, I am hoping you know that statistics can mislead, and machine learning can overfit (*https://en.wikipedia.org/wiki/Overfitting*). That you appreciate that when someone says an experiment is significant to $p = 0.05$ it means that out of every 20 such experiments you read about, *probably* one of them is wrong. A good moment to enjoy Significant, on xkcd (*https://xkcd.com/882/*).

This might also be a good time to mention "my machine," which I sometimes reference for timings. It is a mid-level notebook, a couple of years old, 8GB of memory, four real cores, eight hyper-threads. This is capable of running everything in the book; in fact 4GB of system memory should be enough. However, for some of the grid searches (described in Chapter 5) I "cheated" and started up a cluster in the cloud (covered, albeit briefly, in "Clusters" on page 249 in Chapter 10). I did this just out of practicality: not wanting to wait 24 hours for an experiment to finish before I can write about it.

Conventions Used in This Book

The following typographical conventions are used in this book:

Italic
> Indicates new terms, URLs, email addresses, filenames, and file extensions.

`Constant width`
> Used for program listings, as well as within paragraphs to refer to program elements such as variable or function names, databases, data types, environment variables, statements, and keywords.

`Constant width bold`
> Shows commands or other text that should be typed literally by the user.

`Constant width italic`
> Shows text that should be replaced with user-supplied values or by values determined by context.

 This element signifies a tip or suggestion.

 This element signifies a general note.

 This element indicates a warning or caution.

Using Code Examples

Supplemental material (code examples, exercises, etc.) is available for download at *https://github.com/DarrenCook/h2o/* (the "bk" branch).

This book is here to help you get your job done. In general, if example code is offered with this book, you may use it in your programs and documentation. You do not need to contact us for permission unless you're reproducing a significant portion of the code. For example, writing a program that uses several chunks of code from this book does not require permission. Selling or distributing a CD-ROM of examples from O'Reilly books does require permission. Answering a question by citing this book and quoting example code does not require permission. Incorporating a significant amount of example code from this book into your product's documentation does require permission.

We appreciate, but do not require, attribution. An attribution usually includes the title, author, publisher, and ISBN. For example: "*Practical Machine Learning with H2O* by Darren Cook (O'Reilly). Copyright 2017 Darren Cook, 978-1-491-96460-6."

If you feel your use of code examples falls outside fair use or the permission given above, feel free to contact us at *permissions@oreilly.com*.

O'Reilly Safari

 *Safari* (formerly Safari Books Online) is a membership-based training and reference platform for enterprise, government, educators, and individuals.

Members have access to thousands of books, training videos, Learning Paths, interactive tutorials, and curated playlists from over 250 publishers, including O'Reilly Media, Harvard Business Review, Prentice Hall Professional, Addison-Wesley Professional, Microsoft Press, Sams, Que, Peachpit Press, Adobe, Focal Press, Cisco Press, John Wiley & Sons, Syngress, Morgan Kaufmann, IBM Redbooks, Packt, Adobe Press, FT Press, Apress, Manning, New Riders, McGraw-Hill, Jones & Bartlett, and Course Technology, among others.

For more information, please visit *http://oreilly.com/safari*.

How to Contact Us

Please address comments and questions concerning this book to the publisher:

O'Reilly Media, Inc.
1005 Gravenstein Highway North
Sebastopol, CA 95472
800-998-9938 (in the United States or Canada)
707-829-0515 (international or local)
707-829-0104 (fax)

We have a web page for this book, where we list errata, examples, and any additional information. You can access this page at *http://bit.ly/practical-machine-learning-with-h2o*.

To comment or ask technical questions about this book, send email to *bookquestions@oreilly.com*.

For more information about our books, courses, conferences, and news, see our website at *http://www.oreilly.com*.

Find us on Facebook: *http://facebook.com/oreilly*

Follow us on Twitter: *http://twitter.com/oreillymedia*

Watch us on YouTube: *http://www.youtube.com/oreillymedia*

Acknowledgments

Firstly, a big thanks to the technical reviewers: it is a cliche to say the book is better because of you, but it is certainly true. Another cliche is that the remaining errors are mine, but that is true too. So, to Katharine Jarmul, Yulin Zhuang, Hugo Mathien, Erin LeDell, Tom Kraljevic: thanks, and I'm sorry if a change you suggested didn't get in, or if a joke you scribbled out is still in here. In addition to Erin and Tom, a host of other people at H2O.ai were super-helpful in answering my questions, so a big thank-you to Arno Candel, Tomas Nykodym, Michal Kurka, Navdeep Gill, SriSatish Ambati, Lauren DiPerna, and anyone else I've overlooked. (Sorry!)

Thanks to Nicole Tache for being the editor on the first half of book production, and to Debbie Hardin for taking over when Nicole decided the only way to escape this project was to have a baby. A bit extreme. Thanks to both of you for staying calm when I got so absorbed in building models for the book that I forgot about things like deadlines.

Thanks to my family for quietly tolerating the very long hours I've been putting into this book.

Finally, thanks to everyone else: the people who answer questions on StackOverflow, post blog articles, post video tutorials, write books, keep Wikipedia accurate. They worked around the clock to plug most of the holes in my knowledge. Which brings me full circle: don't hesitate to let me know about the remaining errors in the book. Or simply how anything here can be done better.

CHAPTER 1

Installation and Quick-Start

You will be happy to know that H2O is very easy to install. First I will show how to install it with R, using CRAN, and then how to install it with Python, using pip.[1]

After that we will dive into our first machine learning project: load some data, make a model, make some predictions, and evaluate success. By that point you will be able to boast to family, friends, and the stranger lucky enough to sit next to you on the bus that you're a bit of an expert when it comes to deep learning and all that jazz.

After a detour to look at how random elements can lead us astray, the chapter will close with a look at the web interface, Flow, that comes with H2O.

Preparing to Install

The examples in this book are going to be in R and Python. So you need one of those already installed. And you will need Java. If you have the choice, I recommend you use 64-bit versions of everything, including the OS. (In download pages, 64-bit versions are often labeled with "x64," while 32-bit versions might say "x86.")

You may wonder if the choice of R or Python matters? No, and why will be explained shortly. There is also no performance advantage to using scripts versus more friendly GUI tools such as Jupyter or RStudio.

---

1 Chapter 10 shows some alternative ways to install H2O (see "Installing the Latest Version" on page 248) including how to compile it from source. You might want to do this if you hit a bug that has only been fixed in the latest development version, or if you want to start hacking on H2O itself.

Installing R

On Linux your distro's package manager should make this trivial: `sudo apt-get install r-base` on Debian/Ubuntu/Mint/etc., and `sudo yum install R` on RedHat/Fedora/Centos/etc.

Mac users should head to *https://cran.r-project.org/bin/macosx/* and follow the instructions.

On Windows go to *http://cran.rstudio.com/bin/windows/* and download and run the *exe*, then follow the prompts. On the Select Components page it wants to install both the 32-bit and 64-bit versions; I chose to only install 64-bit, but there is no harm in installing both.

The optional second step of an R install is to install RStudio; you *can* do everything from the command line that you need to run H2O, but RStudio makes everything easier to use (especially on Windows, where the command line is still stuck in 1995). Go to *https://www.rstudio.com/products/rstudio/download/*, download, and install it.

Installing Python

H2O works equally well with Python 2.7 or Python 3.5, as should all the examples in this book. If you are using an earlier version of Python you may need to upgrade. You will also need `pip`, Python's package manager.

On Linux, `sudo apt-get python-pip` on Debian/Ubuntu/Mint/etc.; or for Python 3, it is `sudo apt-get python3-pip`. (Python is a dependency of `pip`, so by installing `pip` we get Python too.) For RedHat/Fedora/Centos/etc., the best command varies by exactly which version you are using, so see the latest Linux Python instructions (*https://packaging.python.org/en/latest/install_requirements_linux/*).

On a Mac, see Using Python on a Macintosh (*http://bit.ly/2gn4HFs*).

On Windows, see Using Python on Windows (*http://bit.ly/1RCJ7VR*). Remember to choose a 64-bit install (unless you are stuck with a 32-bit version of Windows, of course).

 You might also want to take a look at Anaconda (*https://www.continuum.io/downloads*). It is a Python distribution containing almost all the data science packages you are likely to want. As a bonus, it can be installed as a normal user, which is helpful for when you do not have root access. Linux, Mac, and Windows versions are available.

Privacy

H2O has some code[2] to call Google Analytics every time it starts. This appears to be fairly anonymous, and is just for tracking which versions are being used, but if it bothers you, or would break company policy, creating an empty file called *.h2o_no_collect* in your home directory (`"C:\Users\YourName\"` on Windows) stops it. You'll know that works if you see "Opted out of sending usage metrics." in the info log. Another way to opt out it is given in "Running from the Command Line" on page 248 in Chapter 10.

Installing Java

You need Java installed, which you can get at the Java download page (*http://bit.ly/16mhImY*). Choose the JDK.[3] If you think you have the Java JDK already, but are not sure, you could just go ahead and install H2O, and come back and (re-)install Java if you are told there is a problem.

For instance, when testing an install on 64-bit Windows, with 64-bit R, it was when I first tried `library(h2o)` that I was told I had a 32-bit version of the JDK installed. After a few seconds glaring at the screen, I shrugged, and downloaded the latest version of the JDK (*http://bit.ly/16mhImY*). I installed it, tried again, and this time everything was fine.

Install H2O with R (CRAN)

(If you are not using R, you might want to jump ahead to "Install H2O with Python (pip)" on page 5.)

Start R, and type `install.packages("h2o")`. Golly gosh, when I said it was easy to install, I meant it! That command takes care of any dependencies, too.

If this is your first time using CRAN[4] it will ask for a mirror to use. Choose one close to you. Alternatively, choose one in a place you'd like to visit, put your shades on, and take a selfie.

If you want H2O installed site-wide (i.e., usable by all users on that machine), run R as root, `sudo R`, then type `install.packages("h2o")`.

---

2 *http://bit.ly/2f96Hyu* as of June 2016.

3 The "Server JRE" or "JRE" choices *may* work with H2O, but I recommend you always install the JDK.

4 CRAN is R's package manager. See *https://cran.r-project.org/* to learn more about it.

Let's check that it worked by typing `library(h2o)`. If nothing complains, try the next step: `h2o.init()`. If the gods are smiling on you then you'll see lots of output about how it is starting up H2O on your behalf, and then it should tell you all about your cluster, something like in Figure 1-1. If not, the error message should be telling you what dependency is missing, or what the problem is.

```
> h2o.init()

H2O is not running yet, starting it now...

Note:  In case of errors look at the following log files:
    /tmp/Rtmp6btQEF/h2o_darren_started_from_r.out
    /tmp/Rtmp6btQEF/h2o_darren_started_from_r.err

java version "1.7.0_101"
OpenJDK Runtime Environment (IcedTea 2.6.6) (7u101-2.6.6-0ubuntu0.14.04.1)
OpenJDK 64-Bit Server VM (build 24.95-b01, mixed mode)

Starting H2O JVM and connecting: ..... Connection successful!

R is connected to the H2O cluster:
    H2O cluster uptime:         3 seconds 535 milliseconds
    H2O cluster version:        3.8.2.2
    H2O cluster name:           H2O_started_from_R_darren_rge683
    H2O cluster total nodes:    1
    H2O cluster total memory:   1.71 GB
    H2O cluster total cores:    8
    H2O cluster allowed cores:  2
    H2O cluster healthy:        TRUE
    H2O Connection ip:          localhost
    H2O Connection port:        54321
    H2O Connection proxy:       NA
    R Version:                  R version 3.2.5 (2016-04-14)

Note:  As started, H2O is limited to the CRAN default of 2 CPUs.
       Shut down and restart H2O as shown below to use all your CPUs.
           > h2o.shutdown()
           > h2o.init(nthreads = -1)

> |
```

Figure 1-1. Running h2o.init() (in R)

Let's just review what happened here. It worked. Therefore[5] the gods are smiling on you. The gods love you! I think that deserves another selfie: in fact, make it a video of you having a little boogey-woogey dance at your desk, then post it on social media, and mention you are reading this book. And how good it is.

The version of H2O on CRAN might be up to a month or two behind the latest and greatest. Unless you are affected by a bug that you know has been fixed, don't worry about it.

h2o.init() will only use two cores on your machine and maybe a quarter of your system memory,[6] by default. Use h2o.shutdown() to, well, see if you can guess what it does. Then to start it again, but using all your cores: h2o.init(nthreads = -1). And to give it, say, 4GB and all your cores: h2o.init(nthreads = -1, max_mem_size = "4g").

Install H2O with Python (pip)

(If you are not interested in using Python, skip ahead to "Our First Learning" on page 7.)

From the command line, type pip install -U h2o. That's it. Easy-peasy, lemon-squeezy.

The -U just says to also upgrade any dependencies. On Linux you probably needed to be root, so instead type sudo pip install -U h2o. Or install as a local user with pip install -U --user h2o.

To test it, start Python, type import h2o, and if that does not complain, follow it with h2o.init(). Some information will scroll past, ending with a nice table showing, amongst other things, the number of nodes, total memory, and total cores available, something like in Figure 1-2.[7] (If you ever need to report a bug, make sure to include all the information from that table.)

---

5 It is the ability to make inferences like this that separate the common herd from the data scientist.

6 See *http://bit.ly/2gn5h6e* for how to query your Java installation and get the default for your system.

7 You perhaps see some deprecation warnings? For the screenshot I ignored them with import warnings;warnings.filterwarnings("ignore", category=DeprecationWarning), but normally I ignore them by turning a blind eye.

```
In [3]: import h2o

In [4]: h2o.init()
Checking whether there is an H2O instance running at http://localhost:54321..... not found.
Attempting to start a local H2O server...
  Java Version: java version "1.7.0_111"; OpenJDK Runtime Environment (IcedTea 2.6.7) (7u111-
ild 24.111-b01, mixed mode)
  Starting server from /usr/local/h2o_jar/h2o.jar
  Ice root: /tmp/tmpsNCJ_v
  JVM stdout: /tmp/tmpsNCJ_v/h2o_darren_started_from_python.out
  JVM stderr: /tmp/tmpsNCJ_v/h2o_darren_started_from_python.err
  Server is running at http://127.0.0.1:54321
Connecting to H2O server at http://127.0.0.1:54321... successful.
--------------------------  ----------------------------
H2O cluster uptime:         02 secs
H2O cluster version:        3.10.0.7
H2O cluster version age:    5 days
H2O cluster name:           H2O_from_python_darren_a9x6hb
H2O cluster total nodes:    1
H2O cluster free memory:    1.710 Gb
H2O cluster total cores:    8
H2O cluster allowed cores:  8
H2O cluster status:         accepting new members, healthy
H2O connection url:         http://127.0.0.1:54321
H2O connection proxy:
Python version:             2.7.6 final
--------------------------  ----------------------------
```

Figure 1-2. Running h2o.init() (in Python)

If you do indeed see that table, stand up and let out a large whoop. Don't worry about what your coworkers think. They love you and your eccentricities. Trust me.

By default, your H2O instance will be allowed to use all your cores, and (typically) 25% of your system memory. That is often fine but, for the sake of argument, what if you wanted to give it exactly 4GB of your memory, but only two of your eight cores? First shut down H2O with `h2o.shutdown()`, then type `h2o.init(nthreads=2, max_mem_size=4)`. The following excerpt from the information table confirms that it worked:

```
...
H2O cluster total free memory:  3.56 GB
H2O cluster total cores:        8
H2O cluster allowed cores:      2
...
```

 Using `virtualenv` does not work with H2O.[8] To be precise, it installs but cannot start H2O for you. If you really want to install it this way, follow the instructions on starting H2O from the command line in Chapter 10. The `h2o.init()`, and everything else, will then work.

---

8 At least, as of version 3.10.x.x and earlier.

Our First Learning

Now that we have everything installed, let's get down to business. The Python and R APIs are so similar that we will look at them side-by-side for this example. If you are using Python look at Example 1-1, and if you are using R take a look at Example 1-2. They repeat the `import/library` and `h2o.init` code we ran earlier; don't worry, this does no harm.

I'm going to spend a few pages going through this in detail, but I want to just emphasize that this is the complete script: it downloads data, prepares it, creates a multi-layer neural net model (i.e., deep learning) that is competitive with the state of the art on this data set, and runs predictions on it.

The Iris Data Set

If you haven't heard of the Iris data set before, this must be your first machine learning book! It is a set of 150 observations of iris plants, with four measurements (length and width of each of sepal and petal) and the species it belongs to. There are three species represented, with 50 observations each.

It is a very popular data set for machine learning experiments as it is small enough to be quick to learn from, and also small enough to be usefully viewed in a chart, but big enough to be interesting, and it is nontrivial: none of the four measurements neatly divide the data up.

Example 1-1. Deep learning on the Iris data set, in Python

```
import h2o
h2o.init()

datasets = "https://raw.githubusercontent.com/DarrenCook/h2o/bk/datasets/"
data = h2o.import_file(datasets + "iris_wheader.csv")  ❶
y = "class"  ❷
x = data.names
x.remove(y)
train, test = data.split_frame([0.8])  ❸

m = h2o.estimators.deeplearning.H2ODeepLearningEstimator()  ❹
m.train(x, y, train)
p = m.predict(test)  ❺
```

Example 1-2. Deep learning on the Iris dataset, in R

```
library(h2o)
h2o.init(nthreads = -1)
```

```
datasets <- "https://raw.githubusercontent.com/DarrenCook/h2o/bk/datasets/"
data <- h2o.importFile(paste0(datasets, "iris_wheader.csv"))  ❶
y <- "class"  ❷
x <- setdiff(names(data), y)
parts <- h2o.splitFrame(data, 0.8)  ❸
train <- parts[[1]]
test <- parts[[2]]

m <- h2o.deeplearning(x, y, train)  ❹
p <- h2o.predict(m, test)  ❺
```

❶, ❷, ❸ are preparing the data, ❹ is training the model, and ❺ is using that model.

❶ illustrates the first major concept we need to understand when using H2O: all the data is on the cluster (the server), not on our client. *Even when client and cluster are the same machine.*

Therefore, whenever we want to train a model, or make a prediction, we have to get the data into the H2O cluster; we will look at that topic in more depth in Chapter 2. For now, just appreciate that this line has created a *frame* on the cluster called "iris_wheader.hex." It recognized the first line of the *csv* file was a header row, so it has automatically named the columns. It has also realized (from analyzing the data) that the "class" column was categorical, which means we will be doing a multinomial categorization, not a regression (see "Jargon and Conventions" on page 8).

❷ defines a couple of helper variables: y to be the name of the field we want to learn, and x to be the names of the fields we want to learn from; in this case that means all the other fields. In other words, we will attempt to use the four measurements, *sepal_len*, *sepal_wid*, *petal_len*, and *petal_wid*, to predict which species a flower belongs to.

Jargon and Conventions

Your data is divided into *rows* (also called *observations* or *instances*) and *columns*. It is kept in a table, but I will use the word *frame* or *data frame* because that is what H2O calls them. If you are familiar with spreadsheets, or SQL tables, then H2O frames are basically the same thing. In R they are like a data.frame. In Python they are like a DataFrame in pandas (or a dict of equal-length list).

H2O has these column types:

real

> Floating-point numbers; i.e., numeric in R, float in Python, and double in many other languages.

int

> Integers.

---

enum

> A set of categories or classes. Called `factor` in R, or a `categorical` in pandas.

time

> A 64-bit int, milliseconds since Unix epoch (January 1, 1970). Can be parsed from various timestamp formats.

string

> Text. Just about all you can do with them, within H2O, is convert them to enum; they cannot be directly used to build models from.

The decision between using `int` and `real` is made by H2O after analyzing the data in that column; you are only able to specify `numeric` versus `enum`.

In *supervised* machine learning one of these columns will be what we want to predict. It goes by a few names: response, dependent variable, output, correct answer, and others. In this book, I will put the name of this column in a variable called y.[9] (In *unsupervised* learning y will not be set.)

Some or all of the other columns in your data are what we learn from. They go by many names: independent variables, features, attributes, inputs, predictor variables. Our convention will be to put the list of columns to learn from in a variable called x.[10]

More conventions: our complete data will be in a variable called `data`, the subset that is the training frame will be in a variable called `train`, the subset used for validation will be `valid`, and the subset used for testing will be `test`.[11] And remember, each of those are handles (pointers) to the actual data stored on your cluster. (In Python it is a class wrapper around the handle, also storing some summary statistics; in R it is the same idea, implemented as an environment.)

I've kept the names short: this is a book, and word-wrap in listings is ugly; some people might even be reading it on their phone. In your own code I recommend meaningful names, e.g., `premierLeagueScores2005_2015_train` instead of `train`. When your script is a thousand lines long, and you are dealing with a dozen data sets, this will save your sanity.

---

❸ (splitting into training and test data) is another big concept, which boils down to trying not to overfit. Briefly, what we are doing is (randomly) choosing 80% of our data to train on, and then we will try using our model on the remaining 20%, to see

---

9 The R and Python APIs also call it y; in the REST API it is called `response_column`.

10 The APIs also call this x, though if you ever poke your nose into the REST API, you will see it actually receives the complement of x: the list of field names to *not* use, called `ignored_columns`.

11 If you are unfamiliar with these, the difference between validation and test data, and validation and cross-validation, is covered in Chapter 3.

how well it did. In a production system, this 20% represents the gardeners coming in with new flowers and asking us what species they are.

A reminder that the Python code to split the data looked like the following. `split_frame()` is one of the member functions of `class H2OFrame`. The `[0.8]` tells it to put 80% in the first split, the rest in the second split:

```
train, test = data.split_frame([0.8])
```

In R, `h2o.splitFrame()` takes an H2O frame and returns a list of the splits, which are assigned to `train` and `test`, for readability:

```
parts <- h2o.splitFrame(data, 0.8)
train <- parts[[1]]
test <- parts[[2]]
```

The split, being decided randomly for each row, is roughly 120/30 rows, but you may get a few more training rows, or a few more test rows.[12]

Let's quickly recap what we have. As shown in Figure 1-3, the client just has handles (pointers) to the actual data on the H2O cluster.

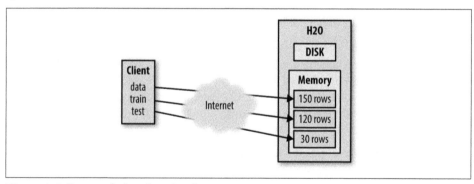

Figure 1-3. Recap of what data is where

Of course, our "cluster" is on localhost, on the same machine as our client, so it is all the same system memory. But you should be thinking as if they are on opposite sides of the globe. Also think about how it might be a billion rows, too many to fit in our client's memory. By adding machines to a cluster, as long as the total memory of the cluster is big enough, it can be loaded, and you can analyze those billion rows from a client running on some low-end notebook.

---

12 Experiment with seed to get an exact split. For example, `h2o.splitFrame(data, 0.8, seed=99)` works for me. In Python: `data.split_frame([0.8],seed=99)`.

Training and Predictions, with Python

At last we get to ❹, the machine learning. In Python it is a two-step process:

1. Create an object for your machine-learning algorithm, and optionally specify parameters for it:

```
m = h2o.estimators.deeplearning.H2ODeepLearningEstimator()
```

2. Tell it to train and which data sets to use:

```
m.train(x, y, train)
```

If you prefer scikit-learn style, you can instead write:

```
from h2o.estimators.deeplearning import H2ODeepLearningEstimator
m = H2ODeepLearningEstimator()
m.train(x, y, train)
```

No parameters to the constructor means the model is built with all defaults, which means (amongst other things): two hidden layers, each with 200 neurons, and 10 epochs of training. (Chapter 8 will define "neurons" and "epochs"—but don't go there yet. The important point is that default settings are usually quite quick to train, just a few seconds on this iris data.)

As with the data frames, m is a class wrapper around a handle, pointing to the actual model stored on the H2O cluster. If you print m you get a lot of details of how the training went, or you can use member functions to pull out just the parts you are interested in—e.g., m.mse() tells me the MSE (mean squared error) is 0.01097. (There is a random element, so you are likely to see slightly different numbers.[13])

m.confusion_matrix(train) gives the *confusion matrix*, which not only shows how many in each category it got right, but which category is being chosen when it got them wrong. The results shown here are on the 120 training samples:

Iris-setosa	Iris-versicolor	Iris-virginica	Error	Rate
42	0	0	0	0 / 42
0	37	1	0.0263158	1 / 38
0	1	39	0.025	1 / 40
42	38	40	0.0166667	2 / 120

In this case I see it matched all 42 setosa perfectly, but it thought one versicolor was a virginica, and one virginica was a versicolor.

---

13 I used h2o.deeplearning(x, y, train, seed = 99, reproducible = TRUE) to get repeatable numbers for this book.

The final line of the listing, ❺, was p = m.predict(test), and it makes predictions using this model, and puts them in p. Here are a few of the predictions. The leftmost column shows which category it chose. The other columns show the probability it has assigned for each category for each test sample. You can see it is over 99.5% certain about all its answers here:

predict	Iris-setosa	Iris-versicolor	Iris-virginica
Iris-setosa	0.999016	0.000983921	1.90283E-019
Iris-setosa	0.998988	0.00101178	1.40209E-020
Iris-versicolor	5.22035E-005	0.997722	0.00222536
Iris-versicolor	0.000275126	0.995354	0.00437055

Just as before, this is a frame on the H2O cluster, so when you see it, you only you see a preview, the first 10 rows. To see all 30 predictions you need to download, which is done with p.as_data_frame(). If you don't have pandas installed, you get a nested list, something like this:

```
[['predict', 'Iris-setosa', 'Iris-versicolor', 'Iris-virginica'],
 ['Iris-setosa', '0.9990160791818314', '9.83920818168421E-4',
  '1.9028267028039464E-19'], ['Iris-setosa', '0.9989882189908829', ...
 ..., ['Iris-virginica', '1.72617432126E-11', '1.0197263306598747E-4',
  '0.9998980273496721']]
```

You could do analysis with that. However, H2O's Python API integrates with pandas (*http://pandas.pydata.org*), and if you are using Python for data work, chances are you already know and use it. (If not, pip install pandas should be all you need to install it.) As long as you have installed pandas, p.as_data_frame() will instead give:

```
      predict   Iris-setosa  Iris-versicolor  Iris-virginica
0   Iris-setosa  9.990161e-01         0.000984    1.902827e-19
1   Iris-setosa  9.989882e-01         0.001012    1.402089e-20
...
```

What else can we do? Chapter 2 will delve into this topic further, but how about (p["predict"] == test["class"]).mean() to tell us the percentage of correct answers? Or p["predict"].cbind(test["class"]).as_data_frame() to give a two-column output of each prediction against the correct answer:

```
         predict           class
0    Iris-setosa      Iris-setosa
1    Iris-setosa      Iris-setosa
...
11   Iris-versicolor  Iris-versicolor
12   Iris-virginica   Iris-versicolor
13   Iris-versicolor  Iris-versicolor
14   Iris-virginica   Iris-versicolor
15   Iris-versicolor  Iris-versicolor
...
```

```
28   Iris-virginica   Iris-virginica
29   Iris-virginica   Iris-virginica
```

Training and Predictions, with R

In R, ❹, the machine learning is a single function call, with parameters and training data being given at the same time. As a reminder, the command was: m <- h2o.deep learning(x, y, train). (In fact, I used m <- h2o.deeplearning(x, y, train, seed = 99, reproducible = TRUE) to get repeatable results, but you generally don't want to do that as it will only use one core and take longer.)

Just like with the data, the model is stored on the H2O cluster, and m is just a handle to it. h2o.mse(m) tells me the mean squared error (MSE) was 0.01097. h2o.confusion Matrix(m) gives the following confusion matrix (on the training data, by default):

```
Confusion Matrix: vertical: actual; across: predicted
           setosa versicolor virginica  Error      Rate
setosa        42          0          0 0.0000 =  0 /  42
versicolor     0         37          1 0.0263 =  1 /  38
virginica      0          1         39 0.0250 =  1 /  40
Totals        42         38         40 0.0167 =  2 / 120
```

So, a perfect score on the setosa, but one versicolor wrong—it thought it was a virginica—and one virginica it thought was a versicolor. The bottom right tells us it therefore had an error rate of 1.67%. (Remember this was on the data it had seen.)

The final line of the listing, ❺ , was p <- h2o.predict(m, test) and it makes predictions using the model m. Again, p is a handle to a frame on the H2O server. If I output p I only see the first six predictions. To see all of them I need to download the data. When working with remote clusters, or big data... sorry, Big Data™, be careful here: you will first want to consider how much of your data you actually need locally, how long it will take to download, and if it will even fit on your machine.

By typing as.data.frame(p) I see all 30 predictions (just a few shown here):

```
predict               Iris-setosa  Iris-versicolor  Iris-virginica
-----------           -----------  ---------------  --------------
Iris-setosa           0.999016     0.0009839        1.90283e-19
Iris-setosa           0.998988     0.0010118        1.40209e-20
Iris-setosa           0.999254     0.0007460        9.22466e-19
...
Iris-virginica        1.5678e-08   0.3198963        0.680104
Iris-versicolor       2.3895e-08   0.9863869        0.013613
...
Iris-virginica        3.9084e-14   2.192105e-06     0.999998
```

The predict column in the first row is the class it is predicting for the first row in the test data. The other three columns show its confidence. You can see it is really sure that it was a setosa. If you explore the predictions you will see it is less sure of some of the others.

The next question you are likely to have is which ones, if any, did H2O's model get wrong? The correct species is in test$class, while deep learning's guess is in p$predict. There are two approaches so, based on what you know so far, have a think about the difference between this:

```
as.data.frame( h2o.cbind(p$predict, test$class) )
```

and:

```
cbind( as.data.frame(p$predict), as.data.frame(test$class) )
```

In the first approach, p$predict and test$class are combined *in the cluster* to make a new data frame *in the cluster*. Then this new two-column data frame is downloaded. In the second approach, one column from p is downloaded to R, then one column from test is downloaded, and then they are combined in R's memory, to make a two-column data frame. As a rule of thumb, prefer the first way.

In my case (your results might differ slightly) this gives (I've put an asterisk by the two cases it got wrong):

```
      predict    class
1     setosa     setosa
2     setosa     setosa
3     setosa     setosa
4     setosa     setosa
5     setosa     setosa
6     setosa     setosa
7     setosa     setosa
8     setosa     setosa
9   versicolor versicolor
10  versicolor versicolor
11  versicolor versicolor
12  versicolor versicolor
13   virginica versicolor  *
14  versicolor versicolor
15   virginica versicolor  *
16  versicolor versicolor
17  versicolor versicolor
18  versicolor versicolor
19  versicolor versicolor
20  versicolor versicolor
21   virginica  virginica
22   virginica  virginica
23   virginica  virginica
24   virginica  virginica
25   virginica  virginica
```

```
26  virginica  virginica
27  virginica  virginica
28  virginica  virginica
29  virginica  virginica
30  virginica  virginica
```

Another way we could analyze our results is by asking what percentage the H2O model got right. In R that can be done with mean(p$predict == test$class), which tells me 0.933. In other words, the model guessed 93.3% of our unseen 30 test samples correctly, and got 6.7% wrong. As we will see in "On Being Unlucky" on page 16, you almost certainly got 0.900 (3 wrong), 0.933 (2 wrong), 0.967 (1 wrong), or 1.000 (perfect score).

Performance Versus Predictions

There is another way we could have found out what percentage it got right. It is to not use predict() at all but instead use h2o.performance(m, test) in R, or m.model_performance(test) in Python. This doesn't tell us what the individual predictions were, but instead gives us lots of statistics:

```
ModelMetricsMultinomial: deeplearning
** Reported on test data. **

MSE: 0.0390774346788
R^2: 0.934384904457
LogLoss: 0.122561507096

Confusion Matrix: vertical: actual; across: predicted
```

Iris-setosa	Iris-versicolor	Iris-virginica	Error	Rate
8	0	0	0	0 / 8
0	10	2	0.166667	2 / 12
0	0	10	0	0 / 10
8	10	12	0.0666667	2 / 30

```
Top-3 Hit Ratios:
k    hit_ratio
---  -----------
1    0.933333
2    1
3    1
```

The hit ratio section at the end tells us the same 0.933 number. (The 1 in the second row means it was 100% accurate if allowed two guesses.) Above that, the confusion matrix tells us that it incorrectly guessed two virginica samples as being versicolor.

If we study the confidence of our predictions we see the correct answers are mostly over 0.99, with the least-confident correct answer being 0.97. What about our incorrect answers? Test row 13 was 0.45 versus 0.55 (the machine-learning version of a teenager's sullen shrug) and test row 15 was 0.07 versus 0.93.

This is great, as it means we can mark results with confidence below 0.97 as suspicious. In a medical application that could mean doing another test to get a second opinion; in a financial trading application (or a poker app) it could mean sit this one out, too risky.

But!! Hopefully you got suspicious as soon as I said, "This is great!" We're choosing our cutoff criteria of 0.97 based on looking at our *test* results, after being told the correct answers. *All* parameters used to interpret the test results *must* only be based on our training data. ("Valid Versus Test?" on page 41 in Chapter 2 will touch on how you could use a validation data set for this, though.)

On Being Unlucky

This is a good time to consider how randomness affects the results. To find out, I tried remaking the model 100 times (using random seeds 1 to 100). 52 times the model got two wrong, and 48 times it got one wrong. Depending on your perspective, the random effect is either minor (93% versus 97%), or half the time it is twice as bad. The result set I analyzed in the previous section was one of the unlucky ones.

What about the way we randomly split the data into training and test data? How did that affect things? I tried 25 different random splits, which ended up ranging from 111/39 to 130/20, and made 20 models on each. (Making these 500 models took about 20 minutes on my computer; sadly this experiment is not so practical with the larger data sets we will use later in the book.)

It seems the randomness in our split perhaps matters more than the randomness in our model,[14] because one split gave a perfect score for all of its 20 models (it had 129 rows to train from, 21 to test on), whereas another only averaged 90% (it had 114 to train from, 36 to test on). You are thinking "Aha! The more training data, the better?" Yet the split that had 130 training rows only managed 90% on almost all its models.

---

14 This is more common with small data sets like Iris; with larger data sets it is less likely to happen unless, for instance, one category in an enum column is much rarer than other categories.

But wait, there's more! The single most important learning from this little experiment, for me at least, was that 85 of the 500 models (17%) gave a perfect score. Typically you will use just *one* split, and make *one* model; 17% of the time you'd be tricked into thinking your model parameters were good enough for perfection.

A year or two ago, it was in the news that 64% of psychology experiments (published in top journals) could not be reproduced. I suspect this kind of bad luck[15] was involved in a few of them.

Flow

Flow is the name of the web interface that is part of H2O (no extra installation step needed). It is actually just another client, written in CoffeeScript (*https://en.wikipedia.org/wiki/CoffeeScript*) (a JavaScript-like language) this time, making the same web service calls to the H2O backend that the R or Python clients are making. It is fully featured, by which I mean that you can do all of the following:

- View data you have uploaded through your client
- Upload data directly
- View models you have created through your client (and those currently being created!)
- Create models directly
- View predictions you have generated through your client
- Run predictions directly

You can find it by pointing your browser to *http://127.0.0.1:54321*. Of course, if you started H2O on a nonstandard port, change the `:54321` bit, and if you are accessing a remote H2O cluster, change the `127.0.0.1` bit to the server name of any node in the cluster (the *public* DNS name or IP address, not the *private* one, if it is a server with both). When you first load Flow you will see the Flow menu, as shown in Figure 1-4.

Data

Let's import the same Iris data set we did in the R and Python examples. From the start screen click the "importFiles" link, or from the menu at the top of the screen choose Data then Import Files. Paste the location of the *csv* file into the search box, then select it, then finally click the Import button; see Figure 1-5.

---

15 Bad luck from the point of view of a healthier, happier, human society. Of course, it was good luck for the person needing a paper accepted by a journal!

Figure 1-4. The Flow menu

Figure 1-5. Import files

Now click "Parse These Files," and it gives you the chance to customize the settings as shown in Figure 1-6, but in this case just accepting the defaults is fine.

If you choose "getFrames" from the main menu, either after doing the preceding steps or after loading the data from R or Python, you would see an entry saying "iris_wheader.hex" and that it has 150 rows and 5 columns. If you clicked the "iris_wheader.hex" link you would see Figure 1-7.

You should see there are buttons to split the data (into training/test frames), or build a model, and also that it lists each column. Importantly it has recognized the "class" column as being of type enum, meaning we are ready to do a classification. (If we wanted to do a regression we could click "Convert to numeric" in the Actions column.)

Click Split (the scissors icon), then change the 0.25 to 0.2. Under "Key," rename the 0.80 split to "train" and the other to "test."

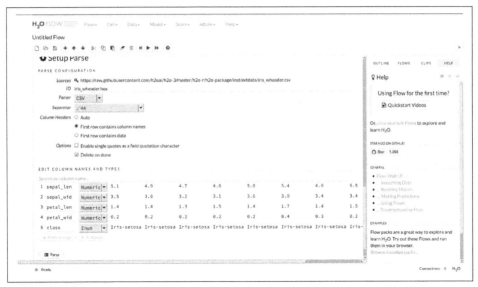

Figure 1-6. Set up file parsing in Flow

Figure 1-7. Data frame view in Flow

Models

Following on from the previous example, click "train," then click "Build Model" (a cube icon). From the algorithms, choose Deep Learning.

Loads and loads of parameters appear. You only need to set one of them, near the top: from the "response_column" drop-down, choose "class." The defaults for everything else are good, so scroll down past them all, and click "Build Model." You should see something like the output in Figure 1-8.

Now click the "View" button (a magnifying glass icon). Alternatively, if you previously made some models (whether in R, Python, or Flow), choose "Model" from the main menu, then "List All Models," and click the one of interest. As you can see in Figure 1-9, you get a graphical output; other options allow you to see the parameters the model was built with, or how training progressed.

Predictions

You can do the full load-model-predict cycle in Flow. From the model view click "Predict" (the lightning icon). (Or, choose "Score" from the main menu, then "Predict," and choose the model from there.)

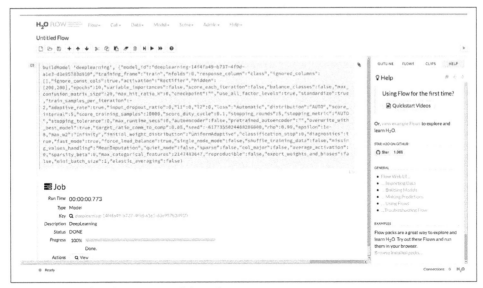

Figure 1-8. A deep learning model in Flow

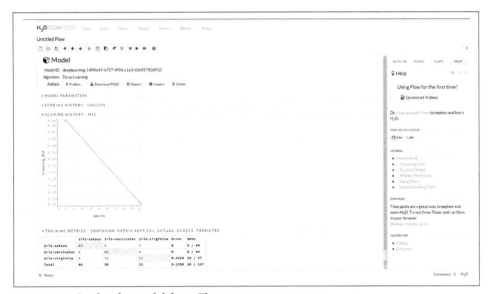

Figure 1-9. Study of a model from Flow

Choose the "test" data frame, and click the Predict button to set it going. You will see results like Figure 1-10.

Figure 1-10. A prediction in Flow

Other Things in Flow

The Flow commands you see can be saved as scripts, and loaded back in later. But, there are some things you can do with the R and Python APIs that you cannot do in Flow, principally, merging data sets (either by columns or by rows), and data manipulation (which we will be taking a look at very soon, in Chapter 2).

So, for some users, Flow can do all you need, but most of us will want to use R or Python. I will not be showing Flow examples in the rest of the book, though the knowledge learned as we look at the algorithm parameters in later chapters can be directly applied to models built in Flow.

Having said that, Flow can be useful to you even if you intend to only use R or Python. If you load data from R/Python you can see it in Flow. If you load data in Flow, you can see it in R/Python. Even better, you can start a long-running model from Python or R, then go over to Flow and get immediate feedback on how the training is going. Seeing unexpected performance, you might realize you forgot something, kill it, and thus avoid wasting hours of CPU time. And the *Water Meter* found under the Admin menu is a very useful way to see how hard each CPU core in your cluster is working.

Summary

In this first chapter we have covered a lot of ground:

- Installing H2O for R and Python
- Importing data, making models, and making predictions...
- ...in any of R, Python, or the browser-based Flow UI

And we had a bit of fun, wearing the shades, and deep learning our data like a boss.

We also glossed over quite a few options, and the next chapter (well, in fact, the whole rest of the book) will start digging in deeper. But keep the shades handy, there is lots of fun still to be had.

CHAPTER 2

Data Import, Data Export

There was a joke going around, recently, that went like this:

> In data science, 80 percent of time is spent in preparing data, 20 percent of time is spent complaining about the need to prepare data.[1]

Sad, but true. H2O provides some functions to make the process a bit easier, but ultimately you are still going to be spending a lot of time finding data sets, understanding them, moaning about them, repairing them, importing them, and more moaning about them. However, it won't be 80% of your time any more... The new 80% is spent tweaking machine learning parameters and drinking tea waiting for your neural nets to overfit. (At least until you read about "Early Stopping" on page 99 in Chapter 4. And "Grid Search" on page 122 in Chapter 5.)

This chapter will cover getting data into H2O, manipulating data in H2O, and getting data out of H2O. The skills will be used, in context, in later chapters.

Memory Requirements

For deciding how much memory your cluster needs, in total, to be able to build models and run predictions against the full data set, H2O recommends four times the size of the data. As an example, you have 100 million rows, which is 5GB when zipped on disk, and maybe takes up 10GB in H2O's memory (it is stored compressed, but not as tightly as a ZIP or GZIP file). So you need about 40GB of memory. If your cluster is made up of machines each with 16GB of memory, you should be looking at using three machines, though you might get away with two.

---

1 Source: tweet by @BigDataBorat.

I will introduce clusters later ("Clusters" on page 249 in Chapter 10), but the largest data set we use in this book is 70,000 rows and takes up 32MB in H2O's memory. However, if you are doing a lot of data munging, or experimenting with a lot of models, you can go through much more than the four times guideline.

 You can use your usual tools, such as w and top on Linux, to monitor server load, but I recommend you take a look at the Water Meter, found under the Admin menu in Flow. It shows how busy each core of each node is. Cluster Status under that same menu is a good one for keeping an eye on memory usage (also available from the R and Python APIs if you have something against using Flow). The key number to pay attention to is the "free" number in the "GC" columns. If it goes below twice the size of a training data set you plan to use to make a model from, it would be worth trying to free up some memory first; and if it is less than the size of the training data, your model is unlikely to build successfully.

Preparing the Data

Before we look at how to get data into H2O, we need to take a step back and consider what we might need to do with our data. Broadly speaking, that means:

- Split it into two or three data sets (train/valid/test)
- Mark field data types (numeric/integer/enum)
- Name fields
- Sort out missing values and other bad data
- Merge data sets
- Add new data columns

Knowledge engineering, aka, The Fun Bit, is part of the last of those items.

For each of those you have an important decision: before loading the data into H2O, or afterwards. The bigger your data the more thought you need to give to this decision, and you will need to factor in such things as your budget, your deadlines, and if this is a one-off or if you are getting new data each month, each day, each hour, each millisecond…

As a rule of thumb, if your data fits in one-eighth of the memory of the best single machine you have, then don't worry about whether to pre-process data before or after loading into H2O; just do the first approach that occurs to you, and fix it if you realize a different way was better. But if it doesn't, either get a bigger boat (to paraphrase *Jaws*), or do all your experiments and planning on a subset of the data, as suggested in the following sidebar.

Scaling and Productivity

However fast your hardware, however much memory your cluster has, if your data is big then you are going to end up sitting around waiting for both data manipulations and models to finish. And each time you get something wrong that was time wasted. Here is my advice: *use the smallest subset of data that is representative.*

Now, the definition of representative can be quite subjective, and can vary by what you want to do with it, but if you can get away with 1000 rows or less, you will be nice and productive. Statistics can help confirm a sample is representative: mean, median, standard deviation (s.d.), etc. If you have 100 million rows of data, how about randomly sampling 1000 from each of the first million, the middle million, and the last million, and confirming the mean and s.d. match on all columns? Also plot a histogram for each column, to be sure the distribution is the same. (There are some normality tests, e.g., `sharipo.test()` in R, which can give you a number if you don't want to trust your eyes.)

Now do all your experiments on that subset. Get the whole pipeline working, so you know how new data is coming in, what you pre-process and what you process in H2O, what reports are needed, which model(s) and model parameters you will be using, how frequently new data arrives. Everything.

Change the subset you work with at least as often as you change your clothes, to make sure you don't make bad assumptions and don't overfit. You there, in the brown shirt, I was thinking daily, not weekly.

Once happy, it is time to test the scaling. Double the amount of data, and test your whole process. Then increase it again, so it takes up nearer to one quarter of the memory of a single machine, and test again. How linearly did it scale? And did results get better or worse? There is more data, so you *should* be getting a better model. But maybe you have a bug, or maybe you need more epochs or more trees (because there are more concepts to learn now).

Next, split it across a cluster of two machines. Then use four machines and double the data again. How did all that affect the scaling? By this point you should have a fair idea of how many machines you will need to handle the whole data set, and (from measuring how the results improved) how much business value you will get from going to that trouble.

Getting Data into H2O

To use the H2O machine-learning algorithms the data must be in the H2O cluster; all that exists on your client is a handle (a pointer) to H2O's data frame. This might frustrate you at times, but it is what allows you to deal with big data sets that won't fit on any single machine in your cluster, let alone on the pokey little notebook you are running the client on. H2O provides quite a few ways to import data, and we will look at each here.

Load CSV Files

In the previous chapter our iris data was in a *csv* file on a remote web server. This is a good approach, because it will work equally well if you are using your local machine or a remote cluster in the cloud. You can use files on S3 (Amazon's cloud file storage) or HDFS (the filesystem of a Hadoop cluster). You can also use files stored on local disk.

When client and H2O cluster are on the same machine, relative file paths usually work. If a relative path import is not working, trying the full path is a good first troubleshooting step. All the online code uses relative paths, by assuming *code* and *datasets* are sibling directories. Start your Jupyter, IPython, RStudio, or R session in the code directory, or edit the scripts to use full paths.

 Python examples are shown in this section; the R API is the same for all these, but use h2o.importFile instead of h2o.import_file. You can also load data (with all the same options) from the browser-based Flow interface; see "Data" on page 17 in Chapter 1.

Here are some of the possible upload paths you can use:

```
df = h2o.import_file("hdfs://namenode/user/path/to/my.csv")
df = h2o.import_file("s3://<AWS_ACCESS_KEY>:<AWS_SECRET_KEY>@mybucket/my.csv")
df = h2o.import_file("https://s3.amazonaws.com/mybucket/my.csv")
df = h2o.import_file("/path/to/my.csv")
```

If the data file is compressed it will be automatically decompressed for you.

If you are interested in what is going on internally when loading, especially when you have a multinode cluster, there are some helpful diagrams (*http://bit.ly/2eKTAFi*) in the H2O architecture documentation.

For S3, you can also specify your AWS credentials when starting *h2o.jar*; see "Running from the Command Line" on page 248 in Chapter 10. If you have a forward slash in your AWS credentials, putting them in the URL won't work. Regenerating your AWS key, until you get one without a slash, is often recommended (the forward slash will stop some command-line tools from working too)! If you have trouble with "s3://" you can also try "s3n://" which is an older version, using a different library under the hood. By the way, when importing to a multinode cluster, each node will be doing a range GET request to S3, for quicker loading.

You can specify a list of file paths,[2] as follows:

```
df = h2o.import_file(["/path/to/my1.csv", "/path/to/my2.csv"])
```

It returns one merged data frame, which means each file must have exactly the same columns. It is equivalent to importing each file individually, then rbind-ing the parts together, but can be considerably quicker[3] and also doesn't leave you with lots of file parts cluttering up your server.

What if the file is on your local machine (which is different to the machine your cluster is on)? Then you have two choices:

- Put the file directly on the cluster machine, or on a web server, S3, a Hadoop cluster, etc., and continue to use h2o.import_file()
- Use h2o.upload_file() instead of h2o.import_file()

If this is a one-off, the second way is simplest. If the data is big, use the first way. If you expect to be regularly starting up the H2O cluster and loading this data, the first way is also superior. If the data is not static, but regularly changing, then use whichever approach is easiest for updating the file.

What about the other situation, when you have a remote multinode H2O cluster, but you want to use the filesystem on it? See "Clusters" on page 249 for that.

You can rename data columns after importing, and you can change column types after importing, but it is more efficient if they are correctly set when doing the import. H2O does a good job of detecting if the first row contains column names, but if your data does not have column names you can set them with col_names (col.names in R). Similarly, you can set the column data types with col_types (col.types in R).[4] (Remember, you don't specify "integer" versus "real": you specify "numeric" and it will analyze the data to decide which it is.)

---

2 It seems you *must* specify full paths when loading multiple files.

3 At least when bandwidth is not the limiting factor, because the reads happen in parallel. For instance, from a small Amazon EC2 cluster, reading a list of 20 *csv.gz* files (each about 15MB) from Amazon S3 took 20 to 25 seconds. Doing them in series literally took an order of magnitude longer.

4 Because H2O analyzes each column as it loads it, you don't often need to use this.

For instance, the next Python example takes a *csv* file that has no header row, and shows how to explicitly specify the column names and the column types:

```
datasets = "https://raw.githubusercontent.com/DarrenCook/h2o/bk/datasets/"
data = h2o.import_file(datasets + "iris.csv",
  col_names=[
    "Sepal length", "Sepal width","Petal length", "Petal width", "Species"
    ],
  col_types=[
    "numeric", "numeric", "numeric", "numeric", "enum"
    ]
  )
```

Here is the same example in R:

```
datasets <- "https://raw.githubusercontent.com/DarrenCook/h2o/bk/datasets/"
data <- h2o.importFile(paste0(datasets, "iris.csv"),
  col.names = c(
    "Sepal length", "Sepal width", "Petal length", "Petal width", "Species"
    ),
  col.types = c(
    "numeric", "numeric", "numeric", "numeric", "enum"
    )
  )
```

When you import or upload a file, the frame is given some unique name. For example, running the preceding code I got "iris.hex_sid_9739_3". If you'd like to have it use meaningful names, then specify `destination_frame` (for once, the argument name is exactly the same in R as in Python).

Another reason you might want to specify `destination_frame` explicitly is because when a frame is uploaded, and the same-named frame already exists, then it is quietly replaced. This is great if you are uploading new versions of the data, because as long as you use the same name, you don't need to worry about the old versions clogging up memory. (Be very careful, as this invalidates any handles that pointed to the previously uploaded version; see "Using as.h2o() in a Function" on page 32.)

Load Other File Formats

H2O also supports a few alternative formats, not just CSV. You import/upload exactly as with *csv* files. If you ever have trouble with the autodetection, you can specify the optional `parse_type` argument, to be one of:

CSV
> Comma-separated (or tab-separated, semicolon-separated, etc.). You can specify `sep`, or leave H2O to work it out.

ARFF

A text-based format, used by WEKA. See *https://weka.wikispaces.com/ARFF* for details on the format.

XLS

Excel files.

SVMLight

A sparse data format. Remember it will be expanded out when loaded into H2O (though H2O's in-memory compression should help).

I'll just briefly mention h2o.import_sql_table() and h2o.import_sql_select() (identical naming in both R and Python), which allow you to bring in data directly from an SQL database. You need to specify the location of the JDBC driver when starting H2O. Please see the online documentation for the exact requirements, the current list of supported SQL systems, and any other restrictions.

Load Directly from R

Say you have some R code to take a data set, analyze it, and add some columns to it. How do you then get that data into H2O? You could either save it to a disk file, then use h2o.uploadFile() as described earlier, or you could use as.h2o().[5] This function takes an R data.frame, turns it into an H2O frame, and returns a handle to the latter.

as.h2o() can handle any other data type that R can convert to a data.frame, such as matrix, xts (time index is quietly dropped), vector (1-column data frame created), array (2D only), list (an N-column, single row, data frame is created), or data.table.

As with h2o.uploadFile() and h2o.importFile(), you can optionally specify a frame name (the name that will be used on the H2O cluster) with destina tion_frame; but the default will be to use the name it is called in R, and that is usually what you want (but see "Using as.h2o() in a Function" on page 32 for when you do need to specify it).

---

5 At the time of writing, as.h2o() is implemented by saving to a temporary file then calling h2o.uploadFile(). So they are equivalent.

Using as.h2o() in a Function

My intention in this next code was to use a function to process each data frame in the same way (to keep this example short, the "processing" is limited to creating a new column c, which is the sum of the other two columns), then upload it to the H2O cluster. What is wrong with this code?

```
uploadIt <- function(d){
 d$c <- d$a + d$b
 as.h2o(d)
 }


d1 <- uploadIt( data.frame(a=1:3, b=2:4) )
d2 <- uploadIt( data.frame(a=9:5, b=5:1) )
```

If you run this and then look at the frames on Flow in your browser (if Flow is new to you, see "Flow" on page 17 in Chapter 1), you will see there is only a single data frame, called d. We've lost one! And if you try to use d1 from inside your R script you will get an error message.

The *it's-a-feature-not-a-bug* that tripped me up is that when you upload a frame with the name of an existing frame, the old version is quietly overwritten. And the local variable name, at the time of the as.h2o() call, is d. Not d1, not d2, but d! What is happening is that we upload our first data frame, call it d, and assign it to our d1 R variable. Then we upload another data frame, also called d, which replaces the previous one, and we assign it to the d2 R variable. d1 is left pointing at a frame that no longer exists.

One solution is to change my function to take an explicit frame name:

```
uploadIt <- function(nm, d){
 d$c <- d$a + d$b
 as.h2o(d, destination_frame = nm)
 }


d1 <- uploadIt("d1", data.frame(a=1:3, b=2:4) )
d2 <- uploadIt("d2", data.frame(a=9:5, b=5:1) )
```

Load Directly from Python

You've got a table of data in your Python script and want to push it to H2O, to generate a model, or bind with other data there. The first solution is to save it to a *csv* file, then use h2o.upload_file() (or h2o.import_file() if the file is somewhere visible to all the nodes in your cluster).

The other way is to use `h2o.H2OFrame()`. For instance, if your data is in a Python dictionary:

```
patients = {
  'height':[188, 157, 175],
  'age':[29, 33, 65],
  'risk':['A', 'B', 'B']
  }
df = h2o.H2OFrame(patients)
```

`df.types` shows it correctly chose `int` for the first two fields, and `enum` for the final field; if it hadn't, well the more powerful function is `h2o.H2OFrame.from_python()`, which takes a Python type, but also allows you to specify `destination_frame`, `column_names`, and `column_types`. Take a look at the next example, which has these changes:

- Set the column types for age to be `enum`. I specified the other two as `None` to let them be autodetected. Note: H2O sees the column names in alphabetical order, so you must specify the types in that order.

- Added 0.1 to one of the heights. `df.types` confirmed it chose `real` instead of `int` for that column.

- Gave the frame a name, so it is much easier to find later. `df.frame_id` confirmed it worked.

```
patients = {
  'height':[188, 157, 175.1],
  'age':[29, 33, 65],
  'risk':['A', 'B', 'B']
  }
df = h2o.H2OFrame.from_python(
  patients,
  column_types=['enum', None, None],
  destination_frame="patients"
  )
df.types
df.frame_id
```

You can also easily upload pandas objects. If `df` is your pandas object, then `h2o.H2OFrame(df)` will do the job:

```
import pandas as pd
patients = pd.DataFrame({
  'height':[188, 157, 175.1],
  'age':[29, 33, 65],
  'risk':['A', 'B', 'B']
  })
df = h2o.H2OFrame(patients)
df.types
df.frame_id
```

However, unlike the dictionary, when you examine df you will see the column names are C1, C2, and C3. So you need to use the more long-winded version:

```
patients = pd.DataFrame({
    'height':[188, 157, 175.1],
    'age':[29, 33, 65],
    'risk':['A', 'B', 'B']
    })
df = h2o.H2OFrame.from_python(
    patients,
    column_names=patients.columns.tolist()
    )
df.types
df.frame_id
```

Data Manipulation

There are a lot of operations you can perform on your data, in situ on the remote H2O cluster, saving you having to download data, modify it, and then upload it again. When the data is too big to fit in your client machine, that can be a lifesaver.

Laziness, Naming, Deleting

There are two key concepts you need to know for successful H2O data manipulation:

- Every change you make involves a data copy. That means the frame name will change, too.

- A lot of operations are lazy, meaning the requested change is recorded, but is not carried out until it has to be.

When you delete a variable in your client session that was pointing to a frame on the H2O server, it should then get deleted on the server. But garbage collection is a complicated topic, and sometimes it doesn't always happen. In R, gc() is often worth calling, to push things along. You can also remove an H2O frame directly with h2o.remove() (Python) or h2o.rm() (in R). You can give a list to remove multiple items at once.

 H2O is built on the assumption of a single user. Sure, you can have multiple clients connected, but be aware that if two clients hold a reference to the same frame, and one of them deletes it, the other client will get an error when it next tries to use it.

Though you can specify a frame name with the load and create frame operations, you cannot with other operations. But proper frame naming can really help—especially when you open Flow and see 300 frames, and have no idea which one is the data you've been working with. h2o.assign() to the rescue. It is used identically in Python and R. This example also shows how a column is deleted—by doing a copy and excluding the column(s) you do not want:

```
import h2o
h2o.init()

datasets = "https://raw.githubusercontent.com/DarrenCook/h2o/bk/datasets/"
data = h2o.import_file(datasets + "iris_wheader.csv")
data.frame_id  #iris_wheader.hex

data = data[:,1:] #Drop column 0. Keep column 1 onwards.
data.frame_id  #py_2_sid_88fe

data = h2o.assign(data, "iris")
data.frame_id  #iris

h2o.ls()  #iris and iris_wheader.hex, no py_2_sid_88fe
h2o.remove("iris_wheader.hex")
h2o.ls()  #Just lists iris
```

Here is the same example in R. Remember that Python counts columns from zero, R counts from 1. I could also have used column names, instead of indices:

```
library(h2o)
h2o.init(nthreads = -1)

datasets <- "https://raw.githubusercontent.com/DarrenCook/h2o/bk/datasets/"
data <- h2o.importFile(paste0(datasets,"iris_wheader.csv"))
attr(data,"id") #iris_wheader.hex_sid_a61b_1

data <- data[, 2:5] #Drop column 1. Keep columns 2 to 5 inclusive.
attr(data,"id")  #RTMP_sid_a61b_2

data <- h2o.assign(data, "iris")
attr(data,"id")  #iris

h2o.ls()  #iris_wheader.hex_sid_a61b_1 and iris, no RTMP_sid_a61b_2
h2o.rm("iris_wheader.hex_sid_a61b_1")
h2o.ls()  #Just iris
```

In both languages you can see that one intermediate frame got deleted, but one didn't and had to be explicitly removed. (gc(), or gc.collect() in Python, did not make any difference in this case.)

I mentioned laziness earlier. Generally, this is a good thing in computing. It might catch you out when you do an operation you expected to be slow and it returns really quickly, and then you do the next operation, which you expected to be quick, and it sits there for *minutes*. But there is something more important to watch out for, which I will come back to when talking about cbind and rbind.

Data Summaries

Whenever H2O imports or creates a frame of data it also creates some summary statistics for each column. You can access these with `data.describe()` in Python, or `h2o.describe(data)` in R. The following is the R output for the iris data:

```
    Label Type Missing Zeros PosInf NegInf Min Max  Mean  Sigma Cardinality
1 sepal_len real       0     0      0      0 4.3 7.9 5.843 0.828       <NA>
2 sepal_wid real       0     0      0      0   2 4.4 3.054 0.434       <NA>
3 petal_len real       0     0      0      0   1 6.9 3.759 1.764       <NA>
4 petal_wid real       0     0      0      0 0.1 2.5 1.199 0.763       <NA>
5     class enum       0    50      0      0   0   2 <NA>  <NA>           3
```

`h2o.summary(data)` is like R's summary function (in fact, `summary(data)` will also work).[6] But if you want more detailed information use `h2o.quantile(data)` and/or `h2o.levels(data)`, with the latter giving you the different categories for each enum column (`data.quantile()` and `data.levels()` in Python).

`dim(data)` tells you the number of rows and columns in the H2O frame, or `nrow(data)` and `ncol(data)` for just one of those values. In Python, they are `data.dim`, `data.nrow`, and `data.ncol`, and notice that they are properties, not function calls.

Operations on Columns

(The examples here follow on from an earlier section, assuming we have 150 iris rows in `data`, and that the sepal length column has been removed.)

Arithmetic and logical operators can be used directly, as well as some common statistical and mathematical functions. (Handling missing data, and data imputation, will be covered much later in this book; see "Missing Data" on page 237.)

```
data["petal_len"] = data["petal_len"] * 1.2
```

Here I've made all the petals 20% longer. New fertilizer. As mentioned earlier, on my client I now have `data` with big petals, but it has been given a new name, and on the H2O server you might see both the new frame and the old one (still with its normal-sized petals). Or the old one might have been garbage-collected.

---

6 `data.summary()` in Python is just the same output as `data.describe()`.

Next I will create a new column, as the ratio of sepal width to petal width, and then calculate the standard deviation of the (20% longer) petal lengths, and how well my new ratio column correlates with those petal lengths:

```
data["ratio"] = data["petal_wid"] / data["sepal_wid"]
data["petal_len"].sd() #2.117
data["ratio"].cor(data["petal_len"])  #0.956
```

The next example creates a new numeric column that is 1 when the petal length is greater than average, and 0 everywhere else. The syntax is something that evaluates to a boolean, followed by ifelse(if_true, if_false):

```
data["islong"] = (data["petal_len"] > data["petal_len"].mean()[0]).ifelse(1,0)
```

You can chain modifications together; here I change the enum to a string, use a regex to strip off the prefix, and assign that to a new *string* column:[7]

```
data["species"] = data["class"].ascharacter().gsub("Iris-", "")
```

Just quickly, here are the R versions of each of the above; you could also have used data[column] or data[,column] instead of the data$column syntax used here:

```
data$petal_len <- data$petal_len * 1.2
data$ratio <- data$petal_wid / data$sepal_wid
h2o.sd(data$petal_len)
h2o.cor(data$ratio, data$petal_len)
data$species <- h2o.gsub("Iris-", "", as.character(data$class) )
data$is_long <- ifelse(data$petal_len > mean(data$petal_len), 1, 0)
```

And, a quick example of when only the square bracket syntax will do the job—taking the mean of two columns:

```
h2o.mean( data[,c("sepal_wid", "petal_wid")] )  #3.054 1.199
```

Aggregating Rows

Carrying on with data from the previous section, when we have an enum column it is natural to want to analyze by groupings, and H2O can do this for us. In this example, I group by iris species, count how many of each, calculate the mean petal length of each group, and then how many in that category of iris got described as long (which you may remember from the previous section was defined as having a length greater than the mean length of all 150 irises):

```
data.group_by("class").count().mean("petal_len").sum("is_long").frame
```

7 Mainly for the sake of example. You cannot actually do much with a string column in H2O. By the way, you can apply gsub() directly to an enum, to alter the category labels.

The results look like this:

class	mean_petal_len	sum_is_long	nrow_sepal_wid
Iris-setosa	2.10816	0	50
Iris-versicolor	6.1344	43	50
Iris-virginica	7.99488	50	50

The available aggregate functions are count, min, max, mean, mode, sd, ss, sum, and var. var calculates variance, ss calculates sum of squares, and sd is standard deviation. You can also group by more than one column.

count() is done as nrow("column") in R, and you give as many aggregate functions as you wish, like this:

```
h2o.group_by(data, by = "class", nrow("class"), mean("petal_len"), sum("is_long"))
```

A different kind of aggregation is putting a numeric column into *buckets*, which is typically used to build a histogram. It is as simple as choosing your column, and calling hist() on it:

```
data["petal_len"].hist()
```

It looks like Figure 2-1.

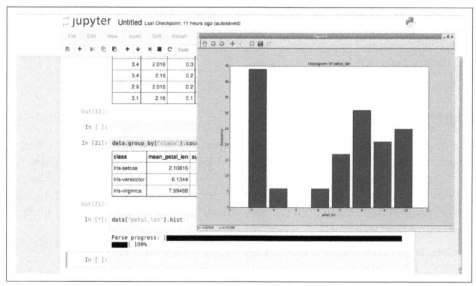

Figure 2-1. How the histogram displays in Jupyter

In R, it is `h2o.hist(data$petal_len)`. Whichever language, you can also specify the optional `breaks` if you don't like how many columns it chooses by default. If you give the `plot` argument as false it will instead return a table of information about where the break points were chosen and the number of elements in each bucket, as well as the mid-point and density of each bar. Remember that all this information is gathered server-side, in a parallel way on big data, and just that summary is being returned to your client.

Indexing

If you `data.show()` in Python you only see the first 10 rows, and `print(data)` in R only gives you the first 6 rows. What if you want to see other rows? What if you want *all* the data to operate on locally?

If you are happy with up to 6 (or 10) at a time, then use row indexing. For example, `data[9:12,:]` in Python gets the 10th, 11th, and 12th rows, while `data[10:12,]` does the same in R. You can still use the bit after the comma to request a subset of columns, as already described.

When you want to fetch more than 6 (or 10) rows, you use `as_data_frame()` in Python or `as.data.frame()` in R to download them. The next examples follow on from earlier ones in this chapter, and assume that `data` contains 150 rows of iris data.

 In Python the behavior depends on if you have pandas installed. If you do, then you will get a pandas `DataFrame`, otherwise you will get a nested list. This book generally assumes you have pandas installed. By the way, if you have pandas installed but would prefer the nested list, use `as_data_frame(use_pandas=False)`.

```
d = data.as_data_frame()
d.info()  #Describes the pandas DataFrame internals
d.corr(method="spearman").round(2)
```

H2O's R and Python bindings try to cover all the common functionality of R and Python, so you should only rarely need to download data. It does indeed have its own `cor()` function, and you could do `data.cor().round(2)`, but H2O doesn't support Spearman correlation, only Pearson, so I chose that for this example.[8]

---

8 Use Pearson correlation when you expect a linear relationship; e.g., doubling x should double y. Use Spearman when you think there is a correlation between their *rankings*, but not a linear one; e.g., if x1 is greater than x2 then y1 should be greater than y2. Spearman will be used when looking at the football data in Chapter 3.

It looks like the following:

	sepal_len	sepal_wid	petal_len	petal_wid	ratio
sepal_len	1.00	-0.16	0.88	0.83	0.76
sepal_wid	-0.16	1.00	-0.3	-0.28	-0.44
petal_len	0.88	-0.3	1.00	0.94	0.9
petal_wid	0.83	-0.28	0.94	1.00	0.97
ratio	0.76	-0.44	0.9	0.97	1.00

Is there a limit on how much data you can download? Maybe. There is the hard limit of the memory on your client machine, of course. But there may also be limits inside your client; I've not personally hit them, but I don't think I've ever downloaded more than 100,000 or so rows at a time. (If you do ever hit a limit, consider getting one column at a time, and combining them afterwards.)

Whether there is a limit or not, I recommend you only ever download what you need. For example, if you have 10 million rows, 100 columns, in a large, remote, H2O cluster, and need the Spearman correlation between age and current credit card debt, only downloading those two columns, not all 100, reduces the load to 1/50th. Also, surely you don't need all 10 million rows to prove your hypothesis,[9] and maybe just a random sample of 1000 is sufficient? If you know the data is already randomly shuffled, that request looks like the first line here, otherwise you need to specify 1000 random indices, which is the rest of this example. The call to sort() is required because indices must be requested in order:

```
d = creditData.as_data_frame(:1000, ["age","ccdebt"]).as_data_frame()

import random
ix = random.sample(xrange(1, creditData.nrow), 1000)
ix.sort()
d = creditData.as_data_frame(ix, ["age","ccdebt"]).as_data_frame()
```

In R, you specify if downloading as a data frame, vector, or matrix. With a matrix, just like in normal R, if the columns are not all numeric, you will end up with a character matrix:

```
#Assumes data contains iris data
d <- as.data.frame(data)
m <- as.matrix(data)
mode(m)  #"character" because of the factor column
```

---

9 I'm assuming you have a hypothesis, a reason to ask the question, such as wanting to justify not giving credit cards to over-40s. If you have no question, and just want to look busy, steam right ahead!

```
m <- as.matrix(data[,c("petal_wid","sepal_wid")])
mode(m)   #"numeric"
```

The R version of the random sampling code is as follows:

```
ix <- sort( sample(1:nrow(creditData), 1000) )
d <- as.matrix(creditData[ix, c("age","ccdebt")])
```

Split Data Already in H2O

We will often want to split our data into either two subsets (train and test) or three subsets (train, valid, and test). See the following sidebar if this concept is unfamiliar.

Valid Versus Test?

If I wanted to know how much mathematics you know, I would give you a test. But if I were to show you the exact questions, and their correct answers beforehand, you are likely to get a higher score than if I give you questions you've not seen before. The machine-learning models we make are no different, which is why we take some of our training data to one side, as a *test set*.

How much? Enough to be representative of the real-world questions the model will be asked once it is in production, and enough so that it will be really hard to get a perfect score just by guessing. Otherwise, as small as possible, because it is stealing our training data and the more training data we use the better our model will be.

Now, let's imagine we make a model and evaluate it on the test set. We tweak one of the parameters and it gets a slightly lower score. We tweak it the other way and get a slightly better score. We repeat this process many times, and proudly present our 187th model as having solved the problem domain because it gets 100%.

Maybe it has. Or maybe we have (indirectly) overfitted on the test data. Even though the model never got to directly see the test data, our decisions about how to tune the model was based on that test data.

The way to avoid this is to do the whole splitting process twice, and create what is called a *validation data set*. If I have 70,000 rows of training data, and I randomly select 10,000 rows to be test data, I then randomly select another 10,000 from the remaining 60,000 rows to be my validation data, leaving me with 50,000 as my training data set.

We train our models with the training data, and score it on the validation data, as indicated in the middle of Figure 2-2. We then tweak the models, and score again on the validation data. Tweaking models also includes trying alternative algorithms (e.g., random forest instead of deep learning, or ensembles). Finally, we choose our model, and declare it ready for production, and then, and only then, do we try it on the test set, as shown at the bottom of the figure.

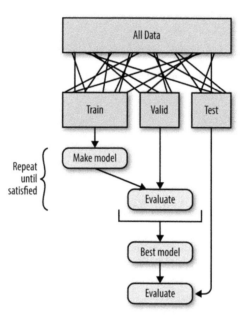

Figure 2-2. Summary of how train, valid, and test data sets are used

Cross-validation is a closely related concept, an alternative to having a validation data set. It is covered in "Cross-Validation (aka k-folds)" on page 104. Briefly, it allows you to use more of your data for training, at the expense of taking longer to build your models.

By the way, the validation data doesn't *have* to be the same size as the test data, it just has to be representative of it: the ideal situation is if a model gets an error of E on the validation data set, that it will get an error of E on the test data set, no higher, no lower. But, yes, that means the same size is usually a good choice. Additional considerations are the expected error and random noise,[10] and also training time: H2O models get evaluated against the validation data regularly while being built so huge validation data sets will cause your models to take longer to build. However, it is also common to have a bigger validation data set than test set: the bigger it is, the harder it is to overfit, and it is that validation data you will be (indirectly) tuning for.

When you go to split data, your first question should *not* be "What split ratio?" but "Am I balanced and independent?" Sorry, not you, I think we all know the answer to that one. Your data.

---

10 In Chapter 11 I briefly introduce models built with over one million training rows and 10,000 test rows, but only 1000 validation rows, because I wanted all the training data I could get my hands on.

First, is it balanced? Meaning, for any column in your data, are some possible values less common? A common example is a gender column. If 90% of the samples are Male, 10% Female, then you want each of your training, validation, and test data sets to also be 90%/10%. But this is not just about enum (categorical) columns; an income column, a numeric field, might have a few very high earners and you want them fairly distributed in each data split. Unbalanced data is more of a problem with small data sets. When you have plenty of data the law of big numbers tends to make sure the data is evenly distributed. By the way, if your data is unbalanced, you will also want to look at the balance_classes parameter (covered in "Data Weighting" on page 106).

Perhaps more important is to ask if the samples (your data rows) are independent. Clinical trials, or iris measurements, or polls conducted in a short time span, are independent. With all these, splitting randomly is exactly what you want. Time-series data is a different beast. If the point of your model will be to predict future events, not ones in the past, then (usually) you would use the oldest data as training data, then the next oldest for validation, with the newest data as test data.

 Often when learning from a time series you will generate features by adding moving average columns, or the difference since some earlier point in time. You will want to add these kinds of columns *before* splitting. But a very important exception is if the calculation uses values from a later row,[11] in other words, from the future. In that case you *must* do the split first, and do the calculation on each split, separately. A good way to tell? Does the calculation leave an NA in the first row (in which case it is best done pre-split) or the final row (in which case it *must* be done after the split)?

Enough talk, time to code. Here is how to create a random 60/20/20 three-way split of an existing H2O data frame (data). Notice how the size of the last split is left implicit:

```
train, test, valid = data.split_frame([0.6, 0.2])
```

And in R:

```
parts <- h2o.splitFrame(data, c(0.6, 0.2) )
train <- parts[[1]]
valid <- parts[[2]]
test <- parts[[3]]
rm(parts) #Optional
```

---

11 ROC (return on capital) in algorithmic trading is a good example of this. It tells us how much money you would have made if you bought on this day and held for one day; obviously we wouldn't know that until we find out the price on the next day.

Do it this way for all data sets that are large and independent. As we saw in the previous chapter, the splits can end up different sizes, which causes a minor issue with small data sets. If, for that reason, or any other, you want splits that are *exactly* the specified size, though there is no single H2O function to do this, we can use `sample()` just as we did earlier in this chapter in "Indexing" on page 39. Like this:

```
ratios <- c(0.6, 0.2, 0.2)
sz <- nrow(data)
indices <- split(1:sz, sample( rep(1:3, sz * ratios) ) )
train <- data[ indices[[1]], ]
valid <- data[ indices[[2]], ]
test <- data[ indices[[3]], ]
```

For instance, if `data` has 10 rows, then `indices` might be:

```
$`1`
[1] 2 3 5 6 7 9

$`2`
[1]  4 10

$`3`
[1] 1 8
```

If we do `data[ c(2, 3, 5, 6, 7, 9), ]` it will create a new data frame (on the H2O server) with only those specified 6 elements. `valid` will be a frame with only rows 4 and 10, and `test` will get rows 1 and 8.

> Using fixed sizes like this is slower; do not use it for large data sets. Always use H2O's split function unless you have a good reason not to.

The same technique can be used for not just random splits, but any arbitrary split you need. For instance, how about if `data` was a time series, and we want the last 10% as `test`, and the 15% before that as `valid`, and all the earlier rows as `train`?

It is just like the preceding code, but without using `sample()`:

```
ratios <- c(0.75, 0.15, 0.1)
sz <- nrow(data)
indices <- split(1:sz, rep(1:3, sz * ratios) )
train <- data[ indices[[1]], ]
valid <- data[ indices[[2]], ]
test <- data[ indices[[3]], ]
```

Another way to split an H2O frame is by using a logical function. Going back to our trusty Iris data set, here is one way to split by petal size:

```
largePetals <- data[ data$petal_len > mean(data$petal_len), ]
smallPetals <- data[ data$petal_len <= mean(data$petal_len), ]
```

Rows and Columns

In "Operations on Columns" on page 36, we added some new columns to H2O frames. But, under the surface, what H2O was doing was copying all the columns from the existing frame, making a new frame with one column, and then *binding* them together. You could have done those steps explictly with cbind().[12] Here is how to do just one of those new columns that way (to save you having to go back to re-create data as it was at that earlier point, this example loads fresh data):

```
import h2o
h2o.init()

datasets = "https://raw.githubusercontent.com/DarrenCook/h2o/bk/datasets/"
data = h2o.import_file(datasets + "iris_wheader.csv")

ratio_frame = data["petal_wid"] / data["sepal_wid"]
ratio_frame.col_names = ["ratio"]
data = data.cbind(ratio_frame)
data = h2o.assign(data, "iris")
ratio_frame.remove()
```

The cbind operation is *lazy*. That means it delays actually joining the frames together until it has to. If I were to move the ratio_frame.remove() up one line, directly after the cbind, doing anything with data would then fail: we've removed part of its data before it got a chance to actually do the copy. That is what the h2o.assign() call is doing (apart from giving a nice name to the new frame, of course). Other functions that will eagerly evaluate the data are nrow(), ncol(), or dim() (to find out how large it is), or any indexing or summarizing command. In fact, printing data would have been enough.

rbind is the equivalent for joining frames together vertically: each frame must have exactly the same columns; just as when cbind-ing, each frame must have exactly the same number of rows.

h2o.merge() is for joining two frames together, based on columns they have in common, just like a join in SQL. The frames can be of different lengths. Here is a simple example where I will merge in my price list for my newly opened flower shop, though currently we only sell (Yep! You guessed it!) irises. The wholesaler has included

---

12 cbind stands for column bind; rbind stands for row bind.

measurements of every iris precise to the millimeter, but my price list is based solely on the petal length in centimeters. My first step is to load my price list into H2O:

```
prices = h2o.H2OFrame({
  'petal_len':[2, 3, 4, 5],
  'price':[4, 5.5, 8, 10]
  })
```

Before I can merge this with `data` (which I assume is already loaded—see the previous example in this section), I need to convert the petal lengths to centimeters. Actually, by huge coincidence, this is not just because I price to the nearest centimeter, but also because H2O's merge refuses to run with floating-point numbers. Integers or enums only. H2O uses a kind of duck-typing for numbers: if all entries in a column are whole numbers it is an int column, but if at least one entry has a fractional part then it is a real column. Therefore, the way to integer-ize a column is to call `round()`. After that, `merge()` with all defaults does the job. Simple.

```
data["petal_len"] = data["petal_len"].round()
iris_prices = data.merge(prices)
```

As Figure 2-3 shows, I get a 99 row frame, because 51 irises, once rounded, were less than 2cm or over 5cm long, and my price list hadn't allowed for them. If I added `all.x=True` to the call to `merge()` then I would have got 150 entries, and a nan in the price column for those 51.

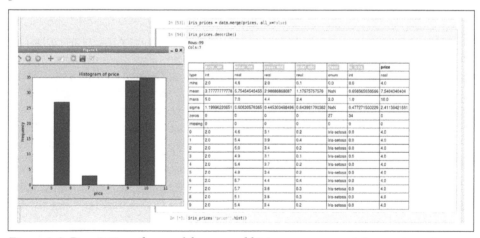

Figure 2-3. Description of merged frame, and histogram summarizing my inventory

Here is the same example in R:

```
prices <- as.h2o( data.frame(list(
  petal_len = 2:5, price = c(4, 5.5, 8, 10)
  ) ) )
data$petal_len <- round(data$petal_len)
irisPrices <- h2o.merge(data, prices)
```

I'll finish this section with a more complex example, in R: Example 2-1. It has a couple of large dependencies, so you cannot run it, but I hope it shows how these functions can be used together. The scripts it is taken from are introduced in a little more detail in "How Low Can You Go?" on page 265 in the last chapter of this book.

Example 2-1. Example of complex data import and manipulation

```
#This helper script is introduced in the next chapter
#It starts H2O, and initializes train/valid/test
source("load.mnist_enhanced.R")

prefix <-"s3://example-bucket/"

#Load data from train
genTrain <- h2o.importFile(paste0(prefix, c(
  "mnist_generated.enhanced.train.501.csv.gz",
  "mnist_generated.enhanced.train.123.csv.gz",
  "mnist_generated.enhanced.train.502.csv.gz",
  "mnist_generated.enhanced.train.499.csv.gz"
  )), destination_frame = "genTrain")

#Load data from valid
genValid <- h2o.importFile(paste0(prefix, c(
  "mnist_generated.enhanced.valid.501.csv.gz",
  "mnist_generated.enhanced.valid.123.csv.gz",
  "mnist_generated.enhanced.valid.502.csv.gz",
  "mnist_generated.enhanced.valid.499.csv.gz"
  )), destination_frame = "genValid")

#Scoop out first 1000 of each file, by specifying
#just the rows to keep.
genValid12_9K <- genValid12[c(
    1001:10000,
   11001:20000,
   21001:30000,
   31001:40000
   )]

genTrain[,y] <- as.factor(genTrain[,y])
genValid_9K[,y] <- as.factor(genValid_9K[,y])

#Just use the first 1000 row, for validating
validSmall <- valid[1:1000,]

#And give the other 9K to training data
train59 <- h2o.rbind(train, valid[1001:10000,])

#Now combine all our training data sources
trainBig <- h2o.rbind(train59, genTrain, genValid_9K)

nrow(trainBig)  #SLOW
```

```
ae_models <- ...  #Load pre-generated auto-encoder models

#generate_data() is a custom function, not shown here.
train_ae <- generate_data(ae_models, trainBig)
valid_ae <- generate_data(ae_models, validSmall)
test_ae <- generate_data(ae_models, test)

#Join columns, deleting old frames as I go
validAll <- h2o.cbind(validSmall, valid_ae)
nrow(validAll)
h2o.rm(validSmall);h2o.rm(valid_ae);gc()

testAll <- h2o.cbind(test, test_ae)
nrow(testAll)
h2o.rm(test);h2o.rm(test_ae);gc()

trainAll <- h2o.cbind(train, train_ae)
nrow(trainAll)  #SLOW
h2o.rm(train);h2o.rm(train_ae)
```

Getting Data Out of H2O

Broadly speaking, there are two things you might want to extract from H2O:

- Frames
- Models

Frames could be data you've previously imported (and possibly modified), or gener-ated, or it might be predictions from a model. Models can be exported in a binary format for re-importing at a later time, or as POJOs (Plain Old Java Objects) for run-ning models without H2O. We will look at each of these.

 When you shut down your H2O cluster, all data and models are lost: nothing is saved to disk unless you explicitly request it. And with a cluster, if even just one node becomes unresponsive, the same thing. For long-running jobs, a regular export is a good idea.

Exporting Data Frames

If you do most of your data preparation in advance of loading into H2O, you may not see the need for this. But, if you have merged and manipulated data frames inside of H2O, you will be looking for a way to get that data out again.

See "Indexing" on page 39 earlier in this chapter for when you are looking to down-load data directly from H2O into a variable in your R or Python client. This section is about saving to files.

The frame sizes reported by H2O are compressed sizes. But the exported files will be uncompressed, so be prepared for that! Also, if exporting to S3, be aware there is a 5GB limit on any one file.

Exported files are in *csv* format, and similarly to the way importing worked, we have two choices for where to export them to:

- To our local machine (where the client runs)
- To the H2O server's local disk, or HDFS or S3

If df is the data frame, for a local download, use h2o.downloadCSV(df, "/path/to/ data.csv") in R, or h2o.download_csv(df,"/path/to/data.csv") in Python.

For saving to a location on the H2O server, use h2o.exportFile() (h2o.export_file() in Python), where the first parameter is the frame to save, and the second is the disk path and filename. To save to HDFS use an "hdfs://" prefix, and to save to s3, use an "s3://" prefix (or try the older "s3n://" if you have problems). As with importing, you can also specify your AWS credentials when starting up *h2o.jar* or in the pathname. Here are some examples:

```
h2o.exportFile(d, "/path/to/d.csv")
h2o.exportFile(d, "s3://mybucket/d.csv")
h2o.exportFile(d, "s3://<AWS_ACCESS_KEY>:<AWS_SECRET_KEY>@mybucket/d.csv")
h2o.exportFile(d, "hdfs://namenode/path/to/d.csv")
```

On the Flow interface, when viewing a frame, there are buttons for both Download and Export.

If you are running on a multinode cluster, there is an optional argument, parts, which can have each node export its own rows from the frame, and can result in quicker exports. It works with all of HDFS, S3, and the local filesystem. This feature is in active development as I type this, so please see the latest documentation.

When exporting from a multinode cluster to the local filesystem the file is written to just one node (either the one your client is connected to, or the first-listed node in cluster info), unless you set parts, in which case the file parts will be written to all nodes (e.g., parts 0 and 1 to node 1, parts 2 and 3 to node 2, and so on).

POJOs

Is it just me, or does POJO sound like something people used to bounce up and down on in the 1970s? Ah, just me. Oh well. POJO stands for Plain Old Java Object. In the context of H2O, it refers to a self-contained Java file with everything needed to use your model. Taking the example of a deep learning model, the POJO file would contain Java code for the algorithms, and Java arrays containing all the weights/biases of all the layers. The idea is that you can run it to make predictions, without having to install the rest of H2O. There is a special *jar* file (*h2o-genmodel.jar*) that you run to use the POJO file.

Writing programs around a POJO is outside the scope of this book (see POJO Quick-Start in the H2O docs (*http://bit.ly/2geZBHO*) for more information on that); in this section we just cover how to export it.

If you view your model on the Flow interface, you'll see a button labeled Download POJO. You will then download an *xxx.java* plain-text file, where *xxx* is the name of your model.

In R, you can fetch the POJO with:

```
m <- h2o.someLearningAlgorithm(...)
h2o.download_pojo(m)

#  ... OR ...

m <- h2o.getModel("my_model_id")
h2o.download_pojo(m)
```

That writes it to your console. What if you wanted it in a string? You could mess around with capturing cat() output. Or, take a peek at the source of down load_pojo() and then use this hack:

```
model_id <- m@model_id
myPojo <- .h2o.__remoteSend(method = "GET",
  paste0(.h2o.__MODELS, ".java/", model_id),
  raw = TRUE)
```

If you look closely you see that all you need is a model ID, not a full model object. If you had a list of 100s of model IDs to fetch POJOs for, wrap the preceding code in a lapply(), and Bob's your uncle.

But, most likely you want to save the POJO. Again, if m is your model, you do that with h2o.download_pojo(m, "/tmp") That will create two files in your */tmp/* directory: *myModel.java* and *h2o-genmodel.jar*. You are likely to only want the *jar* file the first time you do this, so to save downloading it every time, give FALSE as the third parameter: h2o.download_pojo(m, "/tmp/", FALSE).

In Python, the function and arguments are identical, so I'll cut straight to the example of how to save it to your */tmp/* directory: h2o.download_pojo(m, "/tmp") and, again, give the third parameter as False if you don't want the *jar* file each time.

Model Files

The POJO is a Java program, and cannot be imported back into H2O to re-create a model. It doesn't contain any of the information on training statistics, or what parameters it was trained with. For that you need to get the binary model file.

Because the file contents are in a binary format, only of meaning to H2O, you don't download the model file: you just request it be saved. And then later you can request it be loaded.[13]

In R the command to save a model is `fname <- h2o.saveModel(model, "/tmp")` and in Python it is almost the same: `fname = h2o.save_model(model, "/tmp")` (where `model` is a model you've generated or fetched). The model ID will be used as the filename, and it is the full path and filename that is returned. If it already exists, the command will fail; to force it to be overwritten give the third parameter as true: `h2o.save_model(model, "/tmp", True)`.

To load it back in later, you will need the filename you were given. The command is what you expect (R: `h2o.loadModel(fname)`, Python: `h2o.load_model(fname)`). It gets created in H2O with the same model ID it had before. (The model ID cannot be changed; use `h2o.assign()` after loading each model if that creates a conflict.)

The path you specify should not end in a forward slash. The good news is that if the directory does not exist, H2O will create it for you (assuming it has permission to). So, there is no excuse not to use a good naming scheme: `fname <- h2o.saveMo del(model, "/tmp/h2o_models/mnist_tests1")`. (Also consider using a datestamp as a subfolder.)

 A saved model is tied to an H2O version. You cannot load a model in a version later than the one it was saved with. There is also currently no way to convert a model file. That is, if you upgrade H2O you are stuck with having to regenerate your models.

Save All Models

Say you have 30 models stored on H2O, and you want to save them all. The scenario might be that you want to shut down the cluster overnight, but want to use your current set of models as the starting point for better models tomorrow. At the time of writing H2O does not offer this functionality, not even in Flow. So, what you need to do is make a loop to fetch each model, and then save each model.

---

13 On a multinode cluster, load/save will go to the local filesystem of whichever node your client is connected to. You can also save to HDFS or S3.

I have written a blog post (*http://bit.ly/2ge2FnR*) on how to enhance the R API to add functions to do this, including a helper function for loading your models back in. It also shows how to access the internal functions of the R API. (This is useful, though it carries the risk that some future H2O release breaks your code. The best way to prevent that is to do a pull request, and contribute your idea back to the H2O project—it is open source, after all!)

Summary

This chapter has focused on import, manipulation, and export. It is important knowledge to have, even if it is about the "boring 80%" of the data science job. As well as supplying many useful functions (there are too many to cover all of them in this chapter, and they are being expanded all the time—use tab-completion from your editor, or the online documentation, to see the latest list) it also transparently makes them work when the data is too big to fit inside a single machine. Just bear in mind that just about every operation will create a copy, and that before you delete any frames, make sure that lazy operations have been evaluated.

At least a few of the functions introduced here will be seen again in the next chapter, which will introduce the three data sets that we will be using later in the book.

CHAPTER 3

The Data Sets

This chapter will introduce three data sets, how to load and prepare each of them, and some initial analysis. Later chapters will then cover each of the four main supervised machine-learning algorithms that H2O supports (random forest, gradient boosting machines, generalized linear models, and deep learning),[1] and we will try each algorithm on each of these data sets.

The data sets have been chosen to try and introduce something new each time. The first is a regression, the second is a multinomial classification, and the third is flexible but will be used as a binomial classification. The first tests our green credentials, as we try to predict which house designs will be more energy efficient. The second is a well-studied problem in the field of computer vision, trying to recognize hand-written digits. The third is a sports statistics data set, a time series where we will try to predict future events, specifically who will win a football match. All three data sets will fit in the memory of a typical PC, so you will be able to follow along without needing to rent a cluster.

The third data set was compiled for this book, so we spend more time looking at it here, including the process of dealing with messy data. (Even though this takes us away from the core theme of the book, using H2O, at times.)

---

1 There is also naive bayes, covered briefly in "Naive Bayes" on page 252 in Chapter 10, but it is not used on these data sets.

Data Set: Building Energy Efficiency

How much does it cost to heat your house? Or to cool it in summer? Does an extra window make a difference? Is a multifloor building with a small roof cheaper to heat than a bungalow of the same floor area? Maybe you guessed *yes* and *yes*, but by how much?

This will be a regression problem, on a relatively small data set. We have 768 samples, with eight features, and a choice of two responses (heating load, cooling load) to learn.

Example 3-1 is the R code we'll use to load and prepare it for each of our machine-learning algorithms, while Example 3-2 is the equivalent code in Python.

Example 3-1. Loading the ENB data set (in R)

```
library(h2o)
h2o.init(nthreads = -1)

data <- h2o.importFile("../datasets/ENB2012_data.csv")

factorsList <- c("X6", "X8")
data[,factorsList] <- as.factor(data[,factorsList])

splits <- h2o.splitFrame(data, 0.8)
train <- splits[[1]]
```

```
test <- splits[[2]]

x <- c("X1", "X2", "X3", "X4", "X5", "X6", "X7", "X8")
y <- "Y2"  #Or "Y1"
```

Example 3-2. Loading the ENB data set (in Python)

```
import os
import h2o
h2o.init()

#If next line fails, instead set path to datasets location.
path = os.path.dirname(__file__)
fname = os.path.join(path, "../datasets/ENB2012_data.csv")
data = h2o.import_file(fname)

factorsList = ["X6", "X8"]
data[factorsList] = data[factorsList].asfactor()

train, test = data.split_frame([0.8])

x = ["X1", "X2", "X3", "X4", "X5", "X6", "X7", "X8"]
y = "Y2"  #Or "Y1"
```

(See "Jargon and Conventions" on page 8, in Chapter 1, for a reminder of the variable naming conventions being used in this book.)

Setup and Load

In both cases, the first couple of lines load the h2o library, and initialize the connection to the H2O server, starting the server if necessary.

The importFile() (in R) or import_file() (in Python) tells H2O to import the specified data file, as we saw in the previous chapter. By the way, the original data was an *xlsx* spreadsheet file. I loaded it into Open Office, and saved it as a *csv* file instead.

If you didn't download the data sets to your local disk, remember that H2O also supports direct loading from HTTP (as well as Amazon S3, NFS, and HDFS), so you could write (for example):

```
h2o.importFile(
  "https://raw.githubusercontent.com/DarrenCook/h2o/bk/datasets/ENB2012_data.csv")
```

The importFile()/import_file() command returns a handle (a pointer) to the data on the H2O server (wrapped in a class in Python, in an environment in R). You will use that handle in all subsequent operations on it, but remember the data is on the (possibly remote) server's memory, not in your client's memory.

The Data Columns

The next couple of lines in the listing tell H2O which fields are categorical variables. In this case I eyeballed the data, and saw that the "X6" and "X8" columns contained only integers, and only a few distinct values.

Are the "X1" to "X8" labels feeling a bit abstract? Sometimes data is delivered like that, and you have to ask the customer, which can take you through four different contacts, in three different companies, using at least two (human) languages, and involving at least one offshore tax haven. Such fun. Thankfully, in this case, all we had to do was find the paper (*http://bit.ly/2eKPkWo*), by A. Tsanas and A. Xifara (also to be found in the *datasets* directory), and skim it until we get to Table 1. That doesn't just tell us more meaningful names, but looking at the "Number of possible values" column, we also discover that basically all the input variables are categorical! But, for the moment, just the names:

- X1: Relative Compactness
- X2: Surface Area
- X3: Wall Area
- X4: Roof Area
- X5: Overall Height
- X6: Orientation
- X7: Glazing area
- X8: Glazing area distribution
- Y1: Heating Load
- Y2: Cooling Load

 Does it actually matter what the names are, or what the columns mean?

Yes! Once we know that a higher number in X4 means a bigger roof, or that an X6 of 4 means it will be getting more sunlight, we have more chance to spot suspicious data and suspicious results.

What about the meanings for X6, "orientation"? I can see the values range from 2 to 5. This is the rotation of the building shape. The paper is not explicit, but I'm guessing:

- 2: North
- 3: East

- 4: South
- 5: West

Then the other categorical, X8, describes how the windows are distributed:

- 0: No windows
- 1: Uniform, 25% on each side
- 2: 55% on North side, 15% on other sides
- 3: 55% on East side, 15% on other sides
- 4: 55% on South side, 15% on other sides
- 5: 55% on West side, 15% on other sides

I mentioned earlier that, from one point of view, all eight predictor variables are categorical. For instance, X7 ("Glazing area") is how big the windows are, expressed as a percentage of floor area, but there are only three values used: 10%, 25%, 40%. 0% is also used, for when X8 is zero, giving us a total of four values. As another example, there are only two building heights (X5): 3.5m and 7m. That is, single-story or two-story buildings.

This creates an interesting problem. These other six variables are not integers and have been detected as `real` in H2O, so trying to do `as.factor()` on any of them[2] reports `"Categorical conversion can only currently be applied to integer columns."` I *could* try multiplying them through by a large number to turn them into integers, and then into enums. But I'm not going to. For a few reasons.

Firstly, there are factors, and then there are *factors*. To be less enigmatic, I mean that factors (categories) can be either *unordered* or *ordered*. X6 is an unordered factor (you cannot say that East-facing has "more direction" than West-facing), as are things like gender or favorite color. But X7 has an innate ordering (40% windows is more than 25% windows), as do things like income bracket or obesity level. H2O offers no explicit support for ordered factors. And this is fine in this case: X7 = 0.4 versus X7 = 0.1 doesn't just tell me "more" windows, it tells me four times as much sunlight would enter the house. If I changed them to ordered factors I would lose that information.

The second reason is laziness. Bill Gates will tell you that laziness is a fine virtue in a programmer (because laziness inspires creative solutions), but by lazy here I am thinking more of our Donald Knuth's famous: "*Premature optimization is the root of*

---

2 For example, `as.factor(data[,"X7"])` in R, or `data["X7"].asfactor()` in Python.

all evil."[3] I don't know if leaving X3 as a `real` will give me a better model, or if jumping through hoops to turn it into a factor will be better. So, given the choice between doing something and doing nothing I will choose to do nothing, until I find a reason to do otherwise.

The third reason is that linear models, and deep learning, generally prefer numbers to factors. Yes, the tree algorithms prefer categories but, by their nature, they are likely to easily discover the natural split points in features like X7.

Splitting the Data

As you already know, to avoid overfitting it is essential to have some test data that you do not train on, and to be very careful that the test data never influences either the training data or the choice of model and model parameters. (Review "Valid Versus Test?" on page 41 in the previous chapter, if necessary.)

The earlier listing (Example 3-1 or 3-2) splits the data so that `train` is a random 80% of it, and `test` is the other 20% of it (just like we did in the first chapter, with the iris data; also see "Data Manipulation" on page 34). The data set is relatively small, so I have chosen not to have a validation test set, and instead I will use cross-validation (see "Cross-Validation (aka k-folds)" on page 104).

All model building in this book is evaluated on the exact same 20% split,[4] for consistency. However, be aware that this particular data set is sensitive to how it is split: later in this book you will notice a large variance on the results for the 10 cross-validation splits, whichever model is used.

Is my chosen test split an easy one? A hard one? Typical? I cannot say without trying lots of splits and comparing. The Tsanas and Xifara paper, mentioned earlier, took that approach. They had no test set, and instead used 10-fold cross-validation, but for each model they did 100 iterations; i.e., they used 100 different ways to split the data into 10 parts, then took the mean and standard deviation of the results.

I like that idea, but the goals are different: their goal was to see if machine learning could accurately represent the data. Our goal is to compare various machine-learning algorithms, and learn how to tune them. 100 iterations would have slowed us down 100 times. As long as we are consistent it doesn't matter, too much, if we end up with an easy, medium, or hard test set.

---

3 *https://en.wikipedia.org/wiki/Program_optimization#Quotes*

4 Using seed=999 for the call to `split()`.

The last few lines of the listings, shown previously, set x to be the predictor variables, and y to be the response variable. We have two to choose from, and I have chosen Y2, cooling load, simply because the paper mentions that it was harder to predict.

You cannot have more than one response variable in a single H2O model. If there are two things you want to predict, build two models.

Let's Take a Look!

Before you run any kind of machine-learning algorithm, it is well worth your time to run some preliminary analysis on the data.

Remember that the frame we are calling data is *all* the data. If you are going to be making decisions that influence how you model, it is good practice to only look at the train frame, as I do here, and keep the test frame completely untouched.

In Python you can type train.describe() or h2o.describe(train) in R. From a Jupyter notebook the output looks like Figure 3-1. Similar information can be found in the Flow Web UI.

In [10]: train.describe()

Rows:625
Cols:10

	X1	X2	X3	X4	X5	X6	X7	X8	Y1	Y2
type	real	real	real	real	real	enum	real	enum	real	real
mins	0.62	514.5	245.0	110.25	3.5	0.0	0.0	0.0	6.04	10.9
mean	0.760992	674.2008	319.3624	177.4192	5.2192	NaN	0.23616	NaN	22.218176	24.4976
maxs	0.98	808.5	416.5	220.5	7.0	3.0	0.4	5.0	43.1	48.03
sigma	0.104651320939	87.4497158592	44.6793089839	45.0949771316	1.75113040414	NaN	0.1328483809	NaN	10.1449861085	9.57297091374
zeros	0	0	0	0	0	165	37	37	0	0
missing	0	0	0	0	0	0	0	0	0	0
0	0.98	514.5	294.0	110.25	7.0	2	0.0	0	15.55	21.33
1	0.98	514.5	294.0	110.25	7.0	3	0.0	0	15.55	21.33
2	0.98	514.5	294.0	110.25	7.0	4	0.0	0	15.55	21.33
3	0.98	514.5	294.0	110.25	7.0	5	0.0	0	15.55	21.33
4	0.9	563.5	318.5	122.5	7.0	2	0.0	0	20.84	28.28
5	0.9	563.5	318.5	122.5	7.0	5	0.0	0	19.68	29.6
6	0.86	588.0	294.0	147.0	7.0	3	0.0	0	19.95	21.97
7	0.86	588.0	294.0	147.0	7.0	4	0.0	0	19.34	23.49
8	0.82	612.5	318.5	147.0	7.0	2	0.0	0	17.05	23.77
9	0.82	612.5	318.5	147.0	7.0	3	0.0	0	17.41	21.46

Figure 3-1. The output from train.describe()

What to pay attention to? First the type, to make sure X6 and X8 (only) are "enum." The data is not normally distributed (which we will see in a moment), so I am less interested in mean and sigma, aka, standard deviation, but I am paying attention to the min/max of each column, to make sure it matches my expectations. Speaking of which, I had not expected to see the 165 zeros for the X5 column, because in the data they ranged from 2 to 5. But it is fine. What has happened is that the enum has renumbered the levels to be 0 to 3. 165 is just over a quarter of the 625 rows that train contains, so that is about right. Finally, I am comforted to see the "missing" row says zeros for all columns. If this was not the case we would have to investigate further, and decide how we want to deal with missing data.

 Sometimes missing data is not detected as such, because some kind-hearted person has repaired it for you, and unwittingly damaged the data. Watch out for more zeros than expected. (See "Missing Data" on page 237 for an example; as I point out there, mean imputation can also damage the data, but be even harder to spot.)

Another common example, in demographic data, is birthday: you might see no missing data but that 30% of your customers were all born on January 1st. The problem, of course, is we don't know which 0.3% were actually born on that day, and which 29.7% just haven't told us their birthday.

Now let's look at the correlation between variables. I am going to do this all H2O-side, and not download the data. As mentioned in the previous chapter, this means it will be Pearson correlation. (As we will see in a moment, our data is *not* normally distributed, so Spearman correlation would be more appropriate. I did also generate the Spearman correlations and, while the numbers are slightly different, the conclusions we draw are the same.)

In Python run train.cor().round(2) and in R round(h2.cor(train),2). If you run that you will see it has done correlations with the enum columns, which is just noise. (We already discussed how East doesn't have more direction than North, so obviously it cannot correlate with anything.) Here are a few lines of R to exclude those columns (setdiff is an R command to do boolean set logic, i.e., to subtract the contents of one vector from another). I also set some meaningful row names. The output is shown just after:

```
numericColumns <- setdiff(colnames(train),c("X6","X8"))
d <- round( h2o.cor(train[,numericColumns]) ,2)
rownames(d) <- colnames(d)
d

      X1    X2    X3    X4    X5   X7    Y1    Y2
X1  1.00 -0.99 -0.20 -0.86  0.82 0.00  0.61  0.62
X2 -0.99  1.00  0.19  0.87 -0.85 0.00 -0.65 -0.66
```

```
X3 -0.20  0.19  1.00 -0.31  0.29 0.01  0.47  0.44
X4 -0.86  0.87 -0.31  1.00 -0.97 0.00 -0.86 -0.86
X5  0.82 -0.85  0.29 -0.97  1.00 0.01  0.89  0.89
X7  0.00  0.00  0.01  0.00  0.01 1.00  0.28  0.22
Y1  0.61 -0.65  0.47 -0.86  0.89 0.28  1.00  0.98
Y2  0.62 -0.66  0.44 -0.86  0.89 0.22  0.98  1.00
```

We find that X1 and X2 have a perfect negative correlation; i.e., we could get rid of one or the other and we'd still have the same information. X4 and X5 are also very strongly negatively correlated to each other, and X2 and X4 have a very strong positive correlation. (X1 and X4 have the same correlation, but in the negative direction.) All these strong correlations between the *predictor variables* is bad for us: it means we don't have as much information to learn from as we hoped.

Y1 and Y2 are almost perfectly correlated, 0.98, implying that buildings that are expensive to heat in winter are also expensive to cool in summer, and vice versa: if a building is cheap to heat in winter it is cheap to cool in summer. Having said that, the paper said Y2 was harder to learn, and in a moment we will see that they have quite different frequency distributions. And some common sense tells us that breezy houses that are easy to keep cool in summer are rarely easier to keep warm in winter. The moral of the story of this paragraph is that correlations are like politicians: pay attention to them, but never fully trust them.

Some genuine good news is how well each field correlates with our chosen response variable, Y2. As shown in Figure 3-2, X5 and X4 correlate nicely, while X2, X1, and X3 are also all carrying a fair bit of information for us. Here is the Python code used to make it, which assumes train, x, and y are set as shown in Example 3-2:[5]

```python
import pandas as pd
import matplotlib.pyplot as plt

res = train[x].cor(train[y]).as_data_frame()
res.index = x
res.plot.barh()
plt.show()
```

---

5 See *building_energy_correlations.py*, in the online code, for the full Python script used to make this plot.

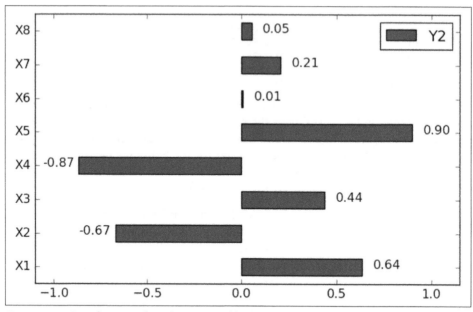

Figure 3-2. Correlations of predictor variables with Y2

Beyond the Maths: U-Values in UK and Greece

Let's leave the mathematical ivory tower of correlations between Xs, and take a moment to think about what they *mean*. X5 is the overall height, and has the highest positive correlation: taller buildings need more energy. X4 is the roof area, and it has the highest negative correlation. So the bigger the roof, the less energy it needs. (The buildings in this study have a constant volume, which is also why X5 and X4 are so strongly correlated.) X2 is surface area: the bigger the surface area of the building the less energy it needs. X3 is wall area: the more wall area the more energy. X7 is glazing area, so bigger windows need more energy.

Most of these were counterintuitive to this Brit, but again we have to go back to the paper to pick up some details, specifically the U-values. A U-value is a heat transfer coefficient; it is a measure of how good a building material is as an insulator. Low values are good. For instance, a single-glazed window might have a U-value of 5.0.[6] A solid brick wall has a U-value of 2.0, while an insulated cavity wall has a U-value of 0.18. An uninsulated roof has a U-value of 2.5, whereas, say, 225mm of sheep wool insulation reduces that to 0.15. Which is why, in the UK, cavity wall insulation and roof insulation have been strongly encouraged since the 1980s.

---

6 What that means is for every degree of difference, in celsius, between the inside and outside, 5W are transmitted per square meter. Modern double-glazing will be under 2.0, while the PassivHaus standard requires tripleglazing with a U-value under 0.8.

When we look at the paper, we see the houses in this study are in Greece and have a low U-value of 0.5 for the roof, but a much worse 1.78 for the walls. In other words, the walls are 3.5 times worse at stopping heat loss. So, tall houses with small roofs will need more heating than shorter houses with larger roofs. (In case you wondered, the U-value for the floors is 0.860, and 2.26 for the windows.) Intuition restored, let's move on.

The last thing I wanted to look at was the distributions, especially looking for bell-shaped curves that tell us a field is normally distributed. I used H2O's built-in histogram function, saving the need to download the data.

I wanted to control the appearance, so I first use `plot = FALSE` to tell `h2o.hist()` not to plot it. It returns a "histogram" object that I can pass to `plot()`, and this extra step allows me to set the main chart title (`main`), remove the x-axis label (`xlab`), which is the same text, and optionally control the y-axis scale (see note). The other thing this code shows is how to use R's `lapply` to loop through the columns. And I set `breaks = 30`, which gives more bars than the default, for a reason I'll come to in a moment:

```
par(mfrow = c(2 ,5))
ylim <- NULL
#ylim <- c(0, 350)
dummy <- lapply(colnames(train), function(col){
  h <- h2o.hist(train[,col], breaks = 30, plot = FALSE)
  plot(h, main = col, xlab = "", ylim = ylim)
  })
```

 Some R-specific things in that listing. The `par(mfrow = c(2, 5))` line tells it to plot them in a 5x2 grid. Also, if you set `ylim` to `c(0, 350)` you will get all 10 y-axes the same height. That is useful when you want to compare across columns, but I find the default y-axis scaling is better for when we are just interested in the shape of each column's histogram (as does setting a higher value for breaks). The `dummy` assignment is to suppress the meaningless output from `lapply()`.

The first thing Figure 3-3 screams at us, if we hadn't already looked at the paper, is the clustering of values, which tells us that most of these variables are more like ordered factors, not continuous numbers. This was why I set breaks higher than the default gave me: with fewer bars this is less clear.

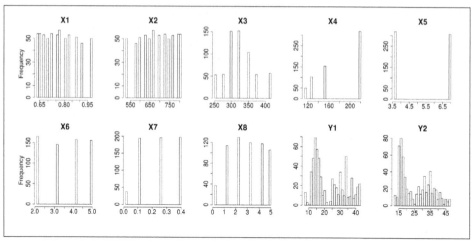

Figure 3-3. Per-column histograms (training data)

X3 (wall area) is the only one that looks even vaguely normally distributed. Looking at the last two charts, which are heating load and cooling load, we see that even these are not normally distributed. Useful knowledge to take with us.

About the Data Set

Data set citation: A. Tsanas, A. Xifara: *Accurate quantitative estimation of energy performance of residential buildings using statistical machine learning tools*, Energy and Buildings, Vol. 49, pp. 560-567, 2012.

It can also be found at: *http://bit.ly/2f8VDRZ.*

A paper studying it can be found at *http://bit.ly/2fAIKkb.*

There is some supplementary information here: *http://bit.ly/2g2Raj3.*

And here: *http://www.designingbuildings.co.uk/wiki/U-values.*

Data Set: Handwritten Digits

Our second data set, called the "MNIST data," dates back to 1998, and the task is to identify handwritten numbers. It is well-known, and there have been many different approaches over the years. It is typical of easy-for-humans-but-hard-for-machine problems. Another reason for choosing it is that there are lots of papers and code you can compare your own attempts with.

This data set is much larger, in all respects, than the previous building energy data set. For starters there are 785 columns. The final column is the correct answer, 0 to 9.

The first 784 are the 28x28 grid of grayscale pixels, and each is 0 (for white) through to 255 (for black).

Figure 3-4 shows the first 60 training samples, in graphical form. This is enough to appreciate the challenge here. 7s with and without a bar. 2s with and without a circle. One of the threes looks more like an "m." Different pen thicknesses. The 7 in the bottom right contains noise lines.

Figure 3-4. The first 60 MNIST training samples

Here is one of the rows (elided):

```
0,0,0,0,0,0,...0,0,26,133,32,0,0,0,0,0,0,0,0,62,220,25,0,0,0,
0,0,0,0,0,0,0,0,0,0,4,127,253,60,0,...,0,157,253,213,20,0,0,
0,0,45,85,167,253,253,229,55,0,...0,117,253,217,0,0,...,0,0,4
```

Most rows are mostly zeros. They are organized row-first, so the grid looks like this:

1	2	3	4	5	6	...	26	27	28
29	30	31	32	33	34	...	54	55	56
57	58	59	60	61	62	...	82	83	84
...	...	...	...	...	...	...	...	...	...
729	730	731	732	733	734	...	754	755	756
757	758	759	760	761	762	...	782	783	784

Another way this data set is larger is that we have 60,000 rows of training data, and 20,000 rows of test data (the data has already been split up). Finally, the files are heavier: 122MB in total, though "only" about 15MB compressed. Happily, H2O can read the compressed files directly. Yay.

Setup and Load

Examples 3-3 and 3-4 show the code to load the MNIST data set into H2O. Again, if using an interactive Python session you will need to set `path` yourself to the location of the data.

Example 3-3. Loading MNIST (in R)

```
library(h2o)
h2o.init(nthreads = -1, max_mem_size = "3G")

train60K <- h2o.importFile("../datasets/mnist.train.csv.gz")
test <- h2o.importFile("../datasets/mnist.test.csv.gz")

x <- 1:784
y <- 785

train60K[,y] <- as.factor(train60K[,y])
test[,y] <- as.factor(test[,y])

parts <- h2o.splitFrame(train60K, 1.0/6.0)
valid <- parts[[1]]
train <- parts[[2]]
rm(parts)
```

Example 3-4. Loading MNIST (in Python)

```
import os
import h2o
h2o.init(max_mem_size="3G")

path = os.path.dirname(__file__)
train60K = h2o.import_file( os.path.join(
  path, "../datasets/mnist.train.csv.gz") )
test = h2o.import_file( os.path.join(
  path, "../datasets/mnist.test.csv.gz") )

x = range(0,784)
y = 784

train60K[[y]] = train60K[[y]].asfactor()
test[[y]] = test[[y]].asfactor()

valid, train = train60K.split_frame([1.0/6.0])
```

This time, the data comes as two files: a training data set and a test data set. But no validation data set. I could use cross-validation, but there is plenty of data, so I have chosen to randomly split off 10,000 rows as validation data, and leave 50,000 as training data. (train60K is all 60,000, train is about 50,000, and valid is about 10,000 samples.)[7]

---

7 To get reproducible results, and exactly a 50K/10K split, I used a ratio of 0.1675 and a seed of 450.

---

x is set to be the first 784 columns, and y to be the final column. The final column looks like an integer, so it needs to be changed to be an enum (and remember to do this in both train60K and test). Notice that I use numeric indices, rather than named indices, for the columns. It is just easier when dealing with so many columns.

Taking a Look

With so many columns, I want to analyze with graphical methods as much as possible. The following couple of lines of R code make the averaged image shown in the left of Figure 3-5, and the next block of code makes the standard deviation representation, shown on the right:

```
avg <- matrix(h2o.mean(train60K[,x]), nrow = 28)
image(avg, col = grey(255:0/255))

avgsd <- matrix(sapply(x, function(x) h2o.sd(train60K[,x]) ), nrow = 28)
image(avgsd, col=grey(255:0/255))
```

The use of sapply() in the second block of code is required because h2o.sd() can only process one column of a data frame at a time. Using h2o.mean() took 0.05 seconds, while h2o.sd() in a loop took 90 seconds. The difference between one function call and 784 function calls! H2O's R API has an R-like apply(), but apply(train60K[,x], 2, sd) won't accept sd as the function.

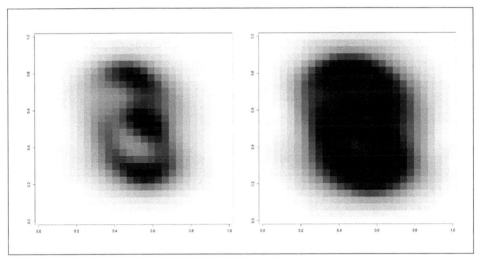

Figure 3-5. Mean (left) and standard deviation (right) of all the MNIST digits

This is telling me there are a lot of unused columns. I estimate we could drop half the columns and not really lose anything: useful to bear in mind if your learning algorithm struggles with lots of inputs. mean(h2o.mean(train2[,x]) > 16) is 0.42, meaning only 42% of the cells have an average value above 16 (on a scale of 0 to 255).

By the way, if you leave `ignore_const_cols` as the default of true, then it will automatically drop columns that are all exactly zero (67 of the 784 columns).

How does the data look if we split it up by each of the 10 digits? Let's show it in Python this time:

```
train60K.group_by(y).count().frame
```

It gives us the number of training samples we have for each digit:

```
C785 nrow_C1
0 5923
1 6742
2 5958
3 6131
4 5842
5 5421
6 5918
7 6265
8 5851
9 5949
```

We have a lot more "1"s than "5"s!

By the way, that one-liner is doing everything on the H2O cluster: `group_by()` does the same as an SQL GROUP BY—dividing the rows in `train60K` into 10 groups, based on the value of y. And then `count()` operates on each of those 10 groups. `.frame` returns a 10-row, 1-column H2O frame. So, even though it only has 10 rows, we should still be keeping in mind that this is data on the remote cluster, not the local client.

`count()` is not the only group operation available. At the time of writing, `count()`, `max()`, `mean()`, `min()`, `mode()`, `sd()`, `ss()`, `sum()`, and `var()` are available. Here is an example that gets the average of each digit:

```
avg = train60K.group_by(y).mean()
avg_pixels = avg.frame[:, 1:785].as_data_frame()
sorted_columns = sorted(avg_pixels.columns, key=lambda x: int(x[6:]))
avg_pixels = avg_pixels.reindex_axis(sorted_columns, axis=1)
```

The second line downloads just the pixel columns. The third and fourth lines are needed because `group_by(y)` does not preserve the order of the columns; normally this won't matter, but if I were to plot them (see Figure 3-6; the Python code to make this figure is online), the ordering becomes critical! The lambda is needed because the column names range from "mean_C1" to "mean_C784," so a normal lexicographic sort will not do the correct thing.

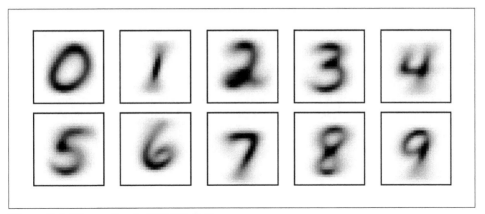

Figure 3-6. Mean of each MNIST digits

Helping the Models

Getting a perfect score on reading handwritten digits is going to be hard (even for Hero Of The Day, Deep Learning!).[8] However there are a couple of ways to help the algorithms get better results on this data set.

The first is to make more data. One of the problems we have is that each data sample is a noisy representation of the digit, and that the unseen test data set is going to contain bad handwriting we've never seen before. How about we take a guess what other types of bad handwriting there might be? We could repeat each of our 60,000 samples but rotated 1° clockwise. Or anticlockwise. Or stretched slightly in the horizontal direction. Or any direction. Or with a bit of random noise added to each pixel. You could make a near-infinite number of additional training samples.

Reasons to not do this? More work to generate those samples, more memory to store them, and then more time to train. But if every drop of quality matters, it is a good investment. "How Low Can You Go?" on page 265 at the very end of this book will look at these ideas again.

 More data samples can be as good as a better algorithm. Think of it as a general rule, and therefore be aware that it is not always the case. For further reading I like this article, More data or better models? (*http://bit.ly/2g08HXw*), as it covers both the reasons why more data can help and why it can hinder, and has good links if you want to study it deeper.

---

8 A good human will have an error rate of 0.2% or higher: some of the handwriting is atrocious, and some samples have extra lines or other noise.

The next thought: those 784 pixels are a 28x28 grid, but for all the machine learning attempts in this book we just give them as 784 inputs. How would *you* do if you were shown a 784-by-1-pixel image and asked to identify the digits? Badly. So we are giving the machines a much harder problem than it might appear—a pattern recognition problem that a human finds challenging. The best models for the MNIST data are those that try to allow for that 2D structure. With that in mind, I am going to do some very simple pre-processing to add some more columns (features). The columns are in four groups:

- 49, from dividing the grid into 4x4 blocks and taking the average of each block
- 36, from dividing the central 24x24 pixels into 4x4 blocks and, again, averaging
- 14, dividing into 2x24 pixel columns, and averaging
- 14, dividing into 24x2 pixel rows, and averaging

The second one differs from the first because I stripped away the 2-pixel border. This wasn't because the border is dull (though it is), or that we save 13 columns (though we do): it was about shifting the 4x4 blocks over 2 pixels and down 2 pixels, to get a different viewpoint. Looking at Figure 3-7 you can see the digits are still readable. If you wonder why the column and row averages might be useful, take a look at the horizontals for the three 7s: they have a pattern distinctive from all the other digits.

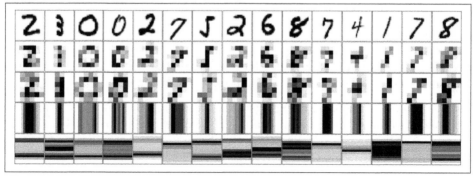

Figure 3-7. Pre-processing the digits

These additional 113 columns were added to the data frames in H2O,[9] then exported as three *csv* files, which you can find in the *datasets* directory:

- *mnist.enhanced_train.csv.gz*
- *mnist.enhanced_valid.csv.gz*

---

9 The code to make this is in *mnist_enhancer.R*, in the online files; that is also where you will find the code used to make the images in this section.

- *mnist.enhanced_test.csv.gz*

You can use them by loading `"load.mnist_enhanced.R"` instead of `"load.mnist.R"`; it is a drop-in replacement, defining `train`, `valid`, `test`, `x`, and `y`.

About the Data Set

Information on the data set, and a link to the 1998 paper (the first study of it) can be found here: *http://yann.lecun.com/exdb/mnist/index.html*.

Searching the Internet for "MNIST" and the name of a machine-learning algorithm will generally find at least one person who has tried that algorithm on the data set.

Data Set: Football Scores

The third data set we will look at here is very different again; a fun theme to allow us to look at some of the special issues when dealing with a time series. This data set will also involve more data preparation, and more knowledge engineering, than the previous two, which both came ready-made.[10]

We will be trying to predict football (soccer) match scores. There will be three main types of input data:

- The first is the match scores and stats.
- The second is the betting odds before the match.
- The third is team strength before each match.

Most of the hard work for the first two has been done by our data source, which is the Football Data repository on GitHub (*https://github.com/jokecamp/FootballData*). Specifically, we will be using the *football-data.co.uk/england* (*http://bit.ly/2flwbX0*) directory.

That repository has data for all the European leagues, in the same format. So it would be interesting to test your best model, built on British football data on, say, the German or Italian leagues. If you try it, let us know how it goes!

---

10 And cause flashbacks to the quote in an earlier chapter: 80% of a data scientist's time is spent on data preparation, the other 20% is spent on moaning about it.

There is data of every football match played in the top four or five divisions in England and Wales, from 1993 to the end of the 2015 season (at the time of writing). Here is what a sample row from *2014-2015/Premier.csv* looks like:

```
E0,16/08/14,Arsenal,Crystal Palace,2,1,H,1,1,D,
J Moss,14,4,6,2,13,19,9,3,2,2,0,1,1.25,6.5,15,
1.25,5.5,12,1.3,5,9,1.25,6,13,1.26,6.45,14.01,
1.25,5.5,12,1.25,5.75,12,1.25,6.25,10.5,50,1.3,
1.25,6.7,5.96,16,12.43,48,1.77,1.72,2.26,2.1,
24,-1.5,1.81,1.78,2.2,2.1
```

That is all one line, and just one match! You can probably work out that it was a match played on August 16th, 2014, between Arsenal (at home) and Crystal Palace. The score was 2-1. But what about all those other columns? Here is the full list (when H is used for "home side," and A for "away side," I've combined them in one entry).

Div
Which division. E0 is the Premier League, E1 is the Championship (previously Division 1), E2 is League 1 (previously Division 2), E3 is League 2 (previously Division 3), and EC is the Conference. Conference data is only available since the 2005/2006 season.

Date
When the match was played. DD/MM/YY format.

HomeTeam
Text string of the team playing at home.

AwayTeam
Text string of the away team.

FTHG/FTAG
Full-Time Home side's Goals. Full-Time Away side's Goals.

FTR
Full-Time Result: H is home team win, A is away team win, and D is draw.

HTHG/HTAG
The score at half-time.

HTR
Who was winning at half-time. Same H/D/A value as for FTR.

Referee
Text string for the name of the referee.

HS/AS
Shots by each side.

HST/AST

Shots on target by each side. Therefore, HST ≤ HS and AST ≤ AS.

HF/AF

Fouls done by each side.

HC/AC

Corners received by each side.

HY/AY

Yellow cards received by each side.

HR/AR

Red cards received by each side.

We're only a third of the way, but take a quick breather. Deep breath. In, 1, 2. And out, 1, 2. The previous columns were all about the match. The remaining ones are all to do with the pre-match betting. I'm deliberately not going into any more details about the odds; all we need to know is that a *lower* number means the bookmakers think that that event is *more* likely to happen:

B365H/B365D/B365A

Bet365 odds of home-win, draw, or away-win.

BWH/BWD/BWA

Bet&Win odds of home-win, draw, or away-win.

IWH/IWD/IWA

Interwetten odds of home-win, draw, or away-win.

LBH/LBD/LBA

Ladbrokes odds of home-win, draw, or away-win.

PSH/PSD/PSA

Pinnacle Sports odds of home-win, draw, or away-win.

WHH/WHD/WHA

William Hill odds of home-win, draw, or away-win.

SJH/SJD/SJA

Stan James odds of home-win, draw, or away-win.

VCH/VCD/VCA

VC Bet odds of home-win, draw, or away-win.

Another breather. These are the odds from eight different bookmakers. That is quite a lot of redundancy, not to mention that any two of the three odds implies the third.

To set their initial odds those bookmakers will be using a model similar to what we are going to build; they will also be looking at each other's odds and adjusting accordingly. However, don't forget this is big business, not sheltered academia, and it is market-driven: if customers (*punters* in British English) are betting on the less favored team the bookmaker will shorten the odds on them; if it gets extreme enough then the weaker team may even become the favorite. For our purposes, this Stupid Punter Effect adds additional noise to the data.

Our bookmaker odds are a snapshot, taken no later than 5 p.m. British local time on the Friday afternoon before the weekend games (and by 3 p.m. Tuesday for mid-week games). That is quite close to the game, so we should expect them to be accurate predictors.

The remaining columns in our data all come from BetBrain (don't feel bad, I hadn't heard of them either), which combines odds from a large number of bookmakers:

Bb1X2
> The number of BetBrain bookmakers used to calculate the following maximum and average columns. The sample row shown earlier had 50 bookmakers.

BbMxH/BbAvH
> The maximum, and average, home-win odds. For the Arsenal versus Crystal Palace row that we showed earlier, the maximum is 1.3, and the average is 1.25.

BbMxD/BbAvD
> The maximum, and average, odds of a draw. Our sample row had 6.7 and 5.96, respectively.

BbMxA/BbAvA
> The maximum, and average, odds of an away win. Our sample row had 16 and 12.43. (These bookies really don't fancy Crystal Palace's chances, do they!)

BbOU
> The number of BetBrain bookmakers used to calculate the following columns.

BbMx>2.5/BbAv>2.5
> Best, and average, odds for more than 2.5 goals[11] in the match.

---

11 Strange terminology, as there are no half-goals in football, but apparently the average game of football has about 2.5 goals per match.

BbMx<2.5/BbAv<2.5

Best, and average, odds for fewer than 2.5 goals in the match. Our sample row had (average) odds of 3+ goals as 1.72, and only 0, 1, or 2 goals being scored as 2.1. Meaning, they think it is close, but 3+ goals is more likely. The final score was 2-1, so they were right. (The bookies were also right about the winner.)

BbAH

Number of BetBrain bookmakers used to calculate the following Asian handicaps (*https://en.wikipedia.org/wiki/Asian_handicap*). Our sample row had 24, half the number of the earlier odds, but still quite a lot.[12]

BbAHh

Size of handicap for the home team. In our sample row this is `-1.5`. That means the away team are given a 1½ goal handicap. (It is never an integer: the purpose of the handicap is to make draws impossible.) Home wins are more common than away wins, so we expect this handicap to be negative more often than it is positive.

BbMxAHH/BbAvAHH

Best, and average, Asian handicap home-team odds. In our sample row the average is 1.78.

BbMxAHA/BbAvAHA

Best, and average, Asian handicap away-team odds. Our row has average of 2.1. This is higher than 1.78, meaning that, even with the 1.5 goal handicap, the home team are still considered more likely to win. (They were wrong this time; after applying the handicap the final score was ½ - 1.)

Correlations

Things will get complex in a moment, but before we get there I want to do some initial analysis on just the 2013-2014 year (2,588 samples).[13] I'm especially curious about the correlations between all those very similar columns.

---

12 Curiously, the first listed match in the relatively unfollowed League Two, Accrington versus Southend, still gets 22 bookmakers following it; football betting has very little to do with football supporting!

13 I've chosen this season as it is recent but also because it is *not* the season I intend to use for test data.

Load the data with Example 3-5; you can find the Python version in the online code (*load.football_2013_2014.py*), and I won't be going through it line by line, here. The bits that look complex are generally about chopping that long *csv* line into the following data sets:

betsH

> The various bookmakers' odds for a home win. It includes both the maximum and average columns.

betsD

> The bookmakers' odds for a draw.

betsA

> The bookmakers' odds for an away win.

abets

> The Asian betting odds.

stats

> The statistics about each game. The half-time and full-time results are converted to a number, where 3 is a home win, 2 is a draw, 1 is an away win. (Conveniently, that can be used as higher means the home team was stronger.)

Example 3-5. Loading raw data for 2013-2014 (in R)

```
library(h2o)
h2o.init(nthreads = -1)

data <- h2o.importFolder("../datasets/england/2013-2014/")
betsH <- data[,c( ((1:8)*3)+21, 49, 50)]
betsD <- data[,c( ((1:8)*3)+22, 51, 52)]
betsA <- data[,c( ((1:8)*3)+23, 53, 54)]
abets <- data[,c(56:59, 61:65)]
stats <- data[,c(5:10, 12:23)]
stats[,c("FTR", "HTR")] <- as.numeric(stats[,c("FTR", "HTR")])
```

betsH, betsD, betsA each have 10 columns, abets has 9 columns, and stats has 18 columns.

We expect strong correlations between betting odds; if not there are *arbitrage* opportunities (*https://en.wikipedia.org/wiki/Arbitrage_betting*), implying the bookmakers are asleep at the wheel. This code gives us all the correlations:

```
d <- as.matrix(betsD)
d <- d[complete.cases(d),]
cor(d)
```

The `as.matrix()` call *downloads* the data from the H2O cluster into an R variable (it is just a thin wrapper around the `as.data.frame()` we've used before). I then use an R idiom to throw away rows that have an NA (missing data) in any column. That is, we only consider matches that were covered by all bookmakers. Rather than show you the output of that, which is just a table of numbers, Figure 3-8 shows the output of R's `pairs()` command.[14] It is showing the correlation in the upper triangle, while the lower triangle shows the scatterplot for each pair of columns.

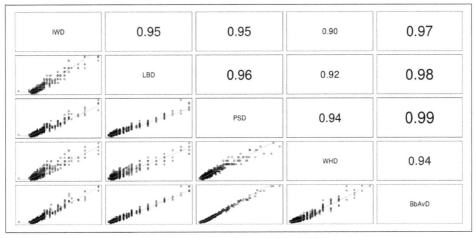

Figure 3-8. Correlations between different bookmakers' odds of a draw

This kind of chart can feel like information overload the first time you see one, but here are some things to pay attention to:

- Perfect correlation is a straight diagonal line. BbAvD (the average of multiple bookmakers) has the neatest lines, and highest correlations. This hints that we could just keep BbAvH, BbAvD, and BbAVA and drop all the other betting odds?
- Most bookmakers correlate well when the odds are low, and less well when the odds get high, as shown by the flaring in the upper-right of each scatterplot.
- IWD has an outlier: the one point on the far left. It appears to be a single bad row, maybe a typo in data entry, not a systematic problem.
- WHD correlates (relatively) poorly. But only for a draw: WHH and WHL are all 0.98s and 0.99s.

---

14 See *analyze_football_bet_correlations.R* in the online code for the exact command that was run.

By the way, I downloaded the data because I wanted to run `pairs()`; if I just wanted the correlations I could have used `h2o.cor(betsD, use="complete.obs")`. I chose `betsD` to show here, as `betsH` and `betsA` were less interesting: all their correlations are 0.97 or above (as expected). And I actually ran `pairs(d[,c(3:6,10)])` as using all 10 bookmakers made the diagram a bit cramped for publication here, and those were the most interesting five.

For reference here is how to do something similar in Python; I've included some lines to load the data, taken from *load.football_2013_2014.py*, so that it is self-contained. I find `scatter_matrix()` less customizable than R's `pairs()`, so all plots in this section were made with the latter:

```
import os, h2o
import pandas as pd
import matplotlib.pyplot as plt
data = h2o.import_file("../datasets/england/2013-2014/")
betsD = data[ range(24, 46, 3) + [50, 51] ]

d = betsD.as_data_frame()
pd.tools.plotting.scatter_matrix(d)
plt.show()
```

What about correlations within `abets`? Figure 3-9 shows:

- The four columns to do with ≥3 goals versus ≤2 goals correlate just about perfectly among themselves, but hardly at all with the other columns.

- The handicap column correlates poorly with all other `abets` columns.

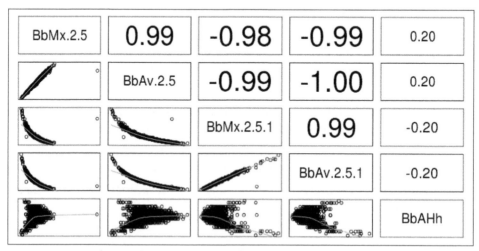

Figure 3-9. Correlations between the Asian betting columns

Home win versus away win of the handicapped result has almost perfect negative correlation (–0.99). It correlates hardly at all with the other columns, which is why I excluded it from the plot.

By the way, notice how the scatterplots, especially in the top left, have a curve. This is why I used method="spearman" for those correlation numbers. For instance, for the average odds of ≥3 and ≤2 goals, it made the difference between –1.00 with the Spearman method and –0.945 with the default Pearson method.

What about the match statistics: cor(stats)? That gives a lot of columns, and a lot of noise, so I'm not even bothering with a diagram. Full-time goals correlates with half-time goals, for each team, with about 0.670. The full-time result and half-time result correlate with 0.587. Shots (AS/HS) and shots-on-target (AST/HST) correlate with 0.630. Everything else gets a bit tenuous.

There is one more I want to try. This looks at correlations between the match result ("FTR" is Full-Time Result), the (average) bookies' expectations of a home win ("BbAvH"), and the Asian Betting handicap ("BbAHh"). Just three columns, so Figure 3-10 is a bit easier on the eyes.

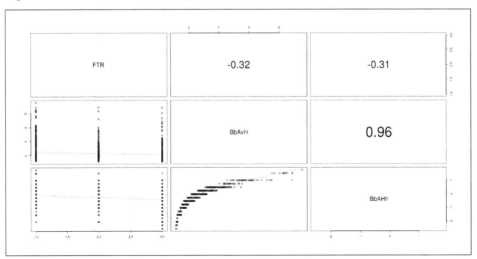

Figure 3-10. Correlations between match odds and final result

The handicap column and other betting odds have a strong positive correlation, but their correlation with the actual result is a mere –0.3. (It is a negative correlation because we used a *higher* FTR to mean the home team was better, but both BbAvH and BbAHh are *lower* when there is a higher probability of a home win.) But that is important: it tells us there is a fair bit of unpredictability in results, and these domain experts get it wrong a lot of the time. Can we make a model that does better?

Missing Data... And Yet More Columns

The most recent files have all the columns shown in the previous section. But the first few rows in *1993-1994/Premier.csv* present a stark contrast:

```
Div,Date,HomeTeam,AwayTeam,FTHG,FTAG,FTR,,,,,,,,,,,,,,,,,,,,,
E0,14/08/93,Arsenal,Coventry,0,3,A,,,,,,,,,,,,,,,,,,,,,
E0,14/08/93,Aston Villa,QPR,4,1,H,,,,,,,,,,,,,,,,,,,,,
```

So, we thought we had over twenty years of rich data, but in fact a third of it is just match results. 1995-1996 adds half-time scores (but only in *Premier.csv*, not the other files). Only when we get to 2000-2001 do we get the full range of columns. But we also get a spanner in the works. Here is the first row of *2000-2001/Premier.csv*:

```
Div,Date,HomeTeam,AwayTeam,FTHG,FTAG,FTR,HTHG,HTAG,HTR,
Attendance,Referee,HS,AS,HST,AST,HHW,AHW,HC,AC,HF,AF,
HO,AO,HY,AY,HR,AR,HBP,ABP,GBH,GBD,GBA,IWH,IWD,IWA,
LBH,LBD,LBA,SBH,SBD,SBA,WHH,WHD,WHA
```

Spot the problem?

Attendance, that's the problem. Not just attendance, but HHW/AHW, HO/AO, and HBP/ABP. Seven new fields not in the 2013-2014 data! It turns out these only appear in 2000-2001 and 2001-2002. They have these meanings:

Attendance
How many people turned up to watch.

HHW/AHW
Hit (the) Woodwork. That is, almost scored, but the ball hit the goal posts or crossbar.

HO/AO
Number of offsides by each side.

HBP/ABP
Team booking points (10 for yellow, 25 for red).

In addition, the odds section is different, with only three bookmakers in common. There is quite a lot of variation in active bookmakers, year to year. All those differences make our life harder, as we shall see shortly in "Setup and Load" on page 81.

How to Train and Test?

Before we look at how to load the data we need to decide what will be our training data, what will be the validation data, and what will be the test data. Take a moment (or two) to ponder the differences, for time-series data, between:

- Random sampling test rows

- Fine-grained stratification (e.g., use every fifth match as test data)
- Test on most recent (e.g., 2014–2015 onwards as test data)

Think about a production system, where we want to predict the result of next weekend's matches. The "test" data equates to what we want our production system to spit out. So, generally, with time-series data, you want to use the third approach: train on the old data, test on the new data. The same thought process applies for validation data, so by keeping training data before validation data before test data, we have the best chance of being kept honest.

Setup and Load

My initial plan was to use H2O's `h2o.importFolder()` function. It will load all files in a directory tree and merge all files into a single data frame. The `pattern` argument allows you to specify only a subset of the files to be loaded. So the code was going to be:

```
data <- h2o.importFolder("/path/to/england", pattern="[.]csv$", header=TRUE )
```

You already saw `h2o.importFolder()` in action in "Correlations" on page 75 (Example 3-5). But, when we try to apply it to *all* years, as here, it complains with `"Column names do not match between files."` If you try with `header=FALSE`, the error is `"Files conflict in number of columns. 21 versus 28."` However, if you look over on Flow you will see the files are all there. I previously glossed over a detail of how H2O loading works: under the surface it is a two-step process. First the file's raw bytes are loaded, then they are parsed. If you have tried importing a file using Flow you will have seen this two-step process made explicit. We can do the two-step process explicitly from our client, and successfully load all files, as follows:

```
fh <- h2o.importFolder("/path/to/england", pattern="[.]csv$", parse=FALSE)
dataList <- lapply(fh, h2o.parseRaw)
```

But, there is a difference between `data` in the first example and `dataList` in the second, and the clue is in the name. When `h2o.importFolder()` does both the load and the parse, it returns a single data frame, a merger of all *csv* files. When you just use it to load, and then run `h2o.parseRaw()` on each file, you get a list: one data frame per file. But we want a single data frame. Therefore we use `h2o.rbind()` to merge them together: `do.call(h2o.rbind,dataList)`. But, then we get `"rbind frames must have all the same columns, found 65 and 28 columns."` and realize we have spent a lot of time and effort getting nowhere.

Yoga, a run in the mountains, gargling your national anthem with a favorite hot beverage... they are all solutions to the stress this creates, but each has its downside (the need to be flexible, the need for nearby mountains, the need for a clean shirt), so let's persevere with a programmatic solution.

We can choose from:

- Merge the *csv* files in advance, with language/tool of choice.
- Add the missing columns in H2O, to each frame, before joining them.
- Get someone else to sort it out for you.

You can use the third option, as there are ready-made files in the *"datasets/"* directory. I gave the second option a try, but gave up. The data manipulation tools in H2O, at least at the moment, are not quite up to the job. The moral of the story is to use the best tool for the job, so reach for Python, R, Excel, or whatever you are most comfortable with. I wrote a script, in PHP (see *code/organize_football_files.php* in the online files[15]), to remake each *csv* file, so they all have the same set of columns; I then used some shell commands to cat them together into train, valid, and test *csv* files. The whole process takes less than three seconds.

The Other Third

Earlier in this chapter, so far back it may be long forgotten, replaced in your mind with new concepts such as Asian Betting and Hitting The Woodwork, I said our third source of data would be team strength. This is where we put our knowledge engineering hat on. There is *so* much that can be done here, from hunting for data sources on players, to sentiment mining social media and the news, to sophisticated moving averages. I will keep it relatively simple. Though I'd be very interested to hear about what features you add.[16]

The first set of fields to add are the match stats from each team's most recent match. I have low expectations of its utility: how many corners a side got as much depends on who they played as it does on some innate team quality. In other words, we are taking the data out of context. But it is relatively easy to get, so let's try.

The second set of fields are recent performance. The first of these is very simple: +1 if they won their last match, 0 if it was a draw, –1 if they lost. Then there are two moving averages (see the sidebar "The Art of the Moving Average" on page 83): over the last 5 matches, and over the last 20 matches. Teams play 38 to 46 matches in a season, so 20 matches is about half a season, and should be a good proxy for underlying team quality. The most recent match is a proxy for star players being injured or banned, and things like the boost to morale that a win can give. Five matches represents approximately the last month, and is a blend of team quality and team morale.

---

15 Check the site for scripts in other languages, and if you write one yourself, please do a pull request so it can be added.

16 Well, that was me being polite. What I really mean is to only let me know if you added features that made the models *better*. Keep your failures to yourself.

By the way, I will treat the entire data history as a single time series. The problem with this approach is that clubs move between leagues at the end of a season. For example, a losing streak leads to demotion. In the new division they are the strongest, but our moving average claims they are the weakest. The alternative is to calculate moving averages on a per-season basis, but then you end up with NAs for the first 5 and 20 matches of each season. You are clever, and your mind is already buzzing with clever workarounds—I can hear it from here. But don't prematurely optimize: if our model's performance is not notably better in the late part of a season compared to the early part, then getting clever here should not be our highest priority.

The Art of the Moving Average

In the world of finance, and in particular the area known as technical trading, moving averages are everywhere. The SMA (simple moving average) is the only one we use in this book, but the EMA (exponential moving average—full data history is used, but the most recent values have most weight) is also popular and there are a whole host of other weighted and smoothed moving averages. My personal rule: use an SMA unless you can come up with a good reason not to.

You will also see the concept of the moving standard deviation. A current value can then be measured in the number of standard deviations it is above or below the moving average over some time span. If you believe a stock is *mean-reverting*, then you should buy when the stock is notably below the moving average, and short when notably above.[17] The other concept used a lot in finance is *crossover*. One type is when a moving average crosses from above or below the current price; another is when moving averages of different periods cross (e.g., a 20-day moving average crosses a 100-day moving average). In both cases they suggest to a trader that a trend has ended, and the price direction will reverse.

Ideally our model will work these concepts out for itself. But such an ideal world often also needs near-infinite data samples, CPU, and memory. So, when dealing with time-series data, keep these concepts in your toolbox; think of them as hints you can give your learning models. If the hint doesn't help (low variable importance) simply remove it again.

I am not going to show the code to create the new columns, but look in the online code repository for the script(s). Hopefully by the time you read this there will be a version in your favorite language (if not, how about contributing one)? If you are using R, look at xts (*https://cran.r-project.org/package=xts*) and its rollMean() func-

---

17 Before you go and lose your life-savings in the stock market, I'll quickly point out that this is the exact opposite of what you want to do if you believe a stock is *trending*. As if that wasn't enough of a challenge, a price stream can be trending at some time scales and mean-reverting at others.

tion; in Python, `convolve()` from the numpy library can be used to make moving averages.

 It has a bug: I foolishly used zero for entries where there was no data (mostly the pre-2000 data), when I should have used a blank field. A blank field would get imported as a NA, a nan in Python, and get ignored, while a zero looks like real data. After some consideration, I left it in as a "deliberate" bug, because in Chapter 9 it gives us a good example and, as we will see there, it turns out not to matter in the end.

Three files have been made: *football.train.csv*, *football.valid.csv*, and *football.test.csv*. Valid and test are the two most recent seasons, and train is all the earlier data. The columns that have been added are:

HS1
The shots by the current home side, in their previous match (whether they were the home or away side in that previous match).

AS1
The shots by the current away side, in their previous match.

HST1/AST1
Shots on target in the previous match.

HF1/AF1
Fouls in the previous match.

HC1/AC1
Corners in the previous match.

HY1/AY1
Yellow cards in the previous match.

HR1/AR1
Red cards in the previous match.

res1H/res1A
The last result for the home and away sides: −1, 0 or +1.

res5H/res5A
Average of the last 5 results: −1.0 to +1.0.

res20H/res20A
Average of the last 20 results: −1.0 to +1.0.

As you should expect (because every winner creates a loser) the res5 and res20 variables are normally distributed, around a mean of zero,[18] with a higher standard deviation for res5.

 As you add new fields, jot down expectations. They are a good way to catch bugs in your models.

Taking that tip further, another good way to check your models for bugs is to add a field that is completely random and make sure it is the least important variable in your model. (You might need to run the models a few times and average the result, to allow for random variation.) If it ends up in with a bunch of other predictor variables, it implies those are also random. I wouldn't be surprised to see HC1 or AY1 there. But if I saw res5H as having no more predictive value than a random variable I would be suspicious and take a deeper look.

Similarly, cheat: add a field that is just some simple mathematical operation of the response variable, and make sure it is not just top of variable importance, but that the model quickly learns perfectly. (Just remember to remove it again!) If not, look for bugs in your scripts. For example, are you training on a different data set by mistake?

Missing Data (Again)

Decision tree machine-learning algorithms cope fairly well with missing data, but deep learning will struggle a bit, and then at the other extreme linear models will simply ignore whole rows where any field is an NA. That is going to cause us problems, because there is quite a lot of missing data.

However, I am not going to explain, here, how the missing data is dealt with, leaving that for "Missing Data" on page 237 in Chapter 9. All I am going to do here is say that in the *datasets* directory you will find alternative versions of our three files that no longer have missing data; the format is the same, no new or removed columns:

- *football.train2.csv*
- *football.valid2.csv*
- *football.test2.csv*

---

18 You might notice the mean is not exactly zero. This is because it is not a closed system: clubs can fall out of the bottom league. Club name changes and bankruptcies also distort the stats.

The code to load either version is shown in a moment. The decision tree variants, random forest, and GBM (gradient boosting machines) use the original data described in this chapter, but GLM (generalized linear models) and deep learning will use these alternative versions.

Setup and Load (Again)

Phew! Almost there! Now that we have a nicely organized data set, what shall we do with it? The obvious one would be to predict the win/draw/loss. But that is three outcomes, and our MNIST data set is also a multinomial classification problem. Instead, I would like to show binomial classification (also called logistic regression) in this book.

We could predict win versus non-win, from the home team's point of view. That is, a draw or away win counts as a failure. To see why we'd do that, here is the breakdown of the FTR column in `train`:

- H:18336 (45%)
- D:11189 (27.5%)
- A:11179 (27.5%)

That is, the home-team advantage is huge (45% versus 27.5%). When we consider home-win versus not-home-win it is 45% versus 55%, so it turns out to be a fairly balanced binomial classification problem. Another idea is to predict *score draws*, those matches where the result is a draw, but not 0-0. This is a harder problem, and is not considered any further in this book. Example 3-6 prepares the ground for any of those three choices: just uncomment the y line for what you want the model to learn.

Something we need to be aware of is the difference in the H/D/A breakdown in the different data sets. The valid and test sets have a notably lower win rate for home sides.[19] What does this mean for us? The simplest possible algorithm that looks at the training data and thinks, always choose not-home-win, and goes away happy with being right 55% of the time, will score an even higher 57.3% on the test data, and 57.9% on the valid data. That imbalance might cause problems.

---

19 Yes, strictly, I shouldn't be looking at the test set here. But I thought it important for interpreting model results.

	train	train2	valid	test
	1993–2013	2000–2013	2013–2014	2014–2015
Home Win	45.0%	44.6%	42.1%	42.6%
Draw	27.5%	27.2%	27.0%	26.2%
Away Win	27.5%	28.2%	30.9%	31.1%

Example 3-6. Loading football data (in R)

```
library(h2o)
h2o.init(nthreads = -1, max_mem_size = "3G")

train <- h2o.importFile("../datasets/football.train.csv")
valid <- h2o.importFile("../datasets/football.valid.csv")
test <- h2o.importFile("../datasets/football.test.csv")

train$HomeWin <- as.factor(train$FTR == "H")
valid$HomeWin <- as.factor(valid$FTR == "H")
test$HomeWin <- as.factor(test$FTR == "H")

train$ScoreDraw <- as.factor(train$FTHG > 0 & train$FTHG == train$FTAG)
valid$ScoreDraw <- as.factor(valid$FTHG > 0 & valid$FTHG == valid$FTAG)
test$ScoreDraw <- as.factor(test$FTHG > 0 & test$FTHG == test$FTAG)

statFields <- c(
  "FTHG", "FTAG", "FTR", "HTHG", "HTAG", "HTR",
  "HS", "AS", "HST", "AST", "HF", "AF",
  "HC", "AC", "HY", "AY", "HR", "AR",
  "HomeWin", "ScoreDraw"
  )
ignoreFields <- c("Date", "HomeTeam", "AwayTeam", statFields)

x <- setdiff(colnames(train), ignoreFields)

xNoOdds <- c(
  "Div", "HS1", "AS1", "HST1", "AST1",
  "HF1", "AF1", "HC1", "AC1", "HY1", "AY1", "HR1", "AR1",
  "res1H", "res1A", "res5H", "res5A", "res20H", "res20A"
  )

#y <- "FTR"   #3-value multinomial
#y <- "ScoreDraw"   #Unbalanced binomial
y <- "HomeWin" #Balanced binomial
```

To load the version without any missing data, just change the three `h2o.import File()` lines to load `"football.train2.csv"` instead of `"football.train.csv"`, and the same for valid and test. The same goes for the Python version (Example 3-7).

I will not go through the listings in detail, because you have seen it all before. I give H2O 3GB of memory, but you can get by with less (I ran out of memory with only

1GB when making many model variations). HomeWin and ScoreDraw get created as enum fields, where 0 means false, 1 means true. For ScoreDraw, the & does a logical AND on two temporary one-column H2O frames, to create another temporary frame, which is then turned into a factor, then copied into our main H2O frame. The extra parentheses shown in the Python version are required.

x is defined to be all fields, except those that would not be known in advance. And then xNoOdds is the same but excludes all the betting odd fields. It ought to be much easier to predict a home win when we have a bank of experts first telling us their prediction, so this sets things up to try it both ways.

Example 3-7. Loading football data (in Python)

```python
import os
import h2o
h2o.init(max_mem_size="3G")

path = os.path.dirname(__file__)
train = h2o.import_file( os.path.join(
  path, "../datasets/football.train.csv") )
valid = h2o.import_file( os.path.join(
  path, "../datasets/football.valid.csv") )
test = h2o.import_file( os.path.join(
  path, "../datasets/football.test.csv") )

train["HomeWin"] = (train["FTR"] == "H").asfactor()
valid["HomeWin"] = (valid["FTR"] == "H").asfactor()
test["HomeWin"] = (test["FTR"] == "H").asfactor()

train["ScoreDraw"] = (
  (train["FTHG"] > 0) & (train["FTHG"] == train["FTAG"])
  ).asfactor()
valid["ScoreDraw"] = (
  (valid["FTHG"] > 0) & (valid["FTHG"] == valid["FTAG"])
  ).asfactor()
test["ScoreDraw"] = (
  (test["FTHG"] > 0) & (test["FTHG"] == test["FTAG"])
  ).asfactor()

statFields = [
  "FTHG", "FTAG", "FTR", "HTHG", "HTAG", "HTR",
  "HS", "AS", "HST", "AST", "HF", "AF",
  "HC", "AC", "HY", "AY", "HR", "AR",
  "HomeWin", "ScoreDraw"
  ]
ignoreFields = ["Date", "HomeTeam", "AwayTeam"] + statFields

x = [i for i in train.names if i not in ignoreFields]

xNoOdds = [
```

```
   "Div", "HS1", "AS1", "HST1", "AST1",
   "HF1", "AF1", "HC1", "AC1", "HY1", "AY1", "HR1", "AR1",
   "res1H", "res1A", "res5H", "res5A", "res20H", "res20A"
   ]

#y = "FTR"  #3-value multinomial
#y = "ScoreDraw"  #Unbalanced binomial
y = "HomeWin" #Balanced binomial
```

About the Data Set

This book's GitHub repository is the canonical data source in this case. The data prior to being manipulated was downloaded from the Football Data repository on GitHub (*https://github.com/jokecamp/FootballData*). All code and data there is under the MIT license. They, in turn, give the following data sources: International Soccer Server, European Football, RSSSF Archive, TBWSport, and Livescore.

Summary

In this chapter we looked at three delightfully different data sets. The first two came to us perfectly formed, but the third was more of a struggle, wasn't it? However, this is more typical of real-world data science. Don't just get used to it, learn to love the struggle.

We built scripts to load each of them, and then did a bit of analysis of the columns (the features) in each data set, and for the handwritten digits and the football data, added some additional features. The latter will hopefully help the models, and the former was to train our intuition, and tell us what to watch out for.

For the building energy data, the main challenge is going to be the small number of data samples, and the way each predictor field is discontinuous. When we take data subsets they can easily become unrepresentative. For the MNIST data the main challenge is that those pesky kids[20] don't all have exactly the same handwriting. And that a row of 784 pixels are very low-level features to learn from; our 113 added features were easy to add but still crude. The biggest challenge with the football data will be that it is just plain hard to predict the outcome of 22 men kicking a ball about for 90 minutes, summed up in Figure 3-10, where we saw that the human experts (the bookmakers) only managed a 0.3 correlation with the match results.

We are almost ready to build models. The next chapter is going to take you on a tour of H2O functionality, and parameters you can tune, common to all the algorithms. Then after that we will have four chapters of machine learning.

---

20 50% of the data came from American high school students.

CHAPTER 4

Common Model Parameters

One of the things that makes the H2O APIs so pleasant to use is that each of the machine learning algorithms have much of their interface in common. Later chapters will look at one algorithm at a time, and show how to use them on each of our example data sets. Rather than repeat the same thing in each of those chapters, a lot of the common functionality will be here.

The Python API is object-oriented, which complicates things for this chapter: most of the parameters described here are given when creating the *estimator* object, but a few are given when calling train() on that object. The latter ones will be pointed out as we go.

The R API (and the underlying REST API) take all parameters in one go.

Each machine learning algorithm will be introduced in its own chapter, but here are their one-line descriptions:

Random Forest
An ensemble (a team) of decision trees. Parameters that apply to it are marked with RF.

GBM
Gradient Boosting Machines. Another ensemble of decision trees, but with a different approach to random forest. Indicated with GBM.

GLM

Generalized Linear Models. A linear model is the idea of drawing the best straight line through data points. The generalized bit allows it to handle some nonlinearity. Indicated with `GLM`.

Deep Learning

Multilayer neural networks, consisting of neurons in layers, and weighted connections between them. The quality improves by showing the training data over and over: each pass of the training data is called an epoch. Parameters are marked with `DL`.

Supported Metrics

H2O supports a number of metrics, ways to measure a model's usefulness. Before we get into parameters it is worth taking a look at them because when we talk about "scoring a model" we mean evaluating on one of these metrics. The only place you specify them directly when making a model is stopping_metric, which is described later in this chapter in "Early Stopping" on page 99. But you have additional choices for sorting grids (described in "Grid Search" on page 122), or when you script custom report views.

Most only apply to either regression (predicting a continuous number) or classification (predicting a category), so they have been organized that way here.

Regression Metrics

There are two choices for early stopping:

MSE

Mean Squared Error. The "squared" bit means the bigger the error, the more it is punished. If your correct answers are 2,3,4 and your algorithm guesses 1,4,3, the absolute error on each one is exactly 1, so squared error is also 1, and the MSE is 1. But if your algorithm guesses 2,3,6, the errors are 0,0,2, the squared errors are 0,0,4, and the MSE is a higher 1.333.

deviance

Actually short for mean residual deviance. If the distribution is gaussian, then it is equal to MSE, and when not it usually gives a more useful estimate of error, which is why it is the default. Needs to be specified as "residual_deviance" when sorting grids.

In reports you might also see:

RMSE

The square root of MSE. If your response variable units are dollars, the units of MSE is dollars-squared, but RMSE is back into dollars.

MAE

Mean Absolute Error. Following on from the MSE example, a guess of 1,4,3 has absolute errors of 1, so the MAE is 1. But 2,3,6 has absolute errors of 0,0,2 so the MAE is 0.667. As with RMSE, the units are the same as your response variable.

R2

R-squared, also written as R^2, and also known as the coefficient of determination. This used to be available as a choice for `stopping_metric`, but has fallen out of favor.[1]

RMSLE

The catchy abbreviation of Root Mean Squared Logarithmic Error. Prefer this to RMSE if an under-prediction is worse than an over-prediction.

Classification Metrics

For multinomial classification, the confusion matrix (an example was shown back in the first chapter) is often the most useful way to evaluate a model, because it shows not just how many it got right, but what category it chose when it guessed wrong. I might see that an MNIST model is getting all the 1s correct, but has a really high error on the 9s because it classifies half of them as 4s. Maybe that gives you an idea of how to improve it, or maybe you just document it to users: "When it guesses 9, be suspicious, it might be a 4."

The first three listed here are valid choices for both multinomial and binomial classifications; AUC is only for binomial classification:

misclassification

This is the overall error, the number shown in the bottom right of a confusion matrix. If it got 1 of 20 wrong in class A, 1 of 50 wrong in class B, and 2 of 30 wrong in class C, it got 4 wrong in total out of 100, so the misclassification is 4, or 4%.

mean_per_class_error

The right column in a confusion matrix has an error rate for each class. This is the average of them, so for the preceding example it is the mean of 1/20, 1/50,

---

1 See *http://data.library.virginia.edu/is-r-squared-useless/* for a good explanation of why.

and 2/30, which is 4.556%. If your classes are balanced (exactly the same size) it is identical to misclassification.

logloss

The H2O algorithms don't just guess the category, they give a probability for the answer being each category. The confidence assigned to the correct category is used to calculate logloss (and MSE). Logloss (*http://bit.ly/2gniKLm*) disproportionately punishes low numbers, which is another way of saying having high confidence in the wrong answer is a bad thing.

MSE

Mean Squared Error. The error is the distance from 1.0 of the probability it suggested. So assume we have three classes, A, B, and C, and your model guesses A with 0.91, B with 0.07, and C with 0.02. If the correct answer was A the error (before being squared) is 0.09, if it is B 0.93, and if C it is 0.98.

AUC

Area Under Curve. Explained next.

Logloss is the default, and is usually the best choice.

Binomial Classification

When you train a binomial model, there are some additional metrics we get, the most commonly used of which is AUC, which normally ranges from 0.5 to 1.0, higher being better. AUC stands for Area Under Curve. What curve? That requires a bit more explanation.

Imagine you are scanning for cancer (or hunting for football wins). You can say yes or no, and the truth can be yes or no, which gives us four possible combinations. Saying yes when it is yes (true positive, TP), and no when it is no (true negative, TN), are the aim, and account for two of those four combinations. The other two are:

- We say cancer when they are healthy (false positive, FP) (Type I errors in statistics).
- We say healthy when it is a cancer (false negative, FN) (Type II errors).

Precision is defined as how many true positives we got, divided by the total number of cancer predictions we gave, which can be written as TP / (TP + FP). If we only give a cancer prediction when we are really sure, precision will be high (but FN might also be high). If we give a cancer prediction at the slightest whiff of tobacco on their clothes, precision will be low (FN will be close to zero, which is good, but FP will be high, which is bad).

Recall is the number of true positives divided by the total number of actual cancer cases. If we got every cancer in the data set, our recall will be high. If we err on the

side of caution, it is likely to be lower. Perfect recall is easy: always say it is cancer…
but that gives a low precision.

Obviously the ideal is perfect precision and perfect recall. But often you will err on
the side of one or the other. This err-ing decision can be represented as a chart, with
false positive rate along the x-axis, and true positive rate up the y-axis. This gives us a
curve, called an ROC curve, something like that shown on the left of Figure 4-1.

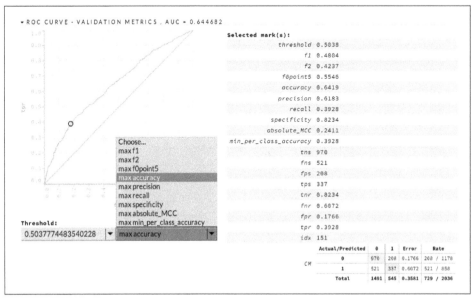

Figure 4-1. Example AUC plot in H2O's Flow interface

You want a high AUC; you can see here it is 0.64. If it was 0.99 you would see the
blue line almost touching the top-left corner. From the drop-down box I chose "max
accuracy," which represents one point along the line, to give the information on the
right of the screenshot.

What about when FP and FN are of equal importance? Then you want to concentrate
on accuracy. *Accuracy* is (TP + TN) / (TP + TN + FN + FP). That is, the total number correct over the total number of cases. Another way of saying that is 1 - error
rate.

By default, H2O uses the F1-optimal threshold; we will instead use the threshold of
maximum accuracy because, with the football predictions, the downside for guessing
a win when it was a loss and for guessing a loss when it was a win are equal. When
evaluating on the test data set, that threshold will be calculated as the average of the
threshold that gave maximum accuracy on the train and validation data.

In Figure 4-2 the solid vertical lines show the threshold for maximum accuracy; the dotted line shows the average of the train and validation thresholds. Not perfect, but close enough.

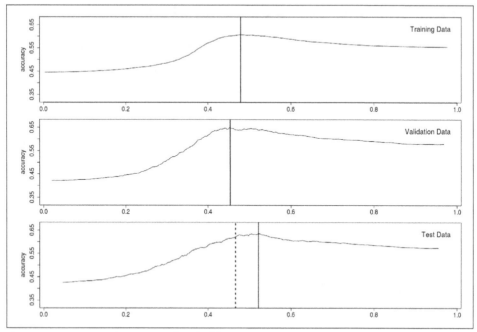

Figure 4-2. Binomial accuracy thresholds

The Essentials

All the machine learning algorithms have fields for *what* is being learned. In Python, the first three are given to train(), not when creating the estimator object:

x

Which fields in training_frame to learn from. The convention in this book is to store them in a variable also called x. **ALL**

y

Which field in training_frame should be learned; in other words, which is the response variable. The convention in this book is to store it in a variable also called y. (When doing unsupervised learning do not set y.) If doing regression this has to represent a numeric field, if doing binomial classification this has to represent a two-level enum, and if doing multinomial classification this has to represent an enum with three or more levels. **ALL**

training_frame

The (handle to the H2O) data set to train from. The convention in this book is to call this `train`. ALL

ignore_const_cols

Defaults to true, meaning if all values in a column are the same value, then ignore that column. You usually only set it to false if you want to see it shown in reports, or they represent a 2D image you will want to plot. ALL

In R, the first three arguments are always x, y, training_frame, in that order, and so you can skip naming them.[2] That is, you can either do h2o.gbm(x, y, train) or h2o.gbm(x = x, y = y, training_frame = train). In Python it is the same: either m.train(x, y, train) or m.train(x=x, y=y, training_frame=train).

Typically, x and y are text: the names of fields. However, if your columns have no names, or there are a lot of columns, you can also use numeric indices, as we did with the MNIST data in the previous chapter. Either way, remember that x and y are column names or column indices, not the column data itself.

When using numeric column indices, in R they count from 1, in Python they count from 0, i.e., exactly what you'd expect in each language. Just be careful if sharing code with someone using a different language!

If you look on Flow, or ever use the REST API directly, you will see only column names are used, never numeric column indices. Also, rather than specifying the column names to use you specify which columns to *ignore*. So response_column on Flow is what we call y, and ignored_columns is the inverse of our x.

For instance, in Examples 4-1 and 4-2 we will try to learn the iris species from just the sepal width. Either of the first two ways is fine, but the third way, in each case, will give errors.

Example 4-1. Ways to give x and y (in R)

```
m1 <- h2o.gbm(2, 5, train)
m2 <- h2o.gbm("sepal_wid", "class", train)
m3 <- h2o.gbm(train["sepal_wid"], train["class"], train)   #BAD
```

---

2 If your coding standards and/or coworkers and/or boss allow it.

Example 4-2. Ways to give x and y (in Python)

```
m = h2o.H2OGradientBoostingEstimator()
m.train(1, 4, train)
m.train("sepal_wid", "class", train)
m.train(train["sepal_wid"], train["class"], train)  #BAD
```

Effort

The first three items here tell their respective algorithms how much work to do:

epochs
> The amount of training cycles a deep learning algorithm should do. `DL`

ntrees
> The number of trees a tree algorithm should do. `RF` `GBM`

max_iterations
> The amount of work a GLM algorithm should do (not applicable in cases when coefficients can be calculated directly). `GLM`

The other couple of parameters allow you to set a random seed to get the exact same results again. Useful for demos, and book authors, but it is better to embrace stochastic diversity the way you would embrace a favorite aunt—without a second thought:

seed
> An integer to control random number generation, which allows you to get exactly the same model if you run the algorithm again. If using deep learning, you also need to set `reproducible`. Perhaps ironically, my main use for `seed` is in grids (a way to tune model parameters, introduced properly in "Grid Search" on page 122 in the next chapter) *not* to allow repeatability, but to allow me to run the same model with the same parameters and see what effect random variation has on the result. (When used for this purpose, you don't need to set `reproducible`.) `ALL`

reproducible
> If true, then deep learning will run on a single thread. This takes away the random element, but of course means it will train more slowly. Set this if also setting a seed, don't set it if not. `DL`

> Setting a seed cannot guarantee you the same model results between different H2O versions. Bug fixes, new bugs, something as simple as a new feature, can be enough.

Scoring and Validation

H2O regularly scores how the model training is doing. If you give a `valida tion_frame` then it will score it on that, if you are using cross-validation, it will score against each fold, and if neither of those it will score against `training_frame`:

validation_frame
> The (handle to the H2O) data set to validate against. The convention in this book is to call this `valid`. (In Python, this is given to `train()`, not when creating the estimator.) `ALL`

score_each_iteration
> This defaults to false; if true it will do the scoring more frequently. `RF` `GBM`

score_tree_interval
> The default of zero disables this. If you set it then the score is evaluated after this many trees. `RF` `GBM`

Deep learning has a large number of additional scoring parameters, which are covered in "Parameters" on page 195 in Chapter 8.

Early Stopping

As described in "Scoring and Validation" on page 99, H2O is regularly scoring your model against the validation, cross-validation, and/or training data. If you are using the Flow interface you can watch how the learning is going. Say you have a deep learning model, which you gave 1000 epochs, and you are regularly watching how it is doing. After 150 epochs you can see it has completely flattened out. You give it another 20 epochs to be sure, but after those it is clear it has learned all it is going to, and is now just wasting time. You yawn, and abort it.

That can get to a person's sanity if you have to do it more than once or twice. Fortunately, H2O has some options to help. The first three are basically doing what you did manually earlier: watching your metric of choice, and when it has not improved for a certain number of scoring rounds, stop.

stopping_metric
> How to decide if the model is improving or not. "Supported Metrics" on page 92 introduced the choices, though you can usually leave it as the default of AUTO ("logloss" for classification and "deviance" for regression). `RF` `GBM` `DL`

stopping_tolerance
> Stop if it (your metric of choice) has not improved by at least this much. For example, 0.01 means you want a 1% improvement, or it should stop. Zero is also

fine: it is saying to keep learning while there is any improvement, however small.
`RF` `GBM` `DL`

stopping_rounds

The scoring history graphs for your models sometimes wobble around a bit. By setting this higher than 1 you make space for things to get worse before they get better. It works by comparing two moving averages; the earliest it can ever stop is after twice this number of scoring rounds. Choosing 1 means the model has to improve on every single scoring round. Set it to zero to not use early stopping at all. `RF` `GBM` `DL`

How responsive your early stopping is depends not just on `stopping_rounds` and `stopping_tolerance` but also on how frequently scoring rounds happen. As an example, if the combination of your model complexity, training data size, and parameters you've set means that it only scores once a minute, and `stopping_rounds` is 5, then the earliest a model can ever stop training is after 10 minutes (twice the number in `stopping_rounds`). If using a grid (see "Grid Search" on page 122) this applies for each model that is made.

There are some other parameters that can stop a model early, though you will use them less often:

max_runtime_secs

The maximum amount of time allowed for model training. The default of zero means no limit. This is cruder than using a stopping metric, but is more predictable: if you are making 50 models in a grid, and you set `max_runtime_secs` to 30 seconds, then you know that (a) it will finish within 25 minutes and (b) each model will get the same amount of CPU resources, which may be the most fair comparison. (In Python, this is given to `train()`, not when creating the estimator.) `ALL`

classification_stop

When the classification error is below this, training will stop. Set it to –1 to not use this. This works independently of `stopping_metric`. `DL`

regression_stop

When the MSE is below this, training will stop. Set it to –1 to not use this. This works independently of `stopping_metric`. `DL`

max_active_predictors

Stops when there are more than this number of active predictors. The default of –1 means no limit. `GLM`

overwrite_with_best_model

True by default, which means the model that is returned will be the best model found during training. If false, then the final model (which may be inferior) will be the one that is returned. I've put it in this section, but this is also used even if not using early stopping. **DL**

H2O has early stopping on by default for deep learning, so explicitly set `stop ping_rounds` to 0 if you don't want it. My suggestion is to always use it for deep learning, if only because the `overwrite_with_best_model` feature means it can go back through the history and choose the best model, not whatever you ended up with at the end of training. For random forest and GBM, I recommend you either use early stopping or checkpoints, explained in a moment, or both.

The following example shows a random forest model that will keep adding trees unless one of three things has happened:

- It uses 100 trees (`ntrees=100`).
- It takes 60 seconds (`max_runtime_secs=60`).
- The value for the misclassification metric has not improved by 2% over the last 3 scoring rounds.

This example uses the same Iris data set we saw back in the first chapter; in fact the first half is exactly the same as Example 1-1. But I'm now splitting off a validation frame, so my training data is reduced to 75% (e.g., 115 rows), and my test data is reduced to 10% (e.g., 16 rows), leaving me 15% for validation (e.g., 19 rows). (The split is random, so will be slightly different each time, unless you use seed.)

```
import h2o
h2o.init()

datasets = "https://raw.githubusercontent.com/DarrenCook/h2o/bk/datasets/"
data = h2o.import_file(datasets + "iris_wheader.csv")
y = "class"
x = data.names
x.remove(y)
train, valid, test = data.split_frame([0.75, 0.15])

from h2o.estimators.random_forest import H2ORandomForestEstimator
m = H2ORandomForestEstimator(
  ntrees=100,
  stopping_metric="misclassification",
  stopping_rounds=3,
  stopping_tolerance=0.02,   #2%
  max_runtime_secs=60,
  model_id="RF:stop_test"
  )
m.train(x, y, train, validation_frame=valid)
```

In fact it stopped after using 8 trees, and 0.024 seconds of training!

When used with cross-validation (explained in a moment) it will use your early stopping criteria on each cross-validation model. But from that it will work out the optimal number of trees/epochs and make the final model *without* using early stopping. (If model quality varies a lot from run to run, randomly, this can sometimes give strange results.)

Checkpoints

Imagine you spend 10 minutes training a neural net. Then you test it and find it has improved over the one you only trained for 5 minutes. So then you wonder how good it would be if you gave it 15 minutes. Altogether it takes you 30 minutes to discover those three things. H2O has this great feature, allowing you to train a model for 5 minutes then stop it and try it out. Then you can train it for another 5 minutes, giving you (approximately) the 10-minute model. And then another 5 minutes to give you the 15-minute model. The same three models, but in half the time.

There are two variables involved:

model_id
    A name for your model. If not given, a random one is chosen. `ALL`

checkpoint
    The ID of a previous model (which must currently be on your H2O cluster) that you would like to use as a starting point. `RF` `GBM` `DL`

Once you start any serious work with H2O, whether using checkpoints or not, I recommend you always set model_id, if only so you can find them in Flow, or find the saved model on disk. POJOs also get named based on the model ID. And for the same reasons, I recommend some convention. For example, "DL:200x200-100" could be a deep learning model with two hidden layers each with 200 neurons, and running for 100 epochs. "GBM:100-5" could be a GBM built with 100 trees, and a max depth of 5.

Don't get carried away with structuring your model IDs: the more information you put in them, the less useful they get. If you find yourself wanting to put more than three parameters in a model ID, maybe it is time to step back and give them names instead. "DL:extra-deep," "DL:big-and-slow," etc. Or even "DL:Tom," "DL:Dick," and "DL:Harry."

The way checkpoints work is you define a new model, with all the same parameters (usually: see the following comment), but give a higher value for epochs (deep learning) or ntrees (GBM, random forest), and then set checkpoint to the ID of the model to use as a starting point. If you give a lower or equal value for epochs/ntrees/max_iterations, then it will return immediately, as there is no new work to be done.

Example 4-3 shows how to build a model "DL:50x50-5" with 5 epochs, then use that as the starting point for a new model "DL:50x50-15", which we give another 10 epochs. When specifying epochs, or the number of trees, specify the *total* amount of training you want if you had started from scratch (epochs=15 here), not how many additional epochs or trees you want.

Example 4-3. Using checkpoints with deep learning (Python)

```
y = "income"
x = ["age", "gender"]

m1 = h2o.H2ODeepLearningEstimator(model_id="DL:50x50-5", hidden=[50,50],
  epochs=5)
m1.train(x, y, train)

m2 = h2o.H2ODeepLearningEstimator(model_id="DL:50x50-15", hidden=[50,50],
  epochs=15, checkpoint="DL:50x50-5")
m2.train(x, y, train)
```

If we look at m1.scoring_history()[3] it looks like this:

```
   duration   epochs training_MSE
0.000 sec 0.000000      NaN
0.156 sec 0.471545   0.224481
0.205 sec 5.048780   0.036641
```

And m2.scoring_history() looks like this:

```
   duration    epochs training_MSE
0.000 sec  0.000000      NaN
0.156 sec  0.471545   0.224481
0.205 sec  5.048780   0.036641
0.261 sec  6.504065   0.096397
0.312 sec 15.455285   0.021673
```

The first three lines are identical! When checkpointing, the new model inherits all that information from the previous model.

One interesting aspect of checkpoints is that you can change more parameters than just how long to train, and thus create models that couldn't be created without checkpoints. For instance, you can use a certain dropout ratio for the first 50 epochs of a deep learning model, then switch to a different dropout ratio for the next 50.

---

3 m1.scoring_history()[['duration','epochs','training_MSE']] was used here; there are lots of other columns telling you how training progressed, but we don't want to see them in this example.

When I started using H2O, I thought checkpoints were the bees knees, and used them a lot. But now (at least when using deep learning and I have a validation data set) I prefer to use "Early Stopping" on page 99 to decide how much to train a model, and instead only use checkpoints for when I feel early stopping has stopped too soon. Or the scenario described in "Model Files" on page 51, where I want to shut down a cluster for the weekend but a model is still learning. (You can export the latest snapshot of a model from Flow, while it is learning.)

Cross-Validation (aka k-folds)

The basic idea behind cross-validation is you chop up your training set into k blocks, then use one of those k blocks as a validation data set, and use the rest for training. Repeat this k times, with a different part of the training set being the validation set each time. The error of the final model is estimated as the average error of the k models and it should therefore be more reliable. The final model that is returned is built again, with all the data, and no validation. The cost of this more reliable estimate of model quality is that it takes more time. Figure 4-3 shows the process for three random folds. m is the final model that is returned.

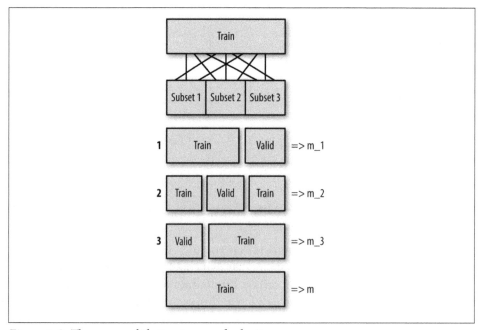

Figure 4-3. The cross-validation process for k=3

In this book I use cross-validation for the building energy data set, but a validation data set for MNIST (as I have enough data) and the football statistics (as I have enough data and it is a time series).

nfolds
> Number of folds. The higher this is the longer training takes, but the more accurate the error estimate, meaning an overfitted model is harder to get past us. However, there are diminishing returns. 5 and 10 are common choices for nfolds. **ALL**

The next two parameters control how the data is split up. Generally there is no need to touch these. However, if doing a classification, and the classes are not balanced, consider fold_assignment="Stratified".

fold_assignment
> How to split up the training data. The choices are "Random," "Modulo," and "Stratified," with the default being "AUTO" (which always means Random, at the moment). Random is what you'd expect, and each fold might end up a slightly different size. If nfolds is 3, Modulo means rows 1, 4, 7, ... go into fold 1, rows 2, 5, 8, ... go into fold 2, and rows 3, 6, 9, ... go into fold 3. Stratified tries to get the same amount of each target class into each fold; this is a good thing but splitting the data might take more time. **ALL**

fold_column
> Allows you complete control. If nfolds is 3, then this column should contain the values 1, 2, and 3 to say which fold you want each row in. (In Python, this is given to train(), not when creating the estimator.) **ALL**

The final two parameters are boolean, to control what information is returned:

keep_cross_validation_fold_assignment
> If set to true then you can find out which rows were in which folds. **ALL**

keep_cross_validation_predictions
> If set to true then the predictions of the test step for each fold are kept. **ALL**

 To use models with h2o.stack(), a technique described in "Ensembles" on page 253 in Chapter 10, you must use cross-validation, and must set fold_assignment = "Modulo" and keep_cross_validation_predictions = TRUE. If you think that is something you might want to do, it can be worth choosing those options on all your models.

Data Weighting

If you have 100 rows of training data, all 100 are considered equally important. H2O provides a few ways to describe that certain rows are more important, without you having to resort to taking a copy of your training data and actually duplicating the rows. All of them can be used with each of the learning algorithms. The first three only apply when doing a classification:

balance_classes

> If false, all data is used evenly. If set to true, then training data class counts (for your response variable) will be used to over/under-sample. For example, assume you are predicting favorite color, and in your 100 training rows 40 people chose red, 30 chose blue, 15 chose black, 10 chose white, 4 chose orange, and only 1 chose green. With `balance_classes` on, each of the blue rows will be made 1.33 times more important than each of the red rows, the black rows will be 2.67 times more important than each of the red rows, and so on, down to the single green row, which will be 40 times more important. `DL` `RF` `GBM`

class_sampling_factors

> Allows explicit control when using `balance_classes`. The default is to balance so that all classes are equally balanced. You should only set this if that equal balancing is not desired. The entries should be in sort order. For example, if you want the same ratio of colors as just shown but also want to limit the maximum weight of any one color to 5.0, you would give: `[2.67, 1.33, 5.0, 5.0, 1.0, 4.0]` (i.e., black, blue, green, orange, red, white is their alphabetic sorted order). Also see the following example, where we happen to know that the training data is not representative. `DL` `RF` `GBM`

max_after_balance_size

> When using `balance_classes`, this allows you to set the maximum relative size of the training data after balancing. Currently this defaults to 5.0, and you are unlikely to need to change it. `DL` `RF` `GBM`

 With h2o.deeplearning() when using `balance_classes`, it is recommended to also set shuffle_training_data to TRUE. (shuffle_training_data is only a parameter for h2o.deeplearning()).

The other two are more general:

weights_column

> The name of a column that says how to weight each row. You can think of this as being how many times to repeat each row when training, so the default is like an invisible column with 1.0 for every row. Fractional values are allowed. Cannot be

used when `balance_classes` is set. (In Python, this is given to `train()`, not when creating the estimator.) **ALL**

offset_column

The name of a column that gives a per-row bias. You can think of the default as being an invisible column with 0.0 for every row. It is like copying and modifying your response variable column by this much, for each row. (In Python, this is given to `train()`, not when creating the estimator.) **ALL**

Here is a full example of using each of the choices for balancing classes:

```
library(h2o)
h2o.init(nthreads = -1)

datasets <- "https://raw.githubusercontent.com/DarrenCook/h2o/bk/datasets/"
data <- h2o.importFile(paste0(datasets,"iris_wheader.csv"))

data <- data[1:120,]   #Remove 60% of virginica
summary(data$class)   #50/50/20

parts <- h2o.splitFrame(data, 0.8)
train <- parts[[1]]
test <- parts[[2]]
summary(train$class)   #41/41/14
summary(test$class)   #9/9/6

m1 <- h2o.randomForest(
  1:4, 5, train, model_id = "RF_defaults"
  )
h2o.confusionMatrix(m1)

m2 <- h2o.randomForest(
  1:4, 5, train, model_id = "RF_balanced",
  balance_classes = TRUE
  )
h2o.confusionMatrix(m2)

m3 <- h2o.randomForest(
  1:4, 5, train, model_id = "RF_class_sampling",
  balance_classes = TRUE, class_sampling_factors = c(1, 1, 2.5)
  )
h2o.confusionMatrix(m3)
```

The first four lines are hopefully familiar by now: start H2O, and load the iris data. I then throw away the last 30 samples (which are all virginica), by keeping just rows 1 to 120. I now have an unbalanced data set: 50 setosa, 50 versicolor, 20 virginica. I chose the seed deliberately when splitting the data, such that my training data has 41 setosa, 41 versicolor, 14 virginica. That is, virginica is 14.58% of the training data and 25% in the test data, compared to 16.67% overall.

I then train three random forest models. m1 is all defaults, and its confusion matrix looks like this:

```
           setosa versicolor virginica  Error      Rate
setosa        41          0         0 0.0000 = 0 / 41
versicolor     0         39         2 0.0488 = 2 / 41
virginica      0          1        13 0.0714 = 1 / 14
Totals        41         40        15 0.0312 = 3 / 96
```

Nothing to see here: it uses the data as it finds it.

Now here is the same output for m2, which switches on `balance_classes`. You can see it has over-sampled the virginica class to get them as balanced as possible (the rightmost column says 41,41,40 instead of 41,41,14 as in the previous output):

```
           setosa versicolor virginica  Error       Rate
setosa        41          0         0 0.0000 =  0 / 41
versicolor     0         41         0 0.0000 =  0 / 41
virginica      0          2        38 0.0500 =  2 / 40
Totals        41         43        38 0.0164 =  2 / 122
```

In m3 we still switch on `balance_classes`, but also tell it the truth of the situation. That is, that the actual data is 16.67% virginica, not the 14.58% it sees in the train data. The confusion matrix for m3 shows that it turned the 14 virginica samples into 37 samples instead of 40 samples:

```
           setosa versicolor virginica  Error       Rate
setosa        41          0         0 0.0000 =  0 / 41
versicolor     0         41         0 0.0000 =  0 / 41
virginica      0          2        35 0.0541 =  2 / 37
Totals        41         43        35 0.0168 =  2 /119
```

How did I know to write c(1, 1, 2.5), and not c(2.5, 1, 1) or c(1, 2.5, 1)? You can find out the correct order with h2o.levels(train$class) which tells me:

```
[1] "setosa"    "versicolor" "virginica"
```

Sampling, Generalizing

The common theme among the parameters in this section is that they try to improve your model's ability to generalize, and they do this by *hiding* some of the data. Generalization is a good thing; it means your model can make a good guess when it sees some combination of inputs that it has never encountered before. But, *hiding* some of the data?! Surely the machine learning is hard enough, and the more data the better?

Imagine you are teaching trigonometry, and you teach the students about sine and tangent, but not about cosine. You then give them a test, and kick out of the class anyone who obviously hasn't worked out the existence of cosine for themselves. This is a good way to make parents angry and get yourself sacked. But it is also a great way to discover who are the budding mathematical geniuses and who merely pay attention in class but don't really *get* it.

Leaving that metaphor behind, it is important to realize that if you hide information, you often need to spend more time learning. With the tree algorithms, you need to give them more trees, and with deep learning you need to give it more epochs. So it will take longer to train, but (hopefully) give a more resilient model.

I only show the parameters for the tree algorithms here. Those for deep learning are in "Deep Learning Regularization" on page 195 and those for GLM are in "GLM Parameters" on page 166. In all cases they are hard to select even with good knowledge of the data, so they are good candidates for a grid search.

For the tree algorithms the parameters are about two things:

- Use all columns?
- Use all training rows?

mtries
>   This is how many variables to randomly choose as candidates at each split, in a random forest. The default is –1, which means $\sqrt{P}$ (rounded down, minimum of 1) for classification, or P/3 (rounded down, minimum of 1) for regression (where P is the number of columns). **RF**

col_sample_rate
>   This is the percentage of columns (from 0.0 to 1.0) to sample from, with GBM. The default is 1. If you multiply `col_sample_rate` by the number of columns in `train`, you get the equivalent of `mtries`. **GBM**

col_sample_rate_change_per_level
>   Relative change of the column sampling rate for every level in each tree. The default is 1.0. If less than 1, then it will have fewer columns to choose from as it gets deeper in the tree. If greater than 1 (maximum 2.0), then it will have more columns to choose from. You might want to experiment with this in a grid, but normally you can just leave it as the default. **GBM** **RF**

col_sample_rate_per_tree
>   This can be from 0.0 to 1.0. It is at the tree level, rather than at the split level as with `mtries` and `col_sample_rate`. The default is 1.0. **GBM** **RF**

sample_rate
>   The default for GBM is 1.0, which means train each tree on all the training data. 0.5 would mean only use half the data. The default for random forest is 0.632. **RF** **GBM**

sample_rate_per_class
> Like `sample_rate` but you give the value for each class. See the description of `class_sampling_factors` under "Data Weighting" on page 106. **RF** **GBM**

max_abs_leafnode_pred
> Maximum absolute value of a leaf node prediction. This is the maximum a leaf node can contribute, so it is a regularization parameter. It defaults to a very large number, but if set lower it stops any one node from dominating the prediction. Generally it can be left as the default, but it might be worth experimenting with in a grid. **GBM**

Regression

Regression is trying to predict a (continuous) number (as different from a classification), and there are a few parameters specifically to control regression.

These first few only apply to deep learning and GBM:

distribution
> Choose the probability distribution of the response variable; the choices are listed in a moment.[4] The default is "AUTO," which is always "gaussian" for a regression. (For binomial classification, distribution is always "bernoulli," and for multinomial classification it is always "multinomial.") **DL** **GBM**

quantile_alpha
> Used when distribution is "quantile." **DL** **GBM**

tweedie_power
> Used when distribution is "tweedie." From 1.0 to 2.0, defaulting to 1.5. Note that 1.0 is equivalent to "poisson," while 2.0 is equivalent to "gamma." **DL** **GBM**

loss
> Certain distributions (gaussian, laplace, huber) allow you to choose a loss function. The default choices for those three being: "Quadratic," "Absolute," "Huber." The final possible value is "CrossEntropy," which is for classification. Give the default of "Automatic" unless you have a good reason not to. You cannot define your own loss function. **DL**

---

4 If you have questions about exactly what a distribution does, the Java source is authoritative. (*http://bit.ly/2gnftvD*)

These ones are for GLM:

family
> As `distribution` but for GLMs. The choices are listed next, but note that only gaussian, poisson, gamma, and tweedie are available (i.e., not huber, laplace, or quantile.) `GLM`

tweedie_link_power
> Used when distribution is "tweedie." Default is 1. `GLM`

tweedie_variance_power
> Used when distribution is "tweedie." Default is 0. `GLM`

Probability Distributions in H2O

Here are the currently available distributions:

gaussian
> This is another name for the normal distribution, the bell curve that I am sure you are familiar with.

poisson
> Use if modeling the number of times an event happens, in a given interval. When the average number of events per interval is high it looks like the normal curve. The per-week intake at a hospital emergency ward might average 200, so could safely be modeled as gaussian (or poisson), but the per-hour intake mean is 1.2, so would be better modeled with poisson.

gamma
> Often used to model the time between events. The exponential decay curve is a special case of the gamma distribution.

tweedie
> A family of distributions. A power of 0 gives you gaussian, 1 gives you poisson, and 2 gives you gamma, but fractional values from 1.0 upwards can give you other distributions.

laplace
> A continuous distribution that looks a bit like two exponential distributions stuck together.

huber
> Specify this to do robust regression (*https://en.wikipedia.org/wiki/Robust_regression*).

---

quantile

Specify this if you want to do quantile regression (*https://en.wikipedia.org/wiki/Quantile_regression*). Used with `quantile_alpha`, where the default of 0.5 is another way of saying the median, but you can set any value from 0.0 to 1.0.

Output Control

In this final group are a few parameters that control what information is reported back to the client. With some it is about controlling verbosity; with others it is about avoiding extra machine load if you do not need the extra information:

max_hit_ratio_k

The maximum number of predictions to report in hit ratios (only applies to multinomial classification). Use 0 to disable (meaning it will make predictions for all classes). `DL`

max_confusion_matrix_size

Maximum number of classes to use when printing confusion matrices in the logs. `DL`

export_weights_and_biases

Set this to true to request to save a deep learning model's weights and biases. They are available afterwards with `h2o.weights()` and `h2o.biases()` (or member functions of those names, in Python). `DL`

variable_importances

The other learning algorithms always tells you relative importance of your input variables, but it can slow down deep learning; therefore it is off by default. Set this to true to have them calculated and returned.[5] `DL`

diagnostics

Enable diagnostics for hidden layers. `DL`

compute_p_values

Request p-values computation for your linear model. Only available when using the IRLSM solver and no regularization. (The latter limits its usefulness more than the former.) `GLM`

---

5 The implementation is based on Gedeon, and the code for `computeVariableImportances()` is in *http://bit.ly/2f8ewED*. It uses the first two layers, so could be inaccurate for very deep networks, but it is only an estimate anyway.

Summary

That was a lot of parameters! But, along the way, we also got a look at some key concepts in machine learning and H2O: cross-validation and validation data sets, early stopping, scoring metrics, checkpoints, dealing with unbalanced data, random sampling to improve model generalization, and probability distributions.

The next chapter starts our four chapter tour of the supervised machine learning algorithms. And, because it is the first of the four, it will also introduce some techniques that apply to all of them, grid search in particular.

CHAPTER 5

Random Forest

In this chapter we will look at the random forest machine learning algorithm. It is a wonderful algorithm: effective on a wide range of data sets, while having relatively few parameters to tune. It is a decision tree algorithm (as is GBM, which we look at it in the next chapter).

I start with a brief look at basic decision trees, then how random forest is different, and then go through the optional parameters that H2O's implementation offers. Then I apply random forest to each of the three data sets: first out-of-the-box, with all defaults, then using a tuning process to find the best single model I can. Each of the subsequent three chapters will follow this same pattern. As the first of the four chapters, grids—a great tool to aid in tuning—are also introduced here. The results of all models are summarized at the end of the book, in Chapter 11.

The tuning process is to try and improve on the default settings. But the H2O implementations tend to have good defaults that adapt to characteristics of your data, so I quickly reach the point of diminishing returns. Have in your mind how much time and effort a certain increase in model accuracy is worth. Maybe your day is better spent on feature engineering than tuning? Maybe $1000 would be better spent on additional data (whether buying data sets, or running your own surveys) than buying 500 node-hours on EC2 to run grids?

Throughout this book, but particularly in the next few chapters, I've deliberately shown some of the bad hunches, the wrong turns, and the just plain (with hindsight) stupidity. I find these just as educational as seeing what worked in the end, and I hope you do too.

Decision Trees

Decision trees, in their simplest form, are perhaps the most easily understandable approach to machine learning. Unlike the black box of neural networks, or the mathematical equations of linear models, decision trees look just like a flow chart.

See Figure 5-1 for an example of a decision tree for classification (these are called *classification trees*).

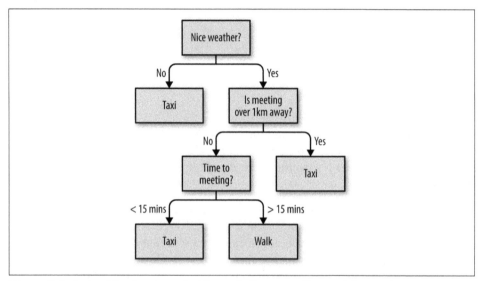

Figure 5-1. A classification tree: deciding whether to walk or catch a taxi

You don't need to know much about how decision trees are built to be able to use them. Basically, the variable at each level that will give the *best* split is chosen, and the most common definition of *best* is *information gain* (*http://bit.ly/2gniT1s*).

They can also be used as *regression trees*, where the value to be learned is a continuous variable. Regression trees are really still just classifying: the value in the leaf nodes is the average of all the training data that matched that branch of the tree. They are built by choosing the variable that gives the greatest reduction in standard deviation at each node. See Figure 5-2.

Random Forest

Random forest is an *ensemble* algorithm, meaning more than one model is made, and their results used together, the aim being to cope better with unseen situations (i.e., to avoid overfitting). This is not the only time we will meet ensemble algorithms in this book.

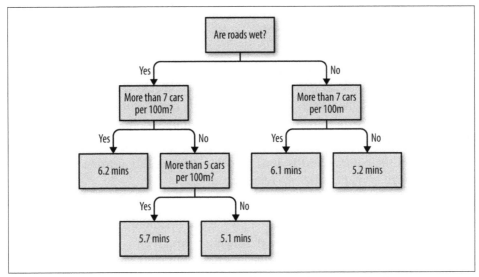

Figure 5-2. A regression tree: estimating how long a car journey will take

If you train a decision tree on a fairly complex data set (and don't take precautions against overfitting), you will find a very deep tree full of fragile rules. The idea behind random forest is to instead have lots of trees. Then, when you use it to predict on new data, you give the new data to each of those trees and ask each for their prediction. If it's a classification you choose the most popular answer, and if it's a regression you take the mean of each tree's answer.

That is the "forest" half. The other half, the "random," says that when training you don't give each tree all the training data; you randomly hold back some rows, or hold back some columns. This makes each individual tree a bit dumber than if it had seen all the data. But when their results are averaged together the whole is more intelligent than any one part.

Parameters

Most of the parameters were introduced in Chapter 4, but there are some specific to random forest. For Python users, all of these are given when creating the object, not when calling train().

The two most important parameters are:

ntrees
How many trees in your forest.

max_depth

> How deep a tree is allowed to grow. In other words, how complex each tree is allowed to be.

Together these two parameters control how big your random forest will be: acres of squat apple trees, or a small grove of giant oaks. The defaults are 50 trees, to a max depth of 20. The training time is going to be roughly proportional to the number of trees times the number of training rows. So you want `ntrees` to be as small as possible... but no smaller.

The control of the random part is done by parameters already introduced in "Sampling, Generalizing" on page 108. To remind you:

mtries

> This is how many variables to randomly choose as candidates at each split. The default is –1, which means $\sqrt{p}$ for classification, or p/3 for regression (where p is the number of columns). Set it to the number of columns in `train` to have it use all variables.

col_sample_rate_change_per_level

> Relative change of the column sampling rate for every level in each tree. The default is 1.0. If less than 1, then it will have fewer columns to choose from as it gets deeper in the tree. If greater than 1 (maximum 2.0) then it will have more columns to choose from.

col_sample_rate_per_tree

> This can be from 0.0 to 1.0. It is at the tree level, rather than at the split level as with `mtries` and `col_sample_rate`.

sample_rate

> The default is 0.632, which means each tree is trained on 63.2% of the training data.

sample_rate_per_class

> Like `sample_rate` but you give the value for each class. See the description of `class_sampling_factors` under "Data Weighting" on page 106.

The next two parameters control *if* splitting is done:

min_rows

> How many training data rows are needed to make a leaf node. The default is 1, meaning that you can have a path through the tree that represents something that was only seen once in the training data. That obviously encourages overfitting. But, if you know you have some cases only represented once in your data, then 1 is what you want.

min_split_improvement
> Each time a split happens there is reduction in the inaccuracy, in the error. This controls how much that error reduction has to be to make splitting worthwhile. The default is zero.

The next set of parameters control *how* the splitting is done:

histogram_type
> What type of histogram to use for finding optimal split points. Can be one of "AUTO," "UniformAdaptive," "Random," "QuantilesGlobal," or "RoundRobin."

nbins
> For numerical columns, build a histogram of (at least) this many bins, then split at the best point. The default is 20.

nbins_top_level
> For numerical columns, build a histogram of (at most) this many bins at the root level, then decrease by factor of two per level. The default is 1024.

nbins_cats
> For categorical columns, build a histogram of (at most) this many bins, then split at the best point. Higher values can lead to more overfitting. The default is 1024.

The next one only applies to binary classification:

binomial_double_trees
> Build one set of trees for each output class. Can give higher accuracy, and the trade-off is that you get twice as many trees. (`ntrees * 2` will be built.)

Finally, when using random forest on a cluster there is a fair bit of network communication. Unless you are using the cluster because you have big data, I recommend you set this to true. With small data sets the communication overhead will destroy any benefit you were hoping to get from using those other nodes.

build_tree_one_node
> Run on one node only. You will only be using the CPUs on that node; the rest of the cluster will be unused.

Building Energy Efficiency: Default Random Forest

This data set has to do with the heating costs of houses (see "Data Set: Building Energy Efficiency" on page 54 if you skipped the earlier introduction to it), and it is a regression problem. If you are following along, run either Example 3-1 (for R) or Example 3-2 (for Python) from the earlier chapter, which sets up H2O, loads the data, and defines `train`, `test`, `x`, and `y`. (See "Jargon and Conventions" on page 8 in Chapter 1 for a reminder of naming conventions.)

There is no valid (i.e., no validation data set); instead we will use k-fold cross-validation. It is a relatively small data set, and is quick for random forest to model, so I have used 10-fold. (Refer back to "Cross-Validation (aka k-folds)" on page 104 if you need a reminder about cross-validation.)

With our train and test data sets prepared, training the random forest is a one-liner, which takes just a couple of seconds to run:

```
m <- h2o.randomForest(x, y, train, nfolds = 10, model_id = "RF_defaults")
```

In Python that looks like:

```
m = h2o.estimators.H2ORandomForestEstimator(model_id="RF_defaults", nfolds=10)
m.train(x, y, train)
```

Now, type m to see how the training went. I will show an extract from an IPython console here (trimmed to fit) but the R client shows all the same figures. By the way, in R, summary(m) shows more information than just printing m:

```
In [23]: m.train(x, y, train)
drf Model Build progress: |████████████████████████| 100%

In [24]: m
Out[24]: Model Details
=============
H2ORandomForestEstimator :  Distributed Random Forest
Model Key:  RF_defaults
Model Summary:
 num_of_trees model_size min_depth max_depth min_leaves max_leaves mean_leaves
 ------------ ---------- --------- --------- ---------- ---------- -----------
 50           133472     20        20        77         364        204.56

ModelMetricsRegression: drf
** Reported on train data. **

MSE: 3.29872615438
RMSE: 1.81623956415
MAE: 1.24760757203
RMSLE: 0.0567712695161
Mean Residual Deviance: 3.29872615438

ModelMetricsRegression: drf
** Reported on cross-validation data. **

MSE: 3.22444719482
RMSE: 1.79567457932
MAE: 1.23071814584
RMSLE: 0.0561318898512
Mean Residual Deviance: 3.22444719482
```

Firstly it says there are 50 trees, and in this case they all used the maximum allowed depth of 20. (You will see some random variation from run to run, unless you set a seed.[1])

Under regression metrics (the ones "Reported on cross-validation data") I see an MSE, mean squared error, of 3.224. Not zero, so our model is not perfect. See "Supported Metrics" on page 92 in the previous chapter for more on the various metrics.

If I look over on Flow I will see 11 models, one for each of the 10 folds, and then one final model on the whole data. The preceding model summary gave me all those metrics on each fold. In this extract notice the wide range—the average MSE was 3.16, but ranged from 2.33 to 4.85:

```
Cross-Validation Metrics Summary:
                   mean       sd          cv_1_valid  ...  cv_9_valid cv_10_valid
------------------ ---------- ----------  ----------  ...  ---------- -----------
mae                1.21774    0.144463    1.00348     ...  1.60152    1.07393
mse                3.16326    0.682396    2.23307     ...  4.85474    2.55511
r2                 0.965288   0.0048532   0.973659    ...  0.955043   0.971501
residual_deviance  3.16326    0.682396    2.23307     ...  4.85474    2.55511
rmse               1.75908    0.185602    1.49434     ...  2.20335    1.59847
rmsle              0.0553582  0.0044408   0.0466292   ...  0.0655638  0.0514496
```

How does it do on the unseen test data? In R you get that with h2o.performance(m, test), in Python m.model_performance(test), and it looks like this:

```
In [25]: m.model_performance(test)
Out[25]:
ModelMetricsRegression: drf
** Reported on test data. **

MSE: 3.62649127211
RMSE: 1.90433486344
MAE: 1.33001699261
RMSLE: 0.0582354639097
Mean Residual Deviance: 3.62649127211
```

A higher MSE than on either our training data, or our cross-validation mean. The square root of MSE (RMSE here) is in real-world units, $kWh/(m^2yr)$—i.e., kilowatt-hours, per square meter of floorspace, per year—so just a reminder that we were trying to predict Y2, the required cooling load. The range on Y2 is from 10.90 to 48.03. The RMSE of 1.90 is not too bad—the guesses are in the right ballpark. The

---

1 I used a seed of 999, both here and for the data split. But you can still see different results if you are using a different version of H2O.

average error, that is. The mean can hide all kinds of sins, so let's also look at the results graphically[2]; see Figure 5-3.

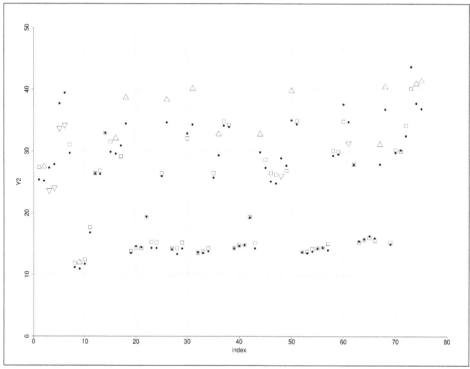

Figure 5-3. Default performance of random forest on test data

The black dots are the correct answers, the squares are relatively close predictions, and the up and down triangles are the worst predictions; for the sake of this plot a bad prediction was defined as 8% above or below the correct answer, and that represents 27 (14 too high, 13 too low) of the 143 test samples here.[3]

Grid Search

All the H2O machine learning algorithms have parameters: knobs, which you can tweak, that will often affect the performance of the model you build. But the interactions between the parameters can be complex.

---

2 See *code/makeplot.building_energy_results.R*, in the online code repository, for the code used to make this chart.

3 To stop this chart from being hopelessly crowded, only the first 75 test samples are plotted.

The labor-intensive way is to try a model, evaluate it, then fiddle with one of the parameters, and repeat. If your intuition is good this may be the most efficient way.

A more systematic way would be to set up nested loops of all the values for each parameter that you think might be important. So, for deep learning you might try 100, 200, and 300 epochs, with three network toplogies (200x200, 64x64x64, 500x50), and L1 regularization of 0 or 0.0001. (The meaning of these parameters will be explained in Chapter 8.) That is 18 combinations, so it takes 18 times as long as making one model.

Alternatively, rather than comprehensively trying all 18 combinations, you might randomly choose 6 of them to try, which only takes one-third of the time, and the hope is that you still get to learn which are best and worst values for the parameters.

When we created the random forest, it used defaults for all the parameters, except for specifying the 10-fold cross-validation. But the results were not as good as they can be. So the question becomes, how can we make it better?

You, at the back, what was that? "Throw a load of trees at it." Brute force, I like your style, sir. And what was that ma'am? Early stopping? (See "Early Stopping" on page 99.) Excellent. You are the yin to his yang. But, you lack depth. No, not you personally, sir, you have plenty of depth.

I mean you could also make *deeper* trees. H2O's random forest defaults to `ntrees=50` trees, with a `max_depth` of 20. Do we want to try 100 trees, keeping depth as 20? Or keep 50 trees, but allow them to grow to a depth of 40? Or both?

Those are the easy ones to tune: higher values are better (well, to the point of diminishing returns, at least). But then there are all the *fiddly* ones. For instance, is `mtries` better nudged a bit higher, or nudged a bit lower? Don't look at me, I don't know. I just work here.

Grids are the solution to this dilemma, and the H2O implementation currently comes in two forms:

- Comprehensive ("Cartesian")
- Random ("RandomDiscrete")

Cartesian

The first, the default, will try all combinations. Here is an example of that type of grid, first in R, then in Python:

```
g <- h2o.grid("randomForest",
  hyper_params = list(
    ntrees = c(50, 100, 120),
```

```
    max_depth = c(40, 60),
    min_rows = c(1, 2)
    ),
  x = x, y = y, training_frame = train, nfolds = 10
  )
```

 If you ever get a 500 Server Error with h2o.grid(), in R, check that you've given the algorithm name correctly! It is case-sensitive.

```
import h2o.grid

g = h2o.grid.H2OGridSearch(
  h2o.estimators.H2ORandomForestEstimator(
    nfolds=10
    ),
  hyper_params={
    "ntrees": [50, 100, 120],
    "max_depth": [40, 60],
    "min_rows": [1, 2]
    }
  )
g.train(x, y, train)
```

In R, you call h2o.grid, telling it which function to run, the hyper-parameters, then the constant parameters. By constant parameter I mean a model parameter that you don't want to experiment with in the grid, so it will have a fixed value in each model. In Python you make the H2OGridSearch object, giving it an instance of the function to use, with most of the constant parameters, then you give the hyper-parameters as a dictionary of arrays; next you call train() just as you do when calling train() on a model object.

hyper_params specifies the combinations we want it to try. So, here I have given three alternatives for ntrees, two for max_depth, and two for min_rows. 3 x 2 x 2 = 12, so 12 models will get made. Because of the combinatorial explosion, each additional hyper-parameter that gets added has a huge effect on the time taken to complete.

Type g (whether using R or Python) to get output like this:

	min_rows	ntrees	max_depth	model_ids	deviance
1	1	120	60	RF_structure1_model_10	3.2616
2	1	120	40	RF_structure1_model_4	3.2616
3	1	100	60	RF_structure1_model_8	3.2724
4	1	100	40	RF_structure1_model_2	3.2724
5	1	50	60	RF_structure1_model_6	3.3210
6	1	50	40	RF_structure1_model_0	3.3210
7	2	120	40	RF_structure1_model_5	3.3518
8	2	120	60	RF_structure1_model_11	3.3518

```
9    2    100    40    RF_structure1_model_3    3.3525
10   2    100    60    RF_structure1_model_9    3.3525
11   2    50     60    RF_structure1_model_7    3.3662
12   2    50     40    RF_structure1_model_1    3.3662
```

It has ordered from best to worst: lower residual deviance (equivalent to MSE here) is what we are after. Though the range of values looks narrow, we've actually learned a lot from this. First, min_rows of 1 is always better than 2. Second, max_depth of 40 and 60 gives exactly the same result.[4] And, third, that more ntrees was always better. Such clear-cut results are unusual—normally you have to piece apart these conclusions.

To seed or not to seed? That is the question: whether 'tis nobler in the mind to suffer the slings and arrows of outrageous random variation, or to take arms against a sea of troubles by setting the same seed each time. Or—and I feel Hamlet overlooked this third choice—you could set seed as one of the grid hyper-parameters, and get a feel for how much random variation is disturbing your conclusions. I use this third approach regularly.

Including nfolds=10 makes the computation much slower (24 seconds instead of 5.5 seconds in this case, so 4x to 5x slower), but the estimate of model performance becomes more consistent. When I tried without nfolds, a couple of the min_rows=1 entries ended up down the bottom, instead of in the middle, and the range of deviance was bigger. Trying nfolds=5 took 17 seconds instead of 24 seconds, but all the deviances were higher; however, it gave the same ordering as for nfolds=10 and that is the important thing.

You can use a different metric to order your grid models; the preceding was using the default of deviance. If you were most interested in how they compare on the R^2 metric, the next code is what you want. Notice how R's h2o.getGrid() takes a grid ID, rather than a grid object:

```
g_r2 <- h2o.getGrid(g@grid_id, sort_by = "r2", decreasing = TRUE)
```

 To find out your sorting options, give sort_by = "xxx" and they are listed in the error message. Refer to "Supported Metrics" on page 92 if some are unfamiliar.

---

4 Probably because I set a random seed: normally you'd expect a bit more variation even when a change of parameter has no effect at all.

In Python you get all models when you print g or g_r2. However, printing a grid in R currently shows just the best 6 and worst 6 models; if you have more than 12 models then you will need to *download* it with this rather clunky idiom:

```
as.data.frame( g_r2@summary_table )
```

Grids in H2O are basically just a set of nested loops (or random parameter selection for the other form), and you could hack your own solution in a few minutes. On the other hand, they get their own top-level menu in Flow, and the g object is a nice container for the models, and the API comes with tables to compare them.

Just bear in mind that if you start craving more flexibility, and don't mind giving up those home comforts, you could write your own loop...

RandomDiscrete

The other mode for grids is "RandomDiscrete." Use this when you have so many hyper-parameters that trying all combinations exhaustively would be, well, exhausting. RandomDiscrete will jump from one random combination to another. It needs some additional parameters to control when it should stop, and you should specify at least one of these:

max_models
Make this many models, then stop.

max_runtime_secs
Run for this long, then stop.

stopping_metric
AUTO, misclassification, etc.

stopping_tolerance
For example, 0.0001, to require at least 0.01% improvement in the given metric.

stopping_rounds
For example, 5. In combination with stopping_tolerance of 0.0001 it means: if none of our last five random models has managed to be 0.01% better than the best random model before that, then stop.

The three stopping choices work just like the ones we saw in "Early Stopping" on page 99, for stopping a model's learning, but they are being applied at the grid level. Note that you can still have these three stopping parameters in your grid's hyper-parameters, or constant parameters, and these will apply to each model that is built.

To see how this works, the next example uses early stopping on both the models and on the grid. The grid search will stop if the best MSE out of the last 10 models is not at least 0.1% better than the best MSE of a model the grid made before those 10. There is also an overall time limit of 120 seconds.

The hyper-parameters being tried are:

- `ntrees`: from 50 to 250.

- `mtries`: the building energy data set has eight predictor columns, so the default of 8÷3, rounded-down, is 2. That feels unreasonably low, so I also try 3, 4, and 5.

- `sample_rate`: the default is 0.632, so a bit below, a bit above, and then quite a lot above (95% of samples).

- `col_sample_rate_per_tree`: the default is 1.0, so a bit below that, then a lot below that (50%).

That is a total of 240 model combinations.

The `max_depth` is fixed at 40 for all models, and 5-fold cross-validation is used (instead of 10-fold, so as to speed things up). Then the per-model early stopping says that if we go four scoring rounds without any improvement at all (`scoring_toler ance=0`) in the deviance, then stop.

 Normally random forest is scored after every tree is added, but `score_tree_interval=3` (which is just a way of telling it to spend more time building trees relative to time spent scoring) combined with four scoring rounds actually means 12 trees have to be added, with zero improvement, before it will stop early.

```
g <- h2o.grid("randomForest",
  search_criteria = list(
    strategy = "RandomDiscrete",
    stopping_metric = "mse",
    stopping_tolerance = 0.001,
    stopping_rounds = 10,
    max_runtime_secs = 120
    ),
  hyper_params = list(
    ntrees = c(50, 100, 150, 200, 250),
    mtries = c(2, 3, 4, 5),
    sample_rate = c(0.5, 0.632, 0.8, 0.95),
    col_sample_rate_per_tree = c(0.5, 0.9, 1.0)
    ),
  x = x, y = y, training_frame = train,
  nfolds = 5, max_depth = 40,
  stopping_metric = "deviance",
  stopping_tolerance = 0,
```

```
    stopping_rounds = 4,
    score_tree_interval = 3
    )
```

For me, it ran for a bit under 90 seconds, and made 61 of the possible 240 models. The early stopping meant it never used all the tree allowance it was given; in fact, the biggest model used 70 trees. This, of course, means it was a waste to have ntrees as a hyper-parameter! On another run, I got just 42 models, with the largest forest having 51 trees.

For mtries the best model used 5, but 3 and 4 were also in the best 3. However, the default of 2 seems to have done relatively poorly. So, for our next grid consider dropping 2. (In another run, the top 10 were all 3 and 4.) For col_sample_rate all the 0.5 models were in the bottom-third, but 9 of the best 10 used 0.9, rather than the default of 1.0. How about 0.85, 0.90, and 0.95 for the next round? sample_rate is less clear-cut, but the top 9 are either 0.632 or 0.8, while 0.95 looks poor. Maybe 0.55, 0.60, 0.65, 0.70, 0.75, 0.80, and 0.85 for the next round? In yet another run 3 of the top 6 were 0.95. So, maybe 0.55, 0.65, 0.75, 0.85, 0.95? Or, maybe this is a sign to stop trying to tune it? That is, your energy is better spent elsewhere.

Certain combinations of parameters can be illegal, and when this happens those models will just fail to build, but the rest of the grid will complete, and you may not realize there was a problem.

If you look on Flow you will see the error messages. To see them in Python, type g.failure_details (you get no output if there are no problems). You can see failures in R by just outputting the grid with g.

Currently H2O's grid implementation is still a bit immature: there is no mode yet that guides its search by which parameters on previous models worked better. There is also no support yet for running models in parallel over a cluster. There is also no way to have dependencies between the parameters, or have one be a function of another. For instance, you might want to try various values of sample_rate, but increase ntrees when learn_rate is lower. If you need that level of flexibility, or any of the other missing features of h2o.grid, you'll need to implement your own version. Alternatively, put a high-level loop on top of multiple calls to h2o.grid(), and combine the results. (You will see this used in Chapter 8, when trying to experiment with differing number of hidden layers, for instance.)

If you use the same grid_id on multiple grid requests, the results get merged! This can allow you to narrow in on your parameters, but still see all the models in one big table.

High-Level Strategy

What is the best way to use grids? I often start with a small exhaustive search, testing the most important few parameters, to get a feel for where it might be going. Then I do a few random searches across more of the parameters (this grid search tutorial (*http://bit.ly/2gmnNMb*) shows the list of parameters that can be tuned, for each algorithm), with relatively short iterations (on the order of a few minutes to complete). After each iteration see if there are any obvious conclusions to use to guide the next iteration. (col_sample_rate=0.5 being bad was a good example.)

As you narrow in on what you think are the best iterations you may switch to cartesian (exhaustive search) mode. This is also a good time to try three or four random seeds, to test the sensitivity to random numbers. And if you reduced the number of k-folds, to speed things up, it is a good idea to increase it again, for a bit more precision.

 Never use the test data set in the grid search phase. Rely on the validation score, or the cross-validation score. Only when you have selected a final model, "ready for production," can you then evaluate it on the test set.

Building Energy Efficiency: Tuned Random Forest

The previous section, "Grid Search" on page 122, has made a good start on improving the parameters. There may not be much more to do.

I've tried using nbins, which is the *minimum* number of levels to divide a numeric predictor column into, when considering how to split on it. It defaults to 20, but most of our numeric fields don't have even 20 distinct values. So I tried values of 8, 12, 16, 20, and 24. The conclusion? All five possible values were used in the top 8 models (out of the 49 that were made in that grid iteration). So that was a failed experiment; best to leave nbins as the default.

If I was trying to get two or three diverse models for an ensemble (see "Ensembles" on page 253) then I would perhaps choose (out of the best models) those with the biggest range of hyper-parameters. But, for the sake of choosing one best model, I did a few more iterations of grids and settled on:

- max_depth = 40
- ntrees = 200
- sample_rate = 0.7
- mtries = 4
- col_sample_rate_per_tree = 0.9

- nbins left as default (20)

The choice of random seed was a big influence, so I chose six seeds, and used the following listing to compare the default model with this tuned model:

```
seeds <- c(101, 109, 373, 571, 619, 999)

defaultModels <- lapply(seeds, function(seed){
  h2o.randomForest(x, y, train, nfolds = 10, seed = seed)
  })

tunedModels <- lapply(seeds, function(seed){
  h2o.randomForest(x, y, train, nfolds = 10, seed = seed,
    max_depth = 40, ntrees = 200, sample_rate = 0.7,
    mtries = 4, col_sample_rate_per_tree = 0.9,
    stopping_metric = "deviance",
    stopping_tolerance = 0,
    stopping_rounds = 5,
    score_tree_interval = 3)
  })

def <- sapply(defaultModels, h2o.rmse, xval = TRUE)
tuned <- sapply(tunedModels, h2o.rmse, xval = TRUE)

boxplot(c(def, tuned) ~ c((rep(1, 6),rep(2, 6)) )
```

Figure 5-4 shows how there does seem to be a distinct improvement, though the best of the default models, and the worst of the tuned models, stop it from being clean.

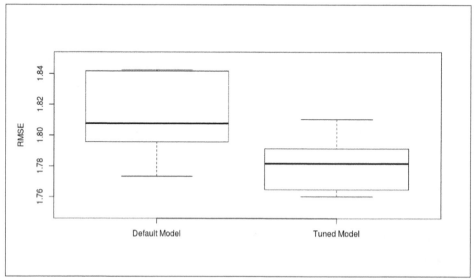

Figure 5-4. Box plot comparing random variation in default and tuned models

I chose RMSE, but MSE gives identical conclusions.[5] I also chose to plot the cross-validation metric, rather than the self-train metric. Oh, and check the y-axis before you get too impressed—notice how far away 0.0 is.

Remaking the same chart from earlier,[6] can you spot the difference? We went from 14 too high, 13 too low, to 8 too high and 17 too low! We come to the same conclusion as the previous box plots: tuning has given us a little improvement, but nothing earth-shattering.

The results of all models on this data set will be compared in "Building Energy Results" on page 259 in the final chapter.

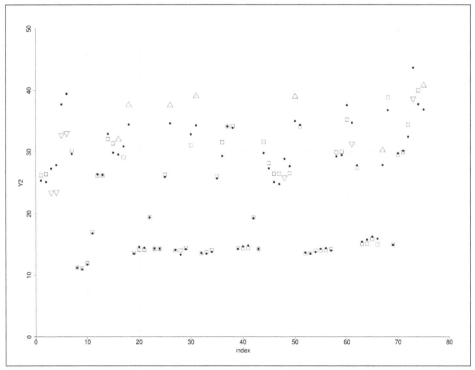

Figure 5-5. Tuned performance of random forest on test data

---

5 I also tried MAE, which gives a more distinct gap between the boxes.

6 Arbitrarily using the first of our six models.

As a follow-up, I tried repeating the grid experiments, but without early stopping: each model got to use all 200 trees. I settled on almost the same parameters, but a higher `sample_rate` of 0.9.

Naturally, training took more time. The cross-validation MSE was slightly better, with a narrower range, but the MSE was notably worse on the test data, suggesting that early stopping was preventing some overfitting?

MNIST: Default Random Forest

This is a pattern recognition problem (see "Data Set: Handwritten Digits" on page 64 for a reminder), and because we are trying to assign one of ten values to each sample, it is a *multinomial* classification problem. If following along, run either Example 3-3 or Example 3-4 from the earlier chapter, which sets up H2O, loads the data, and defines `train`, `valid`, `test`, `x`, and `y`.

Unlike before, with the building energy data set, this time we have a `valid` set, and so won't use cross-validation. Here is the Python code:

```
m = h2o.estimators.H2ORandomForestEstimator(model_id="RF_defaults")
m.train(x, y, train, validation_frame=valid)
```

And the R code:

```
m <- h2o.randomForest(
  x, y, train, model_id = "RF_defaults", validation_frame = valid
  )
```

That code takes about two minutes to run on my machine; all eight cores were used equally at almost 100%.

If you look in the model information you might see it says 500 trees were made—not the 50 that the default settings requested! What is going on is that with a multinomial classification, for both random forest and GBM, one internal tree is built per output class. (Binomial and regression tree models have just the one internal tree per requested tree.) Each internal tree is predicting how likely a value is in that class, and we have 10 classes. Those 10 internal trees each produce a probability. The class with the highest probability is the one that is chosen as the prediction (but all the probabilities are returned if you want to do something more sophisticated with them).

If you look at the confusion matrix (over on Flow, or from R with `h2o.confusionMatrix(m, valid = TRUE)`, or `m.confusion_matrix(valid)` on Python) you will see it has done rather well: it got only 370 out of the 10,000 validation samples wrong.

I use this little MNIST-specific helper in Python, to both quickly view the confusion matrix, and get rid of all the annoying ".0" on the end of the counts:

```
def cm(m, data=valid):
    d = m.confusion_matrix(data).as_data_frame()
    d[list("0123456789")] = d[list("0123456789")].astype(int)
    return(d)
```

	0	1	2	3	4	5	6	7	8	9	Error	Rate
0	1004	0	0	1	1	2	3	1	3	2	0.012783	13 / 1,017
1	0	1083	7	1	2	0	2	3	1	2	0.016349	18 / 1,101
2	4	5	941	4	4	0	3	2	10	2	0.034872	34 / 975
3	0	0	16	976	4	7	0	13	12	5	0.055179	57 / 1,033
4	1	1	3	0	910	0	3	1	4	26	0.041096	39 / 949
5	2	2	3	14	1	897	12	1	5	3	0.045745	43 / 940
6	4	0	1	0	0	12	935	0	2	0	0.019916	19 / 954
7	1	0	13	2	8	1	0	1002	2	17	0.042065	44 / 1,046
8	9	3	7	11	4	7	3	1	931	10	0.055781	55 / 986
9	2	0	2	14	15	2	0	5	8	951	0.048048	48 / 999
10	1027	1094	993	1023	949	928	961	1029	978	1018	0.0370	370 / 10,000

When you look at `h2o.hit_ratio_table(m, valid=TRUE)` (in Python, `m.hit_ratio_table(valid=True)`), it is a bit less impressive:

```
    k  hit_ratio
 1  1  0.963000
 2  2  0.988400
 3  3  0.993100
 4  4  0.996500
 5  5  0.997500
 6  6  0.998000
 7  7  0.998500
 8  8  0.998600
 9  9  0.998600
10 10  1.000000
```

There were 10,000 samples. You can interpret the first value of 0.9630 as: "On the first guess it got 9630 correct and 370 wrong." The second value is 0.9884, and `(0.9884 - 0.9628) * 10000 = 256`, meaning it got another 256 right on its second guess. And so on. The "0.9986" in the ninth row means there were `(1 - 0.9986) * 10000 = 14` that it still hadn't got after nine guesses.

`h2o.performance(m, test)` is how to evaluate it on the test data. Running this it told me 327 wrong, so in fact it did slightly better than the 370 score on the validation test data. And there were only 7, not 14, that it couldn't get after nine guesses (the `h2o.performance()` function outputs all this information).

MNIST: Tuned Random Forest

In our default random forest the `max_depth` of each tree was 20, but almost every tree was banging into that limit. So increasing that parameter is an obvious tuning idea. And giving it more trees is another sensible idea. But both of those mean it will take longer to learn each model. So, I start by adding early stopping, trying to find a compromise between not killing a model before it gets chance to shine, and not taking too long to compute!

```
stopping_tolerance = 0.0001,
stopping_rounds = 3,
score_tree_interval = 3,
```

These say that if it hasn't improved by at least 0.01% over the last 9 trees, then stop and call it a day. With that in place, we can increase `ntrees` from 50 to 500 (and hope it doesn't use all 500 each time).

The other thing for the initial grid is seeing if `min_rows` is important. It wasn't important with the building energy data, but that data set only had 768 rows; now we have 50,000 rows. So I tried `min_rows` of 1, 2, and 5. And `max_depth` of 20, 50, and 120 was tried. I also used two random seeds to get a feel for sensitivity to randomness.

It ran for over an hour before I stopped it early. `max_depth` of 50 and 20 were almost identical, with 50 just a fraction better each time, and the couple of `max_depth = 120` models that completed were exactly identical to the depth 50 ones. The `min_rows = 5` was distinctly worse, while `min_rows = 1` was fractionally better than 2. Each model used between 66 and 132 trees.

The best model from the first grid *is* better than the default model, though not by anything amazing: 96.62% correct on the first guess, compared to 96.3% with default settings; in other words, a net improvement of 32 more samples correctly recognized. (Remember that random variations mean you are likely to see slightly different results.)

What else might we try? The 10 classes are not perfectly balanced, but are not far off, so there should be no need to weight any training rows. What about sampling? `mtries` defaults to the (rounded-down) square root of the number of columns, and the square root of 784 is 28. (With the enhanced data, the square root of 898 columns, rounded down, is 29—close enough not to make much difference.) We could try a higher number. We could try fiddling with `col_sample_rate_per_tree` and `sample_rate` too. And with those changes, maybe different values for `min_rows` and `max_depth` have become more important, so try a couple each for those:

```
g2 <- h2o.grid("randomForest", grid_id = "RF_2",
  search_criteria = list(
   strategy = "RandomDiscrete",
   max_models = 20  #Of the 108 possible
   ),

  hyper_params = list(
    min_rows = c(1, 2),
    mtries = c(28, 42, 56),
    col_sample_rate_per_tree = c(0.75, 0.9, 1.0),
    sample_rate = c(0.5, 0.7, 0.9),
    max_depth = c(40, 60)
    ),

  x = x, y = y, training_frame = train,
  validation_frame = valid,
  ntrees = 500,
  stopping_tolerance = 0.0001,
  stopping_rounds = 3,
  score_tree_interval = 3
  )
```

Altogether that gave 108 possible models, and I set it to stop after 20 models. However, after about 2.5 hours (!) I decided the 17 models were enough so I canceled it at that point. The results are shown next:

sample_rate	min_rows	max_depth	mtries	col...tree	logloss
0.9	2	60	42	0.9	0.21656
0.7	2	60	56	0.9	0.22380
0.7	2	60	56	1	0.22463
0.9	1	40	28	0.75	0.22666
0.9	1	40	28	0.9	0.22854
0.5	2	40	56	1	0.23525
0.5	2	60	56	0.9	0.2388
0.5	1	60	56	0.9	0.24018
0.5	1	60	56	0.75	0.24054
0.7	1	40	28	1	0.24193
0.5	2	60	42	1	0.24331
0.5	1	60	42	0.75	0.25012
0.5	2	60	28	1	0.25705
0.5	1	40	28	1	0.25745
0.5	2	60	28	0.75	0.26080
0.5	1	40	28	0.75	0.26168
0.5	1	60	28	0.75	0.27034

This RandomDiscrete grid search has chosen 0.5 for the `sample_rate` parameter 11 times out of 17 (compared to only three times each for 0.7 and 0.9); these things happen with random processes. But, they have all done worse than than 0.7 and 0.9 so I think we can confidently say `sample_rate=0.5` is a bad choice. If so, I will often mentally remove them, so the grid results now look like this:

sample_rate	min_rows	max_depth	mtries	col...tree	logloss
0.9	2	60	42	0.9	0.21656
0.7	2	60	56	0.9	0.22380
0.7	2	60	56	1	0.22463
0.9	1	40	28	0.75	0.22666
0.9	1	40	28	0.9	0.22854
0.7	1	40	28	1	0.24193

That looks clear-cut! `min_rows` of 2 is better than 1, `max_depth` of 60 is better than 40, *and* `mtries` of 28 is not good? Maybe, but the unfortunate random sampling hurts us here too: every time we had `min_rows` of 1 we also had `max_depth` of 40 and also had `mtries` of 28. Maybe only one of these is significant, and the other two are just along for the ride? Second and third best differ only by the `col_sample_rate_per_tree` value, as do fourth and fifth. So maybe 0.75 is superior to 0.9 is superior to 1.0? But the logloss is very close in each case.

For a third grid I varied `mtries` (42 or 56) and `sample_rate` (0.7 or 0.9) and then tried with two different random seeds, keeping `min_rows` constant at 2 and `max_depth` constant at 40. (The results given here also merge in the best five from the previous grid.)

sample_rate	seed	min_rows	max_depth	mtries	logloss
0.9	999	2	40	56	0.20486
0.9	999	2	40	42	0.21214
0.9	101	2	40	42	0.21454
0.9	300	2	60	42	0.21656
0.9	101	2	40	56	0.22024
0.7	999	2	40	56	0.22317
0.7	350	2	60	56	0.22380
0.7	400	2	60	56	0.22463
0.7	101	2	40	56	0.22358
0.9	450	1	40	28	0.22666
0.9	500	1	40	28	0.22854
0.7	999	2	40	42	0.23153
0.7	101	2	40	42	0.23511

It looks like a `sample_rate` of 0.9 is better than 0.7; the jury is still out on if a higher `mtries` has an effect, but I'm going to go with 56.

I will go with the first model in that grid as the Chosen One. The grid was called g3; I can fetch and evaluate that first model on the test data with:

```
bestModel <- h2o.getModel(g3@model_ids[[1]])
h2o.performance(bestModel, test)
```

It gets 305 wrong out of 10,000, which is 22 better than the default model. (Second guess, third guess, etc. are all slightly better too.)

Enhanced Data

If I repeat the default random forest model, but use the enhanced MNIST data (the extra 113 columns), it gets 355 wrong in the validation set and 326 wrong in the test set. So, only a smidgeon better than on the pixel-only data.

When I tried that final grid with the enhanced MNIST data I got these grid results:

	sample_rate	seed	min_rows	max_depth	mtries	col_sample_rate_per_tree	logloss
1	0.9	999	2	40	56	0.9	0.19946616
2	0.9	101	2	40	56	0.9	0.20147704
3	0.9	101	2	40	42	0.9	0.20494049
4	0.9	999	2	40	42	0.9	0.20636335
5	0.7	101	2	40	56	0.9	0.21045509
6	0.7	999	2	40	42	0.9	0.21215725
7	0.7	101	2	40	42	0.9	0.21510395
8	0.7	999	2	40	56	0.9	0.21713063

We get similar conclusions (0.9 better than 0.7, 56 better than 42), and slightly better logloss results. However, the following confusion matrix on the best model shows it was one *worse*, with an error rate of 306 instead of the earlier 305 when using just the raw pixels. Bad luck?[7]

```
Confusion Matrix: vertical: actual; across: predicted
       0    1    2    3    4   5   6    7   8    9 Error             Rate
0    971    0    0    0    0   1   4    1   3    0 0.0092 =      9 /   980
1      0 1124    3    2    1   1   3    0   1    0 0.0097 =     11 / 1,135
2      7    0  996    7    1   0   1    7  13    0 0.0349 =     36 / 1,032
3      0    0    8  971    0   4   1   14   8    4 0.0386 =     39 / 1,010
4      0    0    3    0  948   0   4    0   6   21 0.0346 =     34 /   982
5      3    0    1   12    1 859   6    2   5    3 0.0370 =     33 /   892
6      4    3    1    0    3   6 937    0   4    0 0.0219 =     21 /   958
7      1    5   12    3    2   0   0  992   2   11 0.0350 =     36 / 1,028
8      6    1    3    7    3   6   4    2 938    4 0.0370 =     36 /   974
9      5    6    4   13   12   2   0    4   5  958 0.0505 =     51 / 1,009
Totals 997 1139 1031 1015 971 879 960 1022 985 1001 0.0306 = 306 / 10,000

Top-10 Hit Ratios:
    k hit_ratio
1   1  0.969400
2   2  0.990900
3   3  0.995200
```

---

7 Yes, actually, it was. If I try with the second best model from the grid, I get an error rate of 288, and would have concluded enhanced data was worth an improvement of 17! The error rate, on test, for the other six models was 310, 292, 312, 308, 320, 313, respectively; so a different random seed can cause a range of at least 18.

```
 4   4  0.998000
 5   5  0.998700
 6   6  0.999300
 7   7  0.999400
 8   8  0.999400
 9   9  0.999400
10  10  1.000000
```

The results of all four learning algorithms will be compared in "MNIST Results" on page 261 in the final chapter of this book.

Football: Default Random Forest

Our third data set is a time series, football results (see "Data Set: Football Scores" on page 71), and we have phrased it as a binomial classification: estimate if the home side will win or not. We have two alternatives for the fields to learn from: with or without the bookmaker odds, that is, with or without expert predictions. It is expected to be tougher without the odds.

If you are following along, run either Example 3-6 or Example 3-7 from the earlier chapter, which sets up H2O, loads the data, and has defined train, valid, test, x, xNoOdds, and y. This is the first time we have met a binomial model, and AUC will be our main metric (see "Binomial Classification" on page 94 for a reminder).

Before we go any further I want to introduce a helper function. Because we are going to be making multiple models, I will often want to analyze them side by side. Example 5-1 shows how to compare metrics for multiple models, on each of our data sets: train, valid, and test. It returns a 3D array, which we can then slice up.

The function is a bit long, but worth studying as it shows both how to use H2O's built-in functions, such as h2o.auc(), as well as how to hack out the information you want when there is no built-in function: I used str(m) to poke around in the objects, to find the variable names I needed.

The information it needs for the train and valid data is found inside of H2O's model object; whereas it has to call h2o.performance() to get the same numbers on the test data. The default for labels uses the model IDs. You will see how to use this function later in this chapter. There is a similar function in Python in the online code.

Example 5-1. Comparing metrics for multiple models (in R)

```
compareModels <- function(models, test, labels = NULL){
#Use model IDs as default labels, if not given
if(is.null(labels)){
  labels <- lapply(models, function(m) m@model_id)
  }
```

```
res <- sapply(models, function (m){
  mcmsT <- m@model$training_metrics@metrics$max_criteria_and_metric_scores
  mcmsV <- m@model$validation_metrics@metrics$max_criteria_and_metric_scores
  maix <- which(mcmsT$metric=="max accuracy")  #4 (at the time of writing)
  th <- mean(mcmsT[maix, 'threshold'], mcmsV[maix, 'threshold'] )

  pf <- h2o.performance(m, test)
  tms <- pf@metrics$thresholds_and_metric_scores
  ix <- apply(outer(th, tms$threshold, "<="), 1, sum)
  if(ix < 1)ix <- 1  #Use first entry if less than all of them

  matrix(c(
    h2o.auc(m, TRUE, TRUE), pf@metrics$AUC,
    mcmsT[maix, 'value'], mcmsV[maix, 'value'], tms[ix, 'accuracy'],
    h2o.logloss(m, TRUE, TRUE), pf@metrics$logloss,
    h2o.mse(m, TRUE, TRUE), pf@metrics$MSE
    ), ncol = 4)
  }, simplify = "array")

dimnames(res) <- list(
  c("train","valid","test"),
  c("AUC","Accuracy","logloss", "MSE"),
  labels
  )

res
}
```

 Close study of that code will show it gets its threshold for test accuracy by averaging the values for train and valid results, but that the train and valid results instead use *maximum* accuracy. This means the accuracy numbers for test and valid will be slightly overstated, compared to those for test. See Figure 4-2 in Chapter 4 to get a feel for the difference.

I will train two models, the first with all fields (x), the second excluding the odds data (xNoOdds). See Examples 5-2 and 5-3.

Example 5-2. Two default random forest models, in R

```
m1 <- h2o.randomForest(x, y, train,
  model_id = "RF_defaults_Odds",
  validation_frame = valid)

m2 <- h2o.randomForest(xNoOdds, y, train,
  model_id = "RF_defaults_NoOdds",
  validation_frame = valid)
```

Example 5-3. Two default random forest models (Python)

```
m1 = h2o.estimators.H2ORandomForestEstimator(model_id="RF_defaults_Odds")
m1.train(x, y, train, validation_frame=valid)

m2 = h2o.estimators.H2ORandomForestEstimator(model_id="RF_defaults_NoOdds")
m2.train(xNoOdds, y, train, validation_frame=valid)
```

It finished relatively quickly: about one-tenth of the time it took random forest to train on the MNIST data. Here is how `compareModels()` can be used to compare the AUC and accuracy scores of each of m1 and m2 on each of the three data sets:

```
res <- compareModels(c(m1, m2), test)
round(res[,"AUC",], 3)
round(res[,"Accuracy",], 3)
```

The results show AUC first, then accuracy underneath: they are easy to confuse on this particular data set, as the numbers are close:

```
      HomeWin HW-NoOdds
train   0.552     0.556
valid   0.637     0.601
test    0.604     0.581

      HomeWin HW-NoOdds
train   0.556     0.561
valid   0.634     0.609
test    0.609     0.599
```

Our benchmark numbers (the linear model, using just the average bookmaker odds) were an AUC of 0.650 and an accuracy of 0.634 on predicting home wins, and we are well below that here. A comparison of how all models did is in the final chapter; see "Football Data" on page 263.

Incidentally, at the top of the summary, it says it made 50 trees, with a `max_depth` of 20, but it also says the `min_depth` is 20. Perhaps we should try allowing deeper trees when we try tuning?

Football: Tuned Random Forest

Out of the box, random forest did not do too great at predicting football scores. For this section I will focus on the easiest problem (predicting a home win, when including the expert opinion fields as input fields), and then hope whatever we learned from that will apply to the other model.

As with the other data sets, the first thing we will do is use early stopping. The following parameters say that if there are four scoring rounds with zero improvement on the AUC metric, then stop:

```
stopping_metric = "AUC", stopping_tolerance = 0, stopping_rounds = 4
```

That gives us the freedom to request lots of trees, and means one less parameter to tune:

```
ntrees = 500
```

The hyper-parameters to try are:

- `max_depth`: I will try 20, 40, and 60.
- `mtries`: There are 58 columns, so the default (the square root, rounded down) is 7 columns. I will try 5, 7, and 10.
- `col_sample_rate_per_tree`: 0.9 or 1.0.
- `sample_rate`: 0.5, 0.75, and 0.95.
- `min_rows`: 1, 2, and 5.

In `search_criteria` I set `strategy = "RandomDiscrete"`, and then set `max_models` to be 54, which is one-third of the combinations, though I interrupted it after 38 models.

By default g1 is giving me logloss, but I want to see AUC, so I will use this code:

```
g1_auc <- h2o.getGrid(g1@grid_id, sort_by="auc", decreasing = TRUE)
range(g1_auc@summary_table$auc)
```

The AUC for the 38 models is quite narrow: from 0.644 to 0.668. However, our default model only managed 0.637. When *all* models in the first grid (which tends to involve quite a bit of guesswork) are better, I get suspicious. The explanation, in this case, is that we moved from the default 50 trees to a generous 500 trees. Even though early stopping means all 500 are never used, it does now get *enough* trees.

I won't show the full grid results, and instead will pick out the highlights:

- The best models use `min_rows = 5`; in contrast the `min_rows = 1` entries are mostly at the very bottom.
- `sample_rate = 0.5` is always in the top half. 0.75 is also good, but 0.95 has consistently done badly.
- There is no obvious pattern for any of `max_depth` (hinting that `max_depth = 20` is sufficient), `mtries`, or `col_sample_rate_per_tree`.

Because our experimental high value for `min_rows` did best, my next grid will try even higher values (10 and 15). Similarly, a `sample_rate` below 0.5 will be tried and the 0.95 value dropped (0.45, 0.55, 0.65, 0.75). It took just over 20 minutes to make 24 models.

I'll save you those results, too, because I found that four of the best five models used `sample_rate = 0.45` and four of the best five models used `min_rows = 15`. So I made another grid, adding two lower `sample_rate` values (0.25, 0.35), and two higher `min_rows` values (20, 25). Again, the highest values of `min_rows` have come out on top, so repeat again! And again 30, 35, and 40 came out on top, so I repeated again. With each new grid I also removed some of the under-performing values, to keep the combinatorial explosion under control.

Even though the best three models come from the highest values of `min_rows` that I tried (50 and 60), so I could keep trying higher values, I decided to stop at this point because the AUC of the top 8 models are all within 0.001, and I'm getting diminishing returns:

	sample_rate	min_rows	mtries	auc
110	0.25	50	7	0.6777874
111	0.35	60	5	0.6776425
112	0.55	60	5	0.6776103
70	0.35	35	5	0.6774847
114	0.35	40	5	0.6774416
71	0.35	30	5	0.6771522
116	0.45	60	5	0.6771512
72	0.35	40	5	0.6768411

What about accuracy? Let's try that `compareModels()` function; here is how to use it to compare just the top models from a grid:

```
d <- as.data.frame(g@summary_table)
topModels <- lapply(head(d$model_ids), h2o.getModel)
res <- compareModels(topModels, test)
round(res[,"AUC",], 3)
round(res[,"Accuracy",], 3)
```

For the best three models, that code gave these results, AUC, then accuracy (I've edited the output to show the hyper-parameters for each model):

sample_rate:	0.25	0.25	0.35
min_rows:	50	40	60
mtries:	5	7	5
train	0.612	0.613	0.612
valid	0.678	0.678	0.678
test	0.646	0.646	0.646
train	0.591	0.591	0.591
valid	0.650	0.649	0.651
test	0.634	0.633	0.635

By the rules, we would choose the third model as it gave the best result on the validation data; luckily that also gave the best result on the test data. The AUC of 0.646 is worse than the benchmark linear model (0.650), but the accuracy of 0.635 just beats the benchmark of 0.634. Not enough to justify the extra effort and complexity of a random forest, but at least it shows it is competitive. And we have significantly improved on the default random forest model results (AUC was 0.604, accuracy was 0.609).

A reminder that "Football Data" on page 263, in the final chapter, will compare the results of all models.

Summary

Random forests models are generally quick to build, and give effective results on most problems. There are not too many tuning knobs and, looking back over this chapter, the most effective technique was to increase `ntrees`, in combination with early stopping. Increasing `max_depth` was also effective.

Random forest is not the only way that the basic decision tree idea has been improved, though, and the next chapter will look at an alternative approach.

CHAPTER 6

Gradient Boosting Machines

A gradient boosting machine (GBM, from now on) is another decision tree algorithm, just like random forest (Chapter 5). If you skipped that chapter, and also don't know what decision trees are, I suggest you go back and at least read some of it; this next section is going to talk more about how GBMs are different, and the pros and cons of their difference. Then, as in other chapters, we'll see how the H2O implementation of GBM performs out-of-the-box on our data sets, and then how we can tune it.

Boosting

Just like random forest, GBM is an ensemble method: we're going to be making more than one tree, then combining their outputs. Boosting is the central idea here. What is getting the "boost" is the importance of the harder-to-learn training data. Imagine a data set with just 10 rows (10 examples to learn from) and two numeric predictor columns (x1, x2), and we are trying to learn to distinguish between two possible values: circle or cross.

The very simplest decision tree we can make has just one node; I will represent it with a straight line in the following diagrams, which divides our training data into two. Unless we get lucky, chances are it has made some mistakes. Figure 6-1 shows the line it chose on its first try.

The truth table from our first decision tree looks like:

```
           Correct
        Circle  Cross
Circle    3       1
Cross     3       3
```

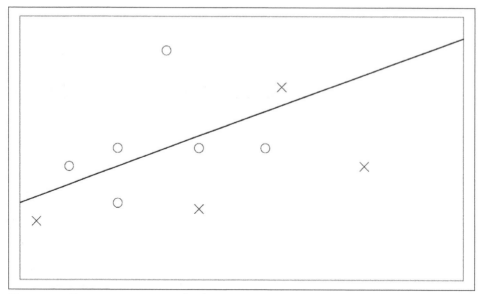

Figure 6-1. First try to partition the data

It scored 60%: six right, four wrong. It called one cross a circle, and there were three circles it thought were crosses. What we do now is train another very simple tree, but first we modify the training data to give the four rows it got wrong a higher weight. How much of a higher weight? That is where the "gradient" bit of GBM comes in (but we don't need to understand it to use and tune GBMs).

In Figure 6-2 I've made the circles and crosses for the wrong items bigger, and our next tree pays more attention to them.

It helped, as it got three of those four right… But it got a different three items wrong, so it still scores 60%. So, for our third tree, we tell it those four are more important; the one it has got wrong twice in a row is the biggest of all. Figure 6-3 shows its third attempt.

If we stop training here, we end up with three weak models that scored 60%, 60%, and 80%, respectively. However, at least one of each of those three trees got every training row correct. You can see how they can work together to cover each other's weaknesses, but hopefully you also got a glimpse of how easy it would be to overfit the data.

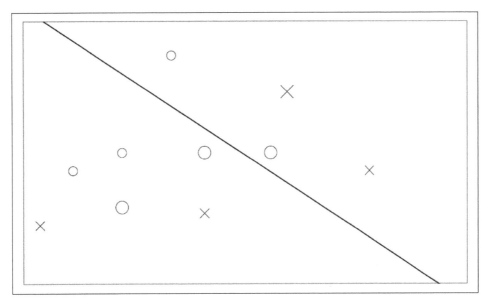

Figure 6-2. Second try to partition the data

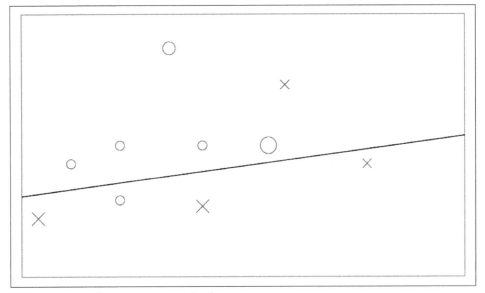

Figure 6-3. Final try to partition the data

The Good, the Bad, and… the Mysterious

GBM naturally focuses attention on the difficult rows in your training data, the ones that are hard to learn. That is good, but it can also be bad. If there is one outlier that each tree keeps getting wrong it is going to get boosted and boosted until it is bigger than the whole universe. If that outlier is real data (an unusual event, a black swan), then this is good, as it will know what to do when it sees one again. If it was bogus (a measuring error, a typo) it is going to distort your accuracy.

The H2O implementation of GBM works well across a cluster if your data is large. However, in my tests, there was not much speed-up from using a cluster on smaller data sets.

The mysterious? Well, unlike (simple) decision trees, which can be really good at explaining their thinking, it becomes a bit of a black box. You have all these dumb little trees, yet quality answers kind of emerge out of them.

Parameters

If you read Chapter 5, you will have seen most of these, but the relevant ones will be shown again here. `learn_rate`, `learn_rate_annealing`, and `max_abs_leaf node_pred` are GBM-specific. What random forest calls `mtries`, GBM calls `col_sam ple_rate`; see "Sampling, Generalizing" on page 108 in Chapter 4—in fact, see the whole of that chapter for the other parameters you can use to control GBM.

For Python users, all of the following parameters are given to the model's constructor, not to the `train()` function.

Just as with random forest, the two most important parameters are:

ntrees
How many trees to make.

max_depth
How deep each tree is allowed to grow. In other words, how complex each tree is allowed to be.

GBM trees are usually shallower than random forest ones, and that is reflected in the lower default of 5 for `max_depth`. `ntrees` defaults to 50 (same as random forest).

These two control the learning rate:

learn_rate
Learning rate (from 0.0 to 1.0). The default is 0.1. Lower takes longer and requires a higher `ntrees`, both of which will increase training time (and query time), but give a better model.

learn_rate_annealing
Scale the learning rate by this factor after each tree (e.g., 0.99 or 0.999). This defaults to 1.0, but allows you to have the `learn_rate` start high, then gradually get lower as trees are added.

The next two parameters control *if* splitting is done:

min_rows

How many training data rows are needed to make a leaf node. The default is 10; if you set it lower you may have more of a problem with overfitting.

min_split_improvement

This controls how much reduction in the inaccuracy, in the error, there has to be for a split to be worthwhile. The default is zero, meaning it is not used.

The next set of parameters control *how* the splitting is done:

histogram_type

What type of histogram to use for finding optimal split points. Can be one of "AUTO," "UniformAdaptive," "Random," "QuantilesGlobal," or "RoundRobin." Can usually be left as AUTO, but worth trying in a grid if you are hunting for ideas.

nbins

For numerical columns, build a histogram of (at least) this many bins, then split at the best point. The default value is 20. Consider a lower value if cluster scaling is poor.

nbins_top_level

For numerical columns, build a histogram of (at most) this many bins at the root level, then decrease by factor of two per level. It defaults to 1024.

nbins_cats

For categorical columns, build a histogram of (at most) this many bins, then split at the best point. Higher values can lead to more overfitting, and also worse performance on a cluster. Like `nbins_top_level`, the default is 1024.

Finally, there is this one for when you are running on a cluster, but find it scaling poorly:

build_tree_one_node

Run on one node only. You will only be using the CPUs on that node; the rest of the cluster will be unused.

Regarding scaling, the communication overhead grows with the number of calculations to find the best column to split, and where to split it. So more columns in your data, higher value for `nbins` and `nbins_cats`, and a higher value for `max_depth` will all make it scale less well.

Building Energy Efficiency: Default GBM

This data set deals with the heating/cooling costs of various house designs (see "Data Set: Building Energy Efficiency" on page 54), and it is a regression problem. If you are following along, run either Example 3-1 or Example 3-2 (from Chapter 3), which sets up H2O, loads the data, and has defined train, test, x, and y. We are using 10-fold cross-validation, instead of a validation set. (See "Cross-Validation (aka k-folds)" on page 104 for a reminder about cross-validation.)

```
m <- h2o.gbm(x, y, train, nfolds = 10, model_id = "GBM_defaults")
```

In Python use:

```
from h2o.estimators.gbm import H2OGradientBoostingEstimator
m = H2OGradientBoostingEstimator(model_id="GBM_defaults", nfolds=10)
m.train(x, y, train)
```

Try m (in R or Python), and see how it did. Fifty trees were made, each of depth 5. On cross-validation data, the MSE (mean squared error) is 2.462, and R^2 is 0.962. (You may see different results due to random variation.)

In the "Cross-Validation Metrics Summary" (seen when printing m) note that the standard deviation on the "mse" row is a high 0.688, and the mse on our 10 folds ranges from 1.471 to 4.369. (You will see slightly different numbers, as the 10 folds are selected randomly.)

Under "Variable Importances" (shown next), which can be seen with h2o.varimp(m) in R, or m.varimp(True) in Python, you will see it is giving X5 way more importance than any of the others; this is typical for GBM models:

variable	relative_importance	scaled_importance	percentage
X5	236888	1	0.796119
X1	19310.6	0.0815178	0.0648979
X3	18540.1	0.0782653	0.0623086
X7	13867.3	0.0585397	0.0466046
X4	4211.8	0.0177797	0.0141548
X8	3442.27	0.0145313	0.0115686
X6	1293.23	0.00545927	0.00434623
X2	0	0	0

When we looked at this data set back in "Let's Take a Look!" on page 59, and especially the correlations, X5 was the most highly correlated with Y2, our response column. Notice how X1 is second most important, but X2 was not used at all—this is good, because those two columns were perfectly (negatively) correlated.

How about on the unseen data? h2o.performance(m, test) (m.model_perfor mance(test) in Python) is saying MSE is 2.318, better than on the training data. By taking the square root of 2.318 (or looking at RMSE) we get 1.522kWh/(m²yr), which is in the same units as Y2. To give that some context, the range of Y2 is from 10.90 to 48.03kWh/(m²yr).

As in the other chapters, let's plot its actual predictions on a chart (see Figure 6-4). The black dots are the correct answers, the small squares are guesses that were quite close, while the up arrows are where it was more than 8% too high, and the down arrows are where it was more than 8% too low. Out of 143 test samples, there are 7 up arrows and 7 down arrows. (Only the first 75 samples are shown on the plot.)

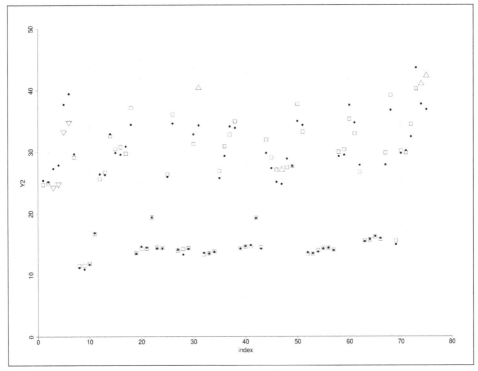

Figure 6-4. Default performance of GBM on test data

Building Energy Efficiency: Tuned GBM

I decided to start, this time, with a big random grid search. If you skipped over the description of grids ("Grid Search" on page 122 in Chapter 5) the idea is to try making lots of models with different sets of parameters, and see which the best performing models are, and therefore which parameters suit this data set best.

The first 50 models that the grid spits out (which were made rapidly: about 10 seconds per model) have MSEs that range from 1.02 to 4.02. Putting that in context, the default model had an MSE of 2.46. Some much better, some much worse. Let's look at each parameter that was tried, and how it did in that small 50-model sample:

max_depth

The default is 5, and I tried 11 different values (5,10,15,20,25,30,40,50,60,75,90). But, four of the top six models were max_depth=5! (The other two in the top 6 were 20 and 10.) Just to muddy the waters a bit, the ninth best model was max_depth=75, so high values may not be *bad*, as such, but they don't appear to help.

min_rows

The default is 10, but because we don't have that much data, and because there is no duplication or noise in it, I guessed lower values might be useful, so tried 1, 2, 5, and 10. I guessed wrong. All but one of the top 28 are either 5 or 10, while the bottom 22 models are all 1 or 2. It is very clear-cut, except for one small detail... the *best* model, the Numero Uno, the Mr. Big of our candidate models, uses min_rows=1. And this is where we have to watch out for random grid search being random: this was the only time it combined min_rows of 1 with max_depth of 5; almost all those poorly performing min_rows = 1 and min_rows = 2 models have high values for max_depth.

sample_rate

I tried 0.67, 0.8, 0.9, 0.95, and (the default of) 1.0, expecting high numbers to perform better. There is no strong pattern, but the top 7 all use one of 0.9, 0.95, and 1.0, so I feel I could narrow it to just those.

col_sample_rate

I tried 0.7, 0.9, and 1.0, which (because there are only eight predictor columns) should correspond to 6, 7, and 8 columns. I see all three values evenly scattered in the results, so it appears the model is not sensitive to this.

nbins

The final hyper-parameter tried was how many groups to divide the values in a column into. The default is 20, and I decided to try 8, 12, 16, 24, and 32. All values are represented in the top quarter of the models, so no conclusion can be drawn yet.

What about ntrees? Isn't that the first parameter you want to be tuning? Instead of trying to tune it, I set it high (1000) and used early stopping, with the following settings: if there is no improvement over 20 trees (which will represent 4 scoring rounds), then stop:

```
ntrees = 1000,
stopping_tolerance = 0,
stopping_rounds = 4,
score_tree_interval = 5,
```

Given that the models were being built so quickly I decided to narrow the parameters slightly (dropped 40 and higher for max_depth and dropped sample_rate of 0.67) and build another 150 models, then merge the results. (A different random seed was also used.)

…time passes (over 40 minutes, in fact)…

More model results just confirmed the first impression: `min_rows` of 1 (or 2) is effective with `max_depth` of 5, but really poor with higher values. `min_rows` of 10 is effective with any value of `max_depth`, but possibly 10 to 20 is best. Curiously `min_rows` of 5 is mediocre. A `sample_rate` of 0.9 or 0.95 looks best, while there is still no clarity for `col_sample_rate` or `nbins`.

So, the remaining grids will be done in two. Think boxing match: in the blue corner, weighing in with `max_depth` of only 5, we have `min_rows` = 1. (The crowd goes wild.) He will be experimenting with sample rates of 0.9 and 0.95, and three `col_sample_rate` values. Over in the red corner, competing at a variable `max_depth` weight of anywhere between 10 and 20, and threatening to go higher if the mood takes him, we have `min_rows` = 10! (Mix of boos and cheers from the crowd.) He says he will be sticking to using all his columns, but will also be experimenting with the same `sample_rate` choices. Both competitors will be switching to 10-fold cross-validation, and a much lower `learn_rate`, for this bout and all tests will done using three random seeds (to make it a fair contest). The two grids use the same `grid_id`, so all the models can be compared in a single table at the end.

Fight!

And we have a clear winner! But the value for seed was the biggest factor, so before I show the results I want to look at how the model performance across the 10 folds varies. (It is a good exercise in extracting values from the individual models when using cross-validation.)

Deep in the model information we have `cross_validation_metrics_summary`, which has 12 columns (one for each of the 10 folds, then two more columns for the mean and standard deviation of the 10 folds, respectively) and three rows (MSE and R^2, and then MSE again under the alias of deviance). Assuming g is the variable representing the grid of interest, then the following three lines of code will append mean and s.d. columns to the grid summary:[1]

```
models <- lapply(g@model_ids, h2o.getModel)
mse_sd <- t( as.numeric( sapply(models, function(m){
  m@model$cross_validation_metrics_summary["mse",c("mean","sd")]
  } ) ) )
cbind( as.data.frame(g@summary_table), mse_sd)
```

---

1 Incidentally, the relative ranking is identical if you instead look at R^2.

That code first extracts the "mean" and "s.d." columns into mse_sd. The call to as.numeric() is because all the data in the H2O object is in character format. The t() call is a matrix transpose; this allows appending the columns to the grid's existing summary.

Here are the results: a clear win for the blue corner!

	sample_rate	seed	min_rows	max_depth	co...rate	deviance	mean	sd
1	0.9	373	1	5	0.9	1.15003	1.15368	0.22753
2	0.9	373	1	5	1	1.15067	1.15349	0.23298
3	0.9	101	1	5	0.9	1.15626	1.15657	0.28437
4	0.9	101	1	5	1	1.16233	1.16137	0.26933
5	0.95	101	1	5	1	1.19692	1.19775	0.26828
6	0.9	373	1	5	0.7	1.22472	1.23143	0.26176
7	0.9	101	1	5	0.7	1.22559	1.22727	0.28405
8	0.95	373	1	5	0.9	1.22681	1.23102	0.27219
9	0.95	373	1	5	1	1.23035	1.23382	0.25511
10	0.95	101	1	5	0.9	1.25170	1.25348	0.28567
11	0.95	101	1	5	0.7	1.27758	1.28178	0.29919
12	0.95	373	1	5	0.7	1.30143	1.30826	0.29126
13	0.9	373	10	10	1	1.31844	1.33174	0.32268
14	0.9	373	10	20	1	1.31936	1.33165	0.31374
15	0.9	101	10	10	1	1.35430	1.34822	0.29901
16	0.95	373	10	20	1	1.35664	1.36992	0.34305
17	0.95	101	10	20	1	1.37336	1.36631	0.30533
18	0.95	101	10	10	1	1.37717	1.37018	0.30708
19	0.95	373	10	10	1	1.38266	1.39670	0.34485
20	0.9	101	10	20	1	1.38350	1.37478	0.33678
21	0.9	999	1	5	1	1.44974	1.37334	0.58270
22	0.9	999	1	5	0.9	1.48146	1.40514	0.58647
23	0.95	999	1	5	1	1.48949	1.41238	0.61211
24	0.95	999	1	5	0.9	1.50276	1.43098	0.58378
25	0.9	999	10	10	1	1.50816	1.45265	0.48877
26	0.9	999	10	20	1	1.54106	1.48196	0.51210
27	0.9	999	1	5	0.7	1.60933	1.53082	0.62574
28	0.95	999	10	20	1	1.62599	1.58178	0.47222
29	0.95	999	10	10	1	1.62983	1.58302	0.48109
30	0.95	999	1	5	0.7	1.65019	1.57151	0.64591

sample_rate of 0.9 consistently beat 0.95. A col_sample_rate of 0.7 was consistently worse; but it was hard to separate col_sample_rate of 0.9 versus 1.0.

Looking at the rightmost column, the lower the s.d. the better it did. However, seed=999 is a little different, with the lower standard deviations coming from the min_rows=10 models.

I'd be tempted at this point to grab half a dozen of these models and use them in an ensemble, to get even lower standard deviation. But let's stick with the game plan of choosing one single model, and go with the top-performing model from this grid (h2o <- h2o.getModel(g@model_ids[[1]])), and see how it does on the test data:

`h2o.performance(m, test)`. 1.640 for me. This is way better than the default GBM's 2.462, and also way better than the best tuned random forest model from the previous chapter.

Plotting the results (Figure 6-5), there are just two up triangles, and four down triangles (indicating when its guess was over 8% from the correct answer).

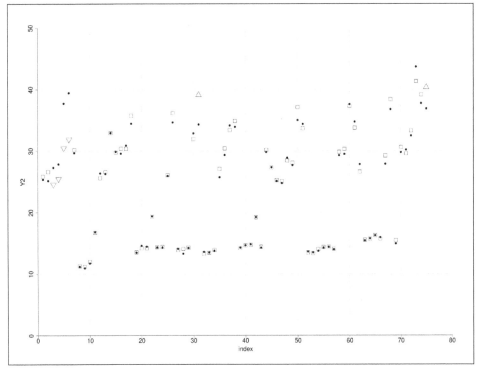

Figure 6-5. Tuned performance of GBM on test data

The results of all models on this data set will be compared in "Building Energy Results" on page 259 in the final chapter.

MNIST: Default GBM

See "Data Set: Handwritten Digits" on page 64 if you need a refresher on this pattern recognition problem. It is a multinomial classification, trying to look at the 784 pixels of a handwritten digit, and say which of 0 to 9 it is.

If you are following along, run either Example 3-3 then Example 6-1, or Example 3-4 then Example 6-2. The first one, from the earlier chapter, sets up H2O, loads the data, and has defined `train`, `valid`, `test`, `x`, and `y`. We have a validation data set, so qw won't be using cross-validation.

Example 6-1. Default GBM model for MNIST data (in R)

```
m <- h2o.gbm(x, y, train, model_id = "GBM_defaults",
  validation_frame = valid)
```

Example 6-2. Default GBM model for MNIST data (Python)

```
m = h2o.estimators.H2OGradientBoostingEstimator(model_id="GBM_defaults")
m.train(x, y, train, validation_frame=valid)
```

This took almost five minutes to run on my machine, and kept the cores fairly busy. The confusion matrix on the *training* data (h2o.confusionMatrix(m)) shows an error rate of 2.08%, while on the *validation* data (h2o.confusionMatrix(m, valid = TRUE)) it is a bit higher at 4.82%. MSE is 0.028 and 0.044, respectively. So we have a bit of overfitting on the training data, but not too much. h2o.performance(m, test) tries our model on the 10,000 test samples. The error this time is 4.44% (MSE is 0.048); in other words, the validation and test sets are giving us similar numbers, which is good.

The following code can be used to compare hit ratios on training, validation, and test data sets, in table format:

```
pf <- h2o.performance(m, test)
cbind(
  h2o.hit_ratio_table(m),
  h2o.hit_ratio_table(m,valid=T),
  pf@metrics$hit_ratio_table
  )
```

Notice that GBM, with default parameters, needs 9 or 10 guesses to get them all correct:

	TRAIN		VALID		TEST
k	hit_ratio	k	hit_ratio	k	hit_ratio
1	0.97922	1	0.95180	1	0.95560
2	0.99540	2	0.98400	2	0.98450
3	0.99828	3	0.99240	3	0.99200
4	0.99924	4	0.99580	4	0.99650
5	0.99972	5	0.99780	5	0.99850
6	0.99996	6	0.99870	6	0.99910
7	0.99998	7	0.99910	7	0.99950
8	0.99998	8	0.99970	8	0.99970
9	1.00000	9	1.00000	9	0.99980
10	1.00000	10	1.00000	10	1.00000

 To give you an idea of random variability, a second run of the preceding code gave an error rate on train of 1.83%, valid of 4.73%, and test of 4.28% (i.e., all slightly better). MSEs were 0.0253, 0.0489, and 0.0464 (slightly better).

MNIST: Tuned GBM

We will switch to using the enhanced data for all these tuning experiments. This change, sticking with default settings, improved the error rate from 4.82% (on the valid test set) to 4.19%. Not huge, but not to be sneezed at.

As usual, the first thing I want to do is switch to using early stopping, so I can then give it lots of trees to work with. I first tried this:

```
stopping_tolerance = 0.0001,
stopping_rounds = 3,
score_tree_interval = 3,
ntrees = 1000,
```

It was very slow, and also was spending a lot of time scoring, so I aborted it and switched to:

```
stopping_tolerance = 0.001,
stopping_rounds = 3,
score_tree_interval = 10,
ntrees = 400
```

These early stopping settings are saying stop if there is less than 0.1% improvement[2] after three scoring rounds, which represents 30 trees.

Just using this, with all other default settings, had some interesting properties:

- Training classification score was perfect after 140 trees (3.3 times the runtime of the default settings, for 2.8 times the number of trees).
- Validation score was down to 2.83% at the point.
- The MSE and logloss of both the training data and validation data continued to fall, and so did the validation classification score.
- Relative runtime kept increasing. That is, each new tree is taking longer.

It finished up with 360 trees, with a very respectable 2.17% error on the validation data.[3]

Well, how can we improve that further? Compared to the building energy data, there is a lot more training data, both in terms of columns and rows, so we expect that lower sample ratios will be more effective. I'm not sure about a low min_rows: there

---

2 In the default metric, which is logloss for a classification.

3 The first time I ran this was with H2O 3.8.2.x, and I got approximately the results shown here. When double-checking results, with version 3.8.3.x, as part of working on Chapter 11, I could not get better than 4% error. Now, in final checking with 3.10.0.8, I get these (good!) results again. A bug must have been introduced, and the bug must have been fixed! I've used the 3.10.0.8 results here and in Chapter 11.

are going to be some bad handwriting examples that only crop up a few times, so we won't want to place an artificial limit on them. Because we have so many columns, I am going to try increasing max_depth, so it can express some complex ideas.

What about learn_rate? Low is slower, but better... and we have a lot of data. So the plan is to use a high (quick) learn_rate for the first grid or two, then lower it later on, once we start to home in on the best parameters.

This is going to be a random grid search, because I'm going to throw loads of parameters into the stew and see what bubbles to the top. The full listing to run the grid is shown next, but I recommend you read the text that follows, rather than running it, as most of my hunches were wrong!

```
g1 <- h2o.grid("gbm", grid_id ="GBM_BigStew",
  search_criteria = list(
    strategy = "RandomDiscrete",
    max_models = 50
    ),

  hyper_params = list(
    max_depth = c(5, 20, 50),
    min_rows = c(2, 5, 10),
    sample_rate = c(0.5, 0.8, 0.95, 1.0),
    col_sample_rate = c(0.5, 0.8, 0.95, 1.0),
    col_sample_rate_per_tree = c(0.8, 0.99, 1.0),
    learn_rate = c(0.1),   #Placemarker
    seed = c(701)   #Placemarker
    ),

  x = x, y = y, training_frame = train, validation_frame = valid,

  stopping_tolerance = 0.001,
  stopping_rounds=3,
  score_tree_interval = 10,
  ntrees = 400
  )
```

My first discovery was that a high max_depth was not just very slow, but no better than a shallow one. And that min_rows=1 seemed poor. I killed the grid very early on, and got rid of max_depth=50 and min_rows=1. I left the updated version to run for a while, and found that max_depth=20 was distinctly worse than max_depth=5 (the default!). I also noticed that min_rows=10 (again, the default!) seemed to be doing best, though it was less clear. Reducing the three sample rates (from their defaults of 1) did seem to help, though there was not enough data to draw a confident conclusion.

So, another try. I'll leave `max_depth` and `min_rows` at their defaults, and just concentrate on testing sampling rates:

```
g2 <- h2o.grid("gbm", grid_id ="GBM_Better",
  search_criteria = list(
    strategy = "RandomDiscrete",
    max_models = 9
    ),

  hyper_params = list(
    max_depth = c(5),
    min_rows = c(10),
    sample_rate = c(0.5, 0.8, 0.95),
    col_sample_rate = c(0.5, 0.8, 0.95),
    col_sample_rate_per_tree = c(0.8, 0.99),
    learn_rate = c(0.1),  #Placemarker
    seed = c(701)  #Placemarker
    ),

  x = x, y = y, training_frame = train, validation_frame = valid,

  stopping_tolerance = 0.001,
  stopping_rounds = 3,
  score_tree_interval = 10,
  ntrees = 400
  )
```

 Even though they have now been reduced to one choice, so they could be moved to normal model parameters, I've left `max_depth` and `min_rows` in the hyper_params section deliberately. This does no harm, and allows me to change my mind later.

That took a while to complete. Measured in number of errors on the 10,000 validation samples, the models ranged from 214 to 239, and used from 350 to 400 trees. (They all scored perfectly on the training data.)

There was not that much clarity in the parameters, but the best two had `col_sample_rate` of 0.8 and `sample_rate` of 0.95. `sample_rate=0.5` was only chosen once, but was the worst of the nine. My default model (all sample rates of 1.0), with just early stopping added, would have come second best in the grid measured on classification error, but fourth on MSE, and seventh on logloss, whereas the "tuned" model is top on all metrics, so I have more confidence in selecting it.

As a final step, I ran the chosen model on the test data and got an error rate of 2.33%. This compares to 4.44% with the default settings. However, most of that improvement came from using early stopping and giving it six times more trees.

A reminder that the results of all four learning algorithms will be compared in "MNIST Results" on page 261 in the final chapter of this book.

Football: Default GBM

Check out "Data Set: Football Scores" on page 71 if you need a reminder of what this one is all about. It is a time series, we added some moving averages of recent results and stats from each team's previous match, and we also have a number of fields of expert opinion (bookmaker odds).

If you are following along, run either Example 3-6 or Example 3-7 from the earlier chapter, which sets up H2O, loads the data, and has defined train, valid, test, x, xNoOdds, and y.

Just as with MNIST, we have a validation data set, so will use that instead of cross-validation. We want to try models using all fields (x), and the harder challenge of not using the bookmaker odds (xNoOdds), to predict a home win (a fairly balanced binomial problem). Let's make both models at once:

```
m1 <- h2o.gbm(x, "HomeWin", train,
  model_id = "GBM_defaults_HomeWin_Odds",
  validation_frame = valid)
m2 <- h2o.gbm(xNoOdds, "HomeWin", train,
  model_id = "GBM_defaults_HomeWin_NoOdds",
  validation_frame = valid)
```

It took about 10 seconds for each model, and during that time my 8 cores were evenly used at about 60–70%. Using the compareModels() function (see Example 5-1) from Chapter 5, these are the AUC scores on each data set:

```
      HomeWin HW-NoOdds
train  0.652    0.633
valid  0.667    0.620
test   0.643    0.613
```

For m1, the accuracy was 0.644 on the validation data, and 0.626 on the test data (compared to 0.650 and 0.634 with the benchmark linear model). For m2 it was 0.607 and 0.602, respectively. No results to write home about. Notice how the expert opinion is making a difference (m1 does better than m2), though not that much. The final chapter ("Football Data" on page 263) compares all the algorithms on this data set.

Football: Tuned GBM

As usual, we start the tuning by giving it loads more trees, in conjunction with early stopping:

```
stopping_metric = "misclassification",
stopping_tolerance = 0,
```

```
       stopping_rounds = 4,
       score_tree_interval = 5,
       ntrees = 500
```

As an experiment, rather than diving into making a grid search, I went ahead and made both models with just that early-stopping change. Hardly any more trees and basically the same results; in one case, it used fewer trees than with the default parameters! (It seems sensitive to the random seed, so your results might vary.)

As a second experiment I went back to default settings, no default stopping, but with 300 trees (instead of the default 50). What I get is *much* better metrics on the training set, but distinctly worse on the validation set, and even worse on the test set. Overfitting. I'm big enough to admit it: early stopping was right, I was wrong.

So, let's go back to early stopping (increasing `score_tree_interval` from 5 to 10), but make a few more changes:

- Use a much lower `learn_rate`. 0.01 instead of the 0.1 default. This should give better results, but take longer to converge.

- Set `balance_classes` to true. It might help, and should not do any harm.

- `col_sample_rate` to 0.9, `col_sample_rate_per_tree` to 0.9, and `sample_rate` to 0.8. This should guard against overfitting.

Again, results that are not so exciting. AUC is a fraction higher for the `valid` data (e.g., 0.678 compared to 0.667 for the home-win model that uses betting odds, and 0.624 versus 0.620 when not using the betting odds), but lower for the `train` data.

Time to pull out a grid? I'm going to concentrate just on the no-odds model, and hope anything we discover generalizes.[4] I'm sticking with `learn_rate=0.01` and `balance_classes=true`, and trying extreme values for each of `max_depth` (5, 12, 40), `min_rows` (2, 10, 40), and then 0.5 and 0.9 for each of the sampling rates (`sample_rate`, `col_sample_rate`, `col_sample_rate_per_tree`). I also put in `seed=c(10)` as a placeholder: this is so we have a column for when we try varying it in the future. That is 72 combinations, and based on earlier models my estimate was it would take 12 minutes, but in fact it took almost half an hour.

---

4 Not a completely arbitrary choice; the no-odds model is building in about two-thirds of the time, because there are fewer columns to deal with.

At this point in the book I made a mistake typing in the grid: I forgot to include `validation_frame`. It spent two hours making 72 models, a lot of which overfitted, and then I wasted an hour writing about how unusual they were. I finally realized when I looked at the best model and saw an AUC of 0.99. We can confidently say that is impossible for this data set: football match prediction is too hard. Even a model that had really detailed player statistics, right down to data from a spy on how each was doing in training the week before the match, would not do that well. So, what I should have immediately done was a sanity check on the best model. Even better would have been to do that while the grid was still making models, using the Flow web interface; then I would have known something was wrong even earlier and could have aborted the grid search.

The most distinct result of the grid search was that `max_depth` of 12 was better than either 5 or 40. Secondly, that `min_rows` of 40 or 2 was good, but not 10. The third thing that stood out was that `sample_rates` of 0.9 did better than 0.5, though this was not as clear-cut as I would have liked.

Extracting Certain Metrics for Each Model in a Grid

If g is a grid, first fetch all the models in it with:

```
models <- lapply(g@model_ids, h2o.getModel)
```

Now, with a list of models, we can pull out any metric we want. To find out the syntax I normally use `str()` on the first model. I want to find out how long the models took to build, and `str(models[[1]])` told me there is something called `$run_time`, which is found inside `@model`. So I use:

```
runTimes <- sapply(models, function(m) m@model$run_time)
```

A useful bonus is that `models` is ordered from best to worst. So `plot(runTimes)` can highlight a relation between model quality and time spent learning it. I might also do `range(runTimes)`, `mean(runTimes)`, `sd(runTimes)`, and so on.

If you return 2+ values from the inner function, you get a matrix. This example code shows how to extract both how long it ran for and how many trees it made (then finds their correlation):

```
timeAndTrees <- sapply(models, function(m) c(
  m@model$run_time,
  m@model$model_summary$number_of_trees
  ) )
cor(timeAndTrees[1,], timeAndTrees[2,])
```

I experimented with a few variations, but surprisingly couldn't improve on the best two from that first grid. I've decided to go with my second best model (as judged on the validation set), which differs from the top model only in min_rows (2 versus 40), for these reasons:

- All the top models have close scores, so all should be good enough.

- The best model used min_rows=2, but five of the top six used min_rows=40.

- Low min_rows are more likely to overfit.

I get my chosen model from the grid, then evaluate it on the test data, with:

```
m <- h2o.getModel(g@model_ids[[2]])
p <- h2o.performance(m, test)
h2o.auc(p)
```

This gets an AUC of 0.607. Our model with default parameters got 0.613 on the test set (this is the model without the help of betting odds, remember). Uh-oh. Our tuning has made things worse. What about accuracy? It has gone from 0.602 to 0.604, basically the same. See "Football Data" on page 263 in the final chapter for the comparison of all models.

Summary

GBM is an interesting alternative to random forest. It has more parameters and requires a bit more effort to tune, but maybe gives slightly better results? Particularly on the regression problem it seemed to outperform random forest. The main danger is that it can happily overfit if you keep giving it more and more trees. GBM was particularly disappointing when given more trees on the noisy football data set.

In the next chapter we will look at GLM (generalized linear models). Linear models might lack the trendiness of GBM and deep learning, but they still have their strengths and are worth studying.

CHAPTER 7

Linear Models

Only one letter different from GBM, GLMs (generalized linear models) take a very different approach. Whereas decision trees are based on logic, and deep learning is a black box inspired by the human brain, GLMs are based on mathematics. The underlying idea is something you almost certainly did at school: make a scatterplot of data points on graph paper, then draw the best straight line through them. And perhaps you have used lm() in R or linear_model.LinearRegression in Python's scikit-learn, or something similar, to have the computer do this for you. Once you progress beyond the graph paper you can apply it to any number of dimensions: each input column in training data counts as one dimension.

Sticking with school memories, when I first heard about Einstein's general and special theories of relativity, I assumed the *special theory* was the complicated one, to handle some especially difficult things that the general-purpose one couldn't deal with. It turns out the *general theory* was called that because it *generalized* both the special theory and some other stuff into one über-complicated theory. And so it is with generalized linear models: they can do your grandfather's linear model (in fact, that is the default behavior), but they can also do other stuff.

That *other stuff* comes down to a couple of things: using link(y) = mx + c instead of y = mx + c (where link() is a function that allows introducing nonlinearity); and specifying the distribution of the response variable. The distributions were described in "Probability Distributions in H2O" on page 111 in Chapter 4. I am not going to go into any more detail, but if you wanted a more mathematical explanation of linear models and/or generalized linear models, the Internet has plenty of them. A good starting point is section 4 of the GLM vignette, Generalized Linear Modeling with H2O (*http://bit.ly/2f8vWOo*), and then that document gives further references if your curiosity still burns bright.

H2O's implementation of GLM is nice and easy to use, and it can be used for both regression (set `family` to one of "gaussian," "poisson," "gamma," or "tweedie") and classification (set `family` to either "binomial" or "multinomial" as appropriate; binomial classification is also called logistic regression). GLM can work with categorical (enum) inputs, by creating one binary input (0 or 1) for each possible value of a category. (This is called *one-hot encoding*, and is covered in a bit more detail in the next chapter, because deep learning uses the same approach.)

 What happens when you have a categorical input, and when using your model to make predictions you give it a value it has never seen before? With H2O's GLM what will happen is that it is ignored: it will be a zero on all known possible values for that category.

GLM Parameters

Many of the parameters to define a GLM are common to most of the H2O algorithms, and those were described in Chapter 4. However, there are a fair few specific to GLM. (Python users: all of the following parameters are given to the model's constructor, not to the `train()` function.)

This first set of parameters are about the type of data it is trying to fit to:

family
>The probability distribution of the response variable (called `distribution` in GBM and deep learning). For regression the choices are gaussian, poisson, gamma, and tweedie; for logistic regression (i.e., binomial classification) you must set this to *binomial*, and for multinomial regression you must set this to *multinomial*. (Note: it currently won't auto-detect when the response variable is an enum, so you must explictly say *binomial* or *multinomial*.) Family defines how the deviance metric is calculated; it is only the same as MSE when the family is gaussian.

tweedie_link_power
>Used when distribution is "tweedie." Default is 1.

tweedie_variance_power
>Used when distribution is "tweedie." Default is 0.

link
>Can be one of "family_default," "identity," "logit," "log," "inverse," or "tweedie." As the name suggests, "family_default" is the default, and is usually best.

The next batch are about regularization, which is a way to avoid overfitting. There are two types: L1 (also called *lasso regularization* or *lasso regression*) and L2 (also called *ridge regularization* or *ridge regression*). Some of the theory behind L1 and L2 regularization can be found on Wikipedia (*http://bit.ly/2g4RZaE*). Briefly, L1 regularization will set some of your coefficients to zero (this can be useful to simplify a problem when you have a lot of predictor columns but don't know which ones are important), whereas L2 regularization tries to keep all the coefficients close to zero, but nonzero, stopping any single coefficient from dominating. If your data is dense (meaning all columns are likely to explain something about the response variable), L2 regularization is likely to be better than L1.

You choose lasso regression by setting `alpha` to 1.0, and you choose ridge regression by setting `alpha` to 0.0. Or you can choose *elastic net*, which is "have your cake and eat it": you set `alpha` between 0.0 and 1.0 to mix them together. The other parameter is `lambda`. While `alpha` decides what type of regularization to use, `lambda` decides how strong to make it.

 The *lambda* here is not what Python (and many other languages) call a lambda, i.e., an anonymous function. It is just "λ," just a variable in a mathematical equation; those mathematicians are trying to impress us with their Greek again. If a programmer had got there first, it might instead have been called `regStrength`. (It is also different to the lambda learning rate of some machine-learning algorithms.)

If you are omniscient then of course you know what value to set `lambda`.[1] I can't even spell omnissiant, let alone be it, so instead I set `lambda_search` to true. This is magic that tells the computer to try lots of different values for lambda and choose the best one. You can use `nlambdas` to control how many distinct lambda values to try, and `lambda_min_ratio` to control how low it should go; intelligent defaults are chosen based on your data, so I normally use those defaults. The lambda search starts high and then goes down, and if you watch it at work in Flow you may see it start very quickly but then slow down. This is because as the lambda decreases there are more coefficients being included in the model, so the model is getting more complex:

alpha

Described earlier, it is how much L1 regularization, and `1-alpha` is how much L2 regularization. The default is 0.5. (If you didn't want either, ignore this parameter and instead set `lambda` to zero.) This is one of the most common parameters to try grid experiments with.

---

1 Or if you previously used lambda search, and made a note of what value it found, and want to save a bit of CPU time.

lambda

Regularization strength. The default is chosen based on `lambda max` (described under `lambda_search`) but, as already mentioned, it is often useful to try lambda search to automatically find a good value. If you want to explicitly choose values for lambda that lambda search should try, specify them as a list here.

lambda_search

If true, then it will try multiple values of lambda for you. It starts with the maximum value of lambda, which is a lambda value such that the regularization causes all coefficients to end up as zero. It then keeps reducing the lambda value until the minimum value (which is decided by `lambda_min_ratio`). Note that when setting `lambda_search` to true you would never also set lambda to a single value. Normally you would not set `lambda` at all, but if you wanted to explicitly give 2+ values for lambda search to try (and no others) you specify them as a list in the `lambda` parameter.

lambda_min_ratio

Minimum lambda used in lambda search, specified as a percentage of the starting (maximum) lambda. Defaults to 0.0001. For example, if lambda search chooses 15 as the starting value, then 0.0015 is the final lambda value it will try. Lambda search will never try a lambda of zero. If you suspect it may be best (e.g., the best value from lambda search was the final and smallest one), you will need to try it separately.

nlambdas

Number of lambdas to be used in a search. The default of –1 normally means it will try 100 lambdas but when doing ridge regression, i.e., `alpha=0.0`, it instead defaults to 30 lambdas. Consider setting this to a lower number if you need to speed things up.

max_active_predictors

The default of –1 means no restriction, but you can set it to have `lambda_search` stop early, once it has reached this number of nonzero coefficients. You might set this just to have it finish more quickly, or because you expect a sparse solution and have an upper limit in mind.

 If that block of parameters seemed complex, I recommend you experiment (in a grid) with three values of `alpha` (0, 0.5, and 1.0) and set `lambda_search` to true, and ignore all the others.

The next parameter to look at, `solver`, decides how GLM will attack the problem. Note that if the family is gaussian, and there is no L1 regularization, the parameters in this section are not applicable because it can be solved analytically. `solver` takes a string that can be any of the following values:

AUTO
> AUTO will set the solver based on given data and the other parameters.

IRLSM
> This stands for Iterative Re-weighted Least Squares Method. If you have only a relatively small number of columns it is usually the best choice. What counts as small? Well, it is mainly to do with memory usage; it is described as usable up to about 500 columns. If you have a lot of columns, but also want to use IRLSM, consider using lambda search, combined with a high `alpha` (to use mostly lasso regression, and therefore force many of your coefficients to zero).

L_BFGS
> The L is for limited memory, and the BFGS is for the Broyden–Fletcher–Goldfarb–Shanno algorithm. Wikipedia (*http://bit.ly/2fNdg87*) describes it as a quasi-Newton method, and that article is a good starting point if you are interested in the details. The limited memory aspect is the reason you would choose it over IRLSM, as it allows large numbers of predictor columns; H2O's implementation handles up to 100,000s of columns.

COORDINATE_DESCENT, COORDINATE_DESCENT_NAIVE
> These two[2] are experimental[3] variants of IRLSM. See Wikipedia (*http://bit.ly/2fNfHb1*) for more details. They are good for up to about 5000 columns.

There are a few parameters the refine how your chosen solver works. Well, not so much how it works as how quickly it will finish:

max_iterations
> This controls how much work the solver will do. It defaults to 50.

beta_epsilon
> This is for the IRLSM solver: if the beta changes less than this, then stop.

gradient_epsilon
> This is for the L-BFGS solver: if the objective changes less than this, then stop.

objective_epsilon
> Stop when the objective value changes less than this.

---

2 The difference between the two is that `COORDINATE_DESCENT_NAIVE` knows less about how the world works, how people can be cruel, how people can make you cry. It also differs in how the inner loop of cyclical coordinate descent is implemented.

3 `COORDINATE_DESCENT` has become the default for when you switch lambda search on, so no longer experimental?

The common theme of the next set of parameters is that they place restrictions on the coefficients. (Yeah, okay, you're right, L1 and L2 regularization are also doing that; stop trying to be clever, I've already talked about them.)

non_negative
Restrict coefficients (not intercept) to be nonnegative.

beta_constraints
Set this to the name of an H2O data frame, with one row per predictor and the following columns: names, lower_bounds, upper_bounds, beta_given, rho. The bounds force a range for each coefficient, while the latter two are starting value and L2 penalty for proximal operators. This parameter feels like one for experts. Or control freaks.

This next bunch have to do with data preparation; they save you having to do this work yourself:

remove_collinear_columns
Remove some of the columns, if any are linearly dependent. False by default. There is no need to set this if using regularization.

standardize
Standardize numeric columns to have zero mean and unit variance. This is true by default. You are unlikely to need to set it to false, but always make sure it is true if using regularization (i.e., `lambda > 0`).

missing_values_handling
The default is "MeanImputation," which gives them the mean value from that column. The alternative is "Skip" to ignore rows with missing values (i.e., not learn from them). If you want something more sophisticated, do it yourself in advance. If you have certain columns with lots of missing data, it is usually better to remove the whole column, because in that case imputation will be useless, and skip will cause you to lose most of your training data.

Then there are parameters to describe something extra about the inputs and the model to make:

interactions
This is a list of columns you want to interact. For example, if you give three columns, such as A, B, and C, then AB, AC, and BC will be added to your model.

intercept
Whether to include a constant term in the model. The default is true, so setting it to false effectively means force an intercept of zero.

obj_reg

An advanced option for when you want to modify the objective function. The default of –1 means it will use 1 divided by the number of rows in your training data set.

prior

Used for binomial classification, and it is the prior probability for the first of the two classes. Being a probability, it must be between 0.0 and 1.0. The default is simply the percentage of samples of the first class in the training data; you only need to set this if you know that the default is wrong.

compute_p_values

Set this to true to have the p-values for each coefficient returned. Only available when using solver="IRLSM" and lambda=0.

Building Energy Efficiency: Default GLM

This is a regression problem, estimating cooling load based on house design features (see "Data Set: Building Energy Efficiency" on page 54). Run either Example 3-1 or Example 3-2 from the earlier chapter, which sets up H2O, loads the data, and has defined train, test, x, and y. We are using 10-fold cross-validation, instead of a validation set. (See "Cross-Validation (aka k-folds)" on page 104, from Chapter 4, for a reminder about cross-validation.)

```
m <- h2o.glm(x, y, train, nfolds = 10, model_id = "GBM_defaults")
```

In Python use:

```
from h2o.estimators.glm import H2OGeneralizedLinearEstimator
m = H2OGeneralizedLinearEstimator(model_id="GLM_defaults", nfolds=10)
m.train(x, y, train)
```

It runs quickly. Type summary(m) (or m.summary() in Python). The first line just summarizes what kind of linear model was being fitted, while the next couple of sections tell us various metrics. The MSE is 10.77. If you've looked at the other chapters you will see this is the worst out-of-the-box performance, by quite a way. The range of the MSE on the 10 folds goes from 6.13 to 14.28.

 Even though GLM has no random element, you might still see slightly different results because of the way the training and test data was split, and because of the random way the 10 folds for cross-validation get made.

The variable importances (available directly with h2o.varimp(m) in R or m.varimp() in Python), shown next, tells us that it thinks X5 is the most useful variable; this agrees with the other models, and also back in "Let's Take a Look!" on page 59 where it had the best correlation (+0.896) with Y2. The variable importances also tell us the sign for X5 is positive, meaning that the more X5 there is, the more Y2 there is. (X5 is height: the taller the building is, the more energy is needed to cool it.)

```
Standardized Coefficient Magnitudes:
              names coefficients sign
1                X5    7.874073  POS
2                X1    3.468041  NEG
3                X4    2.131229  NEG
4              X8.0    1.998280  NEG
5                X7    1.758337  POS
6                X2    1.321006  NEG
7                X3    0.777868  POS
8              X8.1    0.366337  POS
9              X6.5    0.299039  POS
10             X8.3    0.245411  NEG
11             X8.2    0.209615  POS
12             X8.4    0.162054  POS
13             X6.3    0.156978  NEG
14             X8.5    0.000000  POS
15 X8.missing(NA)     0.000000  POS
16             X6.2    0.000000  POS
17             X6.4    0.000000  POS
18 X6.missing(NA)     0.000000  POS
```

The other thing to notice in the variable importances is how our couple of enum (factor) columns are handled: each possible value counts as one input variable, and when one of them is set (has the value 1), all the others will have the value 0.

If you run h2o.performance(m, test) you will see similar metrics to those on the training data (MSE of 9.01). So, finally, let's plot its actual predictions for the test set on a chart (see Figure 7-1). The black dots are the correct answers, the small squares are guesses that were quite close, while the up arrows are where it was more than 8% too high, and the down arrows are where it was more than 8% too low. Out of 143 test samples, there are 27 down arrows and 33 up arrows.[4]

---

[4] I kept the same 8% threshold to allow easier comparison between chapters. Unfortunately here it gives a noisier chart.

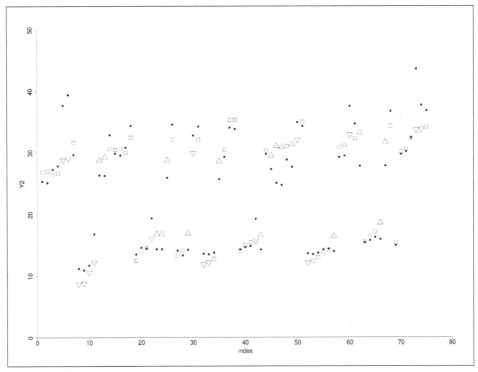

Figure 7-1. Default performance of GLM on test data

Building Energy Efficiency: Tuned GLM

If you understand your data, and the math, you will already know what family and link function you want, and the values for some of the other parameters. But I will start this section by assuming that is not the case. Unfortunately, H2O grids do not support using any of solver, family, and link in a grid. No problem: just fall back on using loops. But then there is another problem: not all the options work together. Even that will not stop us, though it does make things bit more fiddly.

To see how I fiddled it, take a look at Example 7-1. In addition to looping through the legal family/link/solver combinations (tweedie excluded—I'll come back to that in a moment), it does a grid search on four values of alpha. When alpha is 0.0 it is doing ridge regression, when 0.1 it is 90% ridge, 10% lasso regression, 0.5 is half and half, and 0.99 does almost all lasso regression (this is recommended over 1.0, as apparently a small bit of ridge helps stability a lot).

Example 7-1. Trying solver/family/link combinations (in R)

```r
solvers <- c("IRLSM", "L_BFGS", "COORDINATE_DESCENT_NAIVE", "COORDINATE_DESCENT")

families <- c("gaussian", "poisson", "gamma")

gaussianLinks <- c("identity", "log", "inverse")

poissonLinks <- c("log")

gammaLinks <- c("identity", "log", "inverse")
gammaLinks_CD <- c("identity", "log")

allGrids <- lapply(solvers, function(solver){
  lapply(families, function(family){

    if(family == "gaussian")theLinks <- gaussianLinks
    else if(family == "poisson")theLinks <- poissonLinks
    else{
      if(solver == "COORDINATE_DESCENT")theLinks <- gammaLinks_CD
      else theLinks = gammaLinks
      }

    lapply(theLinks, function(link){
      grid_id = paste("GLM", solver, family, link, sep="_")
      h2o.grid("glm", grid_id = grid_id,
        hyper_params = list(
          alpha = c(0, 0.1, 0.5, 0.99)
          ),
        x = x, y = y, training_frame = train,
        nfolds = 10,
        lambda_search = TRUE,

        solver = solver,
        family = family,
        link = link,

        max_iterations = 100
        )
    })
  })
})
```

Something else to notice in the listing is that, rather than specifying lambda (also called *the regularization parameter*), lambda_search is switched on. This is a bit like a built-in grid search, as it means instead of having to know in advance what the best value is, it will try its hardest to find out.[5] We leave the default of `nlambdas=-1`; it will then choose a suitable number (normally 100). `max_iterations` is 100, double the default. We still do 10-fold cross-validation.

It only took 77 seconds to make 27 grids, a total of 104 models. Here are the best 10 models that were found:

```
   alpha       mse                                grid_id
    0.50  9.829750              GLM_IRLSM_poisson_log
    0.50  9.873685             GLM_IRLSM_gaussian_log
    0.00  9.911911  GLM_COORDINATE_DESCENT_poisson_log
    0.10  9.934379              GLM_IRLSM_poisson_log
    0.00  9.937172             GLM_IRLSM_gaussian_log
    0.99  9.953601             GLM_IRLSM_gaussian_log
    0.10  9.963859             GLM_IRLSM_gaussian_log
    0.99  9.979255              GLM_IRLSM_poisson_log
    0.00  9.981798    GLM_COORDINATE_DESCENT_gamma_log
    0.50  9.999247               GLM_IRLSM_gamma_log
```

Approximately half the models had an MSE from 9.8 to 13.3; the other half of the models were *much* worse, ranging from 25.9 to 471.5! Conclusion: these three parameters matter *a lot*! And sometimes the solver is the only thing to blame. One of the worst models (MSE = 91.9) was `GLM_COORDINATE_DESCENT_NAIVE_poisson_log` (`alpha=0.50`), which differs solely in the use of `solver="COORDI NATE_DESCENT_NAIVE"` instead of `solver="GLM_IRLSM"`.

Our default model from the previous section had an MSE of 10.77 (though the 10 folds ranged from 6.13 to 14.28). Our best model so far is distinctly better, though there is still a large range on the 10 folds (from 7.39 to 12.92).

One thing the preceding results should have screamed out at you is that "log" is the best choice for the `link`! I think we can also go with "IRLSM" as the solver. That makes sense, as we only have eight columns, and IRLSM is the recommended choice except when you have lots of columns. (The experimental "GLM_COORDI-NATE_DESCENT," with an alpha of 0.0, i.e., only L1, no L2 penalty, looks promising, but not enough for me to want to double the number of models being made in the next few grids.)

For family, poisson and gaussian both look acceptable, and even gamma is not far behind. That brings us to the other option for family, "tweedie" (*http://bit.ly/ 2fDSdat*). It is a tricky one, as it has another couple of parameters, which can make it act like any of normal (aka gaussian), poisson, or gamma—and some other things too. If you want to run a grid on those special tweedie parameters (`tweedie_var`

---

5 `lambda=0` (no regularization) does not get tried. If you suspect that may give the best model, you will have to try it separately.

iance_power and tweedie_link_power) you should make a dedicated grid for it.[6] By the way, the default values (variance power of 0, link power of 1) make it act like a gaussian. If you just want to try one value, try tweedie_variance_power=1.5 and leave the link as the default.

But trying one value is for losers. The truly heroic data scientist, the one who thirsts for knowledge for the greater good of mankind, the one who, er, has some spare CPU cycles, uses 210 models, as shown in Example 7-2, which tries all combinations of tweedie_variance_power from 1.0 (aka poisson) through 2.0 (aka gamma) to 4.0, with all combinations of tweedie_link_power from 0.0 to 2.0. Yes, tweedie_var iance_power=1.0 and tweedie_variance_power=2.0 duplicate models we've already made (poisson and gamma, respectively), but the difference here is link power also gets varied.

Example 7-2. Tweedie experiments (in R)

```
g_tweedie <- h2o.grid("glm", grid_id = "GLM_tweedie",
  hyper_params = list(
    tweedie_variance_power =
      c(1.0, 1.25, 1.50, 1.75, 2.0, 2.33, 2.67, 3.0, 3.5, 4.0),
    tweedie_link_power =
      c(0, 0.33, 0.67, 1.0, 1.33, 1.67, 2)
    ),
  x = x, y = y, training_frame = train,
  nfolds = 10,
  lambda_search = TRUE,

  solver = "IRLSM",
  family = "tweedie",
  alpha = 0.5,

  stopping_tolerance = 0,
  stopping_rounds = 5,
  max_iterations = 100
  )
)
```

That was 70 models, and I repeated it three times to get a feel for random variance (the only random element is how the 10 folds get split up); 210 models sounds like a lot, but it only took 5 minutes. I found that higher values for tweedie_var iance_power when combined with higher values for tweedie_link_power are bad (they give a very high mean squared error). However, seeing which values are good is a bit harder, so I first filtered out those definitely bad results, then made the chart shown in Figure 7-2.

---

6 That is, those parameters have no meaning for the other families, so you would be wasting time.

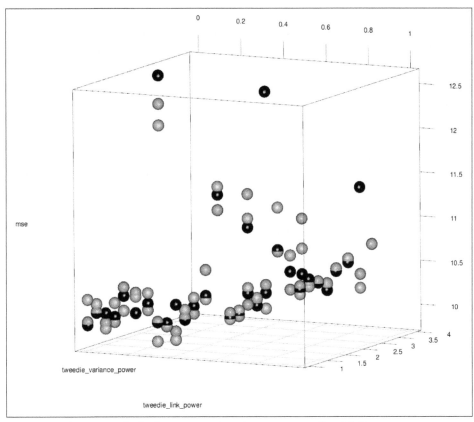

Figure 7-2. How tweedie link power and variance power affect MSE

This works much better as an interactive 3D color chart than a static grayscale chart in a book; you might just have to believe me when I tell you it shows that link_power of 0 or 0.33 is best, but that the best value for variance_power could be anywhere from 1.0 to 2.67, and that this is due to the large amount of random variance.[7]

To be honest there is not much more to try; most of the other parameters are for trying to speed up the model generation, but for this relatively small data set that is not an issue. However, I did give interactions=x a try, where x, if you remember, is the list of all eight of the predictor variables. By setting it to all eight columns it added all combinations, e.g., X1_X2, X1_X3, all the way up to X7_X8. It did terribly, even with trying a range of values for alpha (i.e., with each of ridge regression, lasso regression, and elastic net).

---

7 If I had to choose one, at this stage, I'd go with tweedie_variance_power = 1.5 and twee die_link_power=0.0, as it has the best "worst of the three runs."

As the random variation was quite noticeable, I decided to do the final tests 10 times, and then use the mean. I made four gaussian models and four poisson models, using `alpha` of 0.2, 0.3, 0.4, and 0.5; for tweedie the grid made 96 models: variance power from 1.25 to 1.60 in 0.05 increments, link power chosen from 0.0, 0.2, 0.33, and 0.4, and finally alpha chosen from 0.33, 0.5, and 0.67.[8]

See the online code for how the grids were run, and results merged. The result was that the best models were all tweedie; going by the mean, the best parameters were variance power of 1.55, link power of 0.0, and alpha of 0.33. This got a mean MSE of 9.919 on the training data, compared to 10.77 with GLM default settings. When I run this best model on the unseen `test` data set I get an MSE of 8.922, compared to 9.01 from the earlier default model.

When plotting the points (Figure 7-3), we find 26 are 8% or more below the correct answer, and 27 are over 8% above (the down and up triangles, respectively).

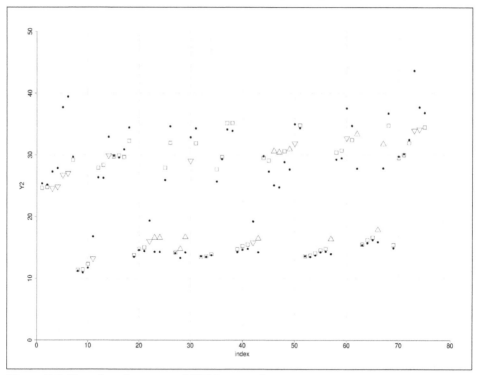

Figure 7-3. Tuned performance of GLM on test data

---

8 There may be a small bit of optimization to be wrung out by trying other alpha values near 0.33.

That is a slim improvement for so much effort. The tuned GLM is considerably worse than the out-of-the-box default settings for any of the other three algorithms (random forest, GBM, or deep learning). Obviously this data set is not well-suited to linear models, but I hope the tuning process gave you some ideas. A reminder that the results of all models on this data set will be compared in "Building Energy Results" on page 259 in the final chapter.

MNIST: Default GLM

This is a pattern recognition problem (see "Data Set: Handwritten Digits" on page 64, in Chapter 3), and even with all its smarts, I am expecting GLM to be the worst performer on this data set. It is a multinomial classification, with 784 inputs, and the output being a digit from 0 to 9.

If you are following along, run either Example 3-3 or Example 3-4 from the earlier chapter, which sets up H2O, loads the data, and defines train, valid, test, x, and y. (We are not using cross-validation this time, as valid is set.) Then run either Example 7-3 or Example 7-4.

Example 7-3. Default GLM on MNIST (Python)

```
m = h2o.estimators.H2OGeneralizedLinearEstimator(
    model_id="GLM_defaults", family="multinomial")
m.train(x, y, train,validation_frame=valid)
```

Example 7-4. Default GLM on MNIST (in R)

```
m <- h2o.glm(x, y, train, model_id = "GLM_defaults",
  validation_frame = valid, family = "multinomial")
```

It took about four minutes to run, for me, and kept all eight cores toasty-warm.[9]

 This is a multinomial problem, and so we must explicitly set fam
ily="multinomial". If we don't it will return a meaningless model
(rather than an error).

---

9 The 3.8.3.x and 3.10.0.x versions appeared to have a bug that means only one core is kept busy. It is fixed in 3.10.0.8, so if you see this problem, upgrade to at least that version.

It has done better than I expected, getting only 6.25% wrong on the training data, and only 7.82% wrong on the unseen validation set. Here is the full confusion matrix for the validation data:[10]

```
Confusion Matrix: vertical: actual; across: predicted
           0    1    2    3    4    5    6     7    8    9  Error            Rate
0        988    0    4    2    3    5    8     3    2    2 0.0285 =    29 / 1,017
1          0 1069    6    2    2    4    0     2   13    3 0.0291 =    32 / 1,101
2          4   17  867   13   15    3   20     7   23    6 0.1108 =   108 /   975
3          3    4   25  923    2   35    3    10   21    7 0.1065 =   110 / 1,033
4          2    6    3    2  883    1    8     3    6   35 0.0695 =    66 /   949
5         10    4    3   28   13  833   17     2   22    8 0.1138 =   107 /   940
6          7    2    6    0    7   14  912     5    0    1 0.0440 =    42 /   954
7          1    2   13    4   11    1    0   976    3   35 0.0669 =    70 / 1,046
8          9   19   11   19    6   29    5     2  876   10 0.1116 =   110 /   986
9          5    3    4   12   40    1    0    33   10  891 0.1081 =   108 /   999
Totals  1029 1126  942 1005  982  926  973  1043  976  998 0.0782 =   782 /10,000
```

It is interesting to see that a linear model can tell the difference between handwritten zeros and ones rather well. It has the most trouble telling the difference between 4s and 9s, and 7s and 9s.

On the 10,000 test samples the error is 746, about the same as on the validation data. You get this with p <- h2o.performance(m, test) in R (then h2o.confusionMatrix(p) and h2o.hit_ratio_table(p)), and with p = m.model_performance(test) in Python (then p.confusion_matrix() and p.hit_ratio_table()):

```
k    hit_ratio
---  -----------
1    0.9254
2    0.9708
3    0.9849
4    0.9912
5    0.995
6    0.9973
7    0.9988
8    0.9995
9    1
10   1
```

That hit ratio table shows it is having trouble on some numbers even if you give it eight or nine guesses, but this is no different than all the other algorithms.

The last thing I want to point out about this (almost) out-of-the-box model: the default parameters are different to that on the previous data sets. When making the building energy data set models we were assigned a default of 50 iterations, and used

---

10 m.confusion_matrix(valid) in Python, or h2o.confusionMatrix(m, valid=TRUE) in R. Also part of the output when you print m.

none. This time we were given a default of 500 iterations, and used 180 of them. The value chosen for lambda is also different. This wasn't anything I chose: H2O looked at the data and chose these defaults.

MNIST: Tuned GLM

There are two things to try here that immediately jump to mind. First, how much better does it do with the extended data set (the extra 113 rows we add in "Helping the Models" on page 69 in Chapter 3), and secondly as we have quite a lot of columns, which solver is going to be best?

Then there are the questions I always have with a GLM: which value for alpha (0, 0.5, 0.99, i.e., L1, elastic net, or L2), and for lambda (lambda_search will be set to true, to have it find the best one for us).

How about we first try with the same default settings, but using the extended data? I won't bore you with either the code or the detailed results, and will just say it took slightly longer to run and gave near-identical results (6.35% error on training data, 7.96% error on validation data, 7.45% error on the test data).

The identical results are not so surprising as five of the top six coefficients (as extracted with h2o.varimp(m)) are for raw pixels, not the new columns that were added. How about trying a model that *only* uses those new, richer columns?

```
m <- h2o.glm(1:113, y, train,
  validation_frame = valid,
  model_id = "GLM_first113",
  family =" multinomial"
  )
```

This model builds in approximately one-eigth of the time, but has a 7.88% error rate on the training data, and 8.67% on the validation data. In other words, the performance is distinctly worse. These richer columns seem harder for a linear model to get to grips with.

So, I went back to using all columns, and set up a grid to try and answer my earlier question of which solver is best, while also answering the question of the best alpha and lambda values.

By the way, Figure 7-4 is a screenshot from Flow during this grid building process. This was done on two 36-core nodes, and the mostly-50% CPU usage shown in the Water Meter is typical for GLM, at least on a data set of this size.

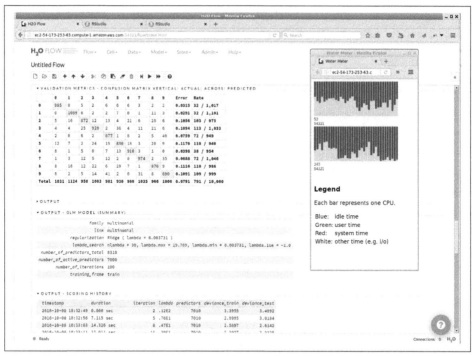

Figure 7-4. Viewing one model in Flow, while another is building

Example 7-5. Running a grid for each possible solver

```
solvers <- c("IRLSM", "L_BFGS", "COORDINATE_DESCENT_NAIVE", "COORDINATE_DESCENT")
system.time(
allGrids <- lapply(solvers, function(solver){
  grid_id = paste("GLM",solver,sep="_")
  cat("GRID:",grid_id,"\n")
  h2o.grid("glm", grid_id=grid_id,
    hyper_params = list(
      alpha = c(0, 0.5, 0.99)
      ),
    x = x, y = y, training_frame = train,
    validation_frame = valid,
    lambda_search = TRUE,

    solver = solver,
    family = "multinomial",

    max_iterations = 100
    )
  })
)
```

I got errors when I tried `COORDINATE_DESCENT_NAIVE`, but the rest of the results are interesting:

solver	alpha	MSE	logloss	error
IRLSM	0	0.075	0.292	0.0791
COORDINATE_DESCENT	0	0.077	0.297	0.0802
L_BFGS	0	0.08	0.31	0.0839
IRLSM	0.99	0.098	0.343	0.0931
COORDINATE_DESCENT	0.5	0.101	0.352	0.0941
IRLSM	0.5	0.101	0.352	0.0942
COORDINATE_DESCENT	0.99	0.1	0.35	0.0953
L_BFGS	0.5	0.81	2.302	0.8899
L_BFGS	0.99	0.81	2.302	0.8899

While the differences of the parameters is interesting, all of them are worse than our default model, which scored 0.0782! So, in this case, I think the default GLM model parameters cannot be beaten.

The results of all four learning algorithms will be compared in "MNIST Results" on page 261 in the final chapter of this book.

Football: Default GLM

This is the most challenging of our data sets: predicting football match results, based on a combination of recent performance and expert predictions in the form of bookmaker odds. (See "Data Set: Football Scores" on page 71 in Chapter 3 for how it was prepared.) If you are following along, run either Example 3-6 or Example 3-7 from the earlier chapter, but make sure you change it to use *football.train2.csv*, *football.valid2.csv*, and *football.test2.csv*, because those are the files where the missing values have been either removed or filled in,[11] and GLM does not handle missing values very well. The aforementioned scripts set up H2O, load the data, and define `train`, `valid`, `test`, `x`, `xNoOdds`, and `y`. We have a validation data set, so we will use that instead of cross-validation.

As a first step, let's make a linear model with all default settings, except it will be given just a single input, rather than all of them. The single input will be the average bookmaker odds of a win, and the model is therefore the simplest one possible. The

---

11 See "Missing Data" on page 237 in Chapter 9 for how this was done. All data prior to August 2000 got removed, because too many columns were missing.

result it gives is a good baseline with which to evaluate the other models; in fact, you will already have seen this result referenced in the other chapters.

Here is the R code:

```
mAvH <- h2o.glm("BbAvH", "HomeWin", train,
  model_id = "GLM_defaults_HomeWin_BbAvH",
  validation_frame = valid, family = "binomial")
```

First, the AUCs:

```
      HomeWin
train   0.618
valid   0.675
test    0.650
```

Then, the accuracy:

```
      HomeWin
train   0.589
valid   0.650
test    0.634
```

Okay. With that baseline number in mind, let us make both models we are interested in: predicting home win, first using all fields (x), and the harder challenge of not using the bookmaker odds (xNoOdds):

```
m1 <- h2o.glm(x, "HomeWin", train,
  model_id = "GLM_defaults_HomeWin_Odds",
  validation_frame = valid, family = "binomial")
m2 <- h2o.glm(xNoOdds, "HomeWin", train,
  model_id = "GLM_defaults_HomeWin_NoOdds",
  validation_frame = valid, family = "binomial")
```

Each of those ran quickly. I'm going to use the compareModels() that was introduced in Chapter 5 (see Example 5-1 for the code) to take a look at their AUC, and their accuracy:

```
res <- compareModels(c(m1,m2), test)
round(res[",AUC",], 3)
round(res[",Accuracy",], 3)
```

I get this output for AUC:

```
      Odds    NoOdds
train 0.636   0.595
valid 0.678   0.625
test  0.645   0.612
```

And this output for accuracy:

```
      Odds    NoOdds
train 0.607   0.582
valid 0.650   0.615
test  0.622   0.605
```

On accuracy, 0.634 was our target for HomeWin (0.650 for valid), so adding more fields has made the model worse. Sigh. If we take a look at the most useful input variables, with `h2o.varimp(m1)` it tells me the first 24 variables are all betting odds; number 25 is `res5a`. So it is strange it didn't give an identical result, rather than a worse one.

Without betting odds to help, we naturally score worse, though not terribly so. Here are the top five variables for m2:

```
  names coefficients sign
1 res20A     0.199159  NEG
2 res20H     0.183050  POS
3 Div.E0     0.098531  POS
4    HS1     0.080411  POS
5  res5H     0.062600  POS
```

The top two were the "long-term team strength" estimates, based on the results of the previous 20 matches: the away team's strength is a negative influence, and the home team's strength is a positive influence. That makes sense. The third one shows how GLM deals with factors: it is saying "if the match is a top-division match then a home win is more likely." Unlikely, but could the home-team effect be bigger for the most heavily supported teams? The fourth one says that the number of shots made by the home team in their most recent match is an influence: the higher it is, the more chance they will win.

Football: Tuned GLM

So, having seen that using all columns gave us a worse result than just using one, the question becomes can we tune GLM to do better? I am going to concentrate on just the first of our two variations: using all available columns, and trying to predict home wins. We have quite a lot of columns, 79, but that is still comfortably below the 500 columns guideline for the IRLSM solver, so I am going to stick with that solver. With a binomial classification, you set `family = "binomial"`, and there is no choice for the link function (it is always "logit").

I will use early stopping, lambda search on, and try the three main values of alpha (0.0 to get ridge regression, 1.0 to get lasso regression, and 0.5 to get elastic net). The only grid hyper-parameter is `alpha`, and the following code runs nice and quickly:

```
g <- h2o.grid("glm", grid_id = "GLM_1",
  hyper_params = list(
    alpha = c(0, 0.5, 0.99)
  ),
  x = x, y = "HomeWin", training_frame = train,
  validation_frame = valid,
  family = "binomial",

  lambda_search = TRUE,
```

```
stopping_metric = "AUC",
stopping_tolerance = 0,
stopping_rounds = 4,
max_iterations = 100
)
```

To three decimal places, the AUC turned out to be identical (0.645 on test set) for all values of alpha, and therefore slightly worse than the benchmark model. Results for accuracy were similarly unexciting.

The best value of alpha was 0.0. I tried again with some more low values of alpha, 0.05 and 0.15, but 0.0 came out top again. The difference between the models is minor.

And the exciting conclusion is that there is nothing else worth tuning, and that our best model performs exactly the same as our default model. The AUC on the test set is 0.645! The final chapter ("Football Data" on page 263) compares all the models on this data set.

Summary

Linear models are great when there is a linear relationship between your predictor variables (even if hundreds or even thousands are involved) and your response variable. It is less well-suited to more nonlinear data, and to the kind of pattern matching problems that humans are good at.

But when the data suits the problem it can generally give a good model with less effort than the other algorithms, and the H2O implementation can work very quickly on really large data sets. I will use GLM when imputing missing data in Chapter 9, because of these *good enough* and *quick* properties.

The next chapter is the last of this block of four, and looks at deep learning. This has almost the opposite benefits of linear models: deep learning is good at pattern-matching problems, but is usually the slowest model to build.

CHAPTER 8

Deep Learning (Neural Nets)

Deep learning is the new and trendy name for neural networks, and it sure is trendy! But deservedly so, as it is behind some of the most spectacular advances in AI and machine learning at the moment. Deep learning algorithms tend to be the best performers at problems that humans find easy yet (other) machine learning approaches find difficult, such as pattern recognition. Theoretically they can solve any problem, but they have their downsides too: they can be slow, they are black boxes and cannot explain their thinking, and they struggle a bit with categorical inputs. If your problem is to take a company's annual transactions and calculate how much tax is owed, a neural net is not the right choice.

If you've used another library for neural nets or deep learning, one complaint you won't have about H2O's implementation is ease of use. As we saw back in Chapter 1, it takes care of most of the details for you, and you can get good results with a oneliner. Yes, there are still a huge number of parameters to tune but, as we will see in this chapter, the majority of them never need to be touched.

As in the other chapters, we will take look at how they work, but only the parts you need to understand to effectively tune them, then we will go through the parameters, and then dive into using deep learning on each of our data sets, first with defaults, then going through the tuning process.

However, a few special points to note. First, the use of deep learning as an autoencoder, i.e., unsupervised deep learning, is instead in Chapter 9. Second, there are so many parameters that some of them (the ones I have never needed to touch) are in an appendix at the end of this chapter. Third, deep learning grids can be slow. If you have faithfully followed along with every code example to this point, you may need more patience or more hardware.

Even if you are sure deep learning is the model for you, it can be worth making some quick models with the other algorithms, if only to get an idea of what a good score on your data set will be. If deep learning is doing better than all the other algorithms, but you seem to have hit a wall, maybe that is just the best that can be done without overfitting. But if it is doing worse, chances are there is still some parameter you can tweak to improve performance.

What Are Neural Nets?

I am supposed to mention the human brain here, but let's cut to the chase: a neuron is a function that takes multiple numeric inputs and gives out one numeric output. These neurons are organized into layers, and the outputs from all the neurons in one layer become the inputs for each neuron in the next layer.

I am only describing the implementation in H2O, which is called a feed-forward neural network. The H2O implementation is designed to be run in parallel across a cluster on very large data. At the time of writing, H2O does not support GPUs.[1]

As Figure 8-1 shows, the very first layer is your data: a training sample, or a test sample, or real inputs once you are in production. And the very last layer is your outputs: the answer. If you are doing a regression (learning a single value) then the output layer will have one neuron. If you are doing a classification then the output layer will have one neuron for each possible answer (and each output value will be a probability for that answer: the answer with the highest probability for your set of inputs is chosen). The layers between the input layer and the output layer are called the hidden layers.

Each neuron in each hidden layer has a weight for each of its inputs, and modifying those weights is how the network learns. (There is also a "bias" input to each neuron, which can be thought of as a weight connected to a constant input; it is also tuned during training.) The functions inside the neuron are discussed later, in "Activation Functions" on page 193.

---

[1] The Deep Water project, under development as I write this, will allow leveraging other deep learning libraries, such as Tensorflow, Caffe, and Mxnet, and so will gain GPU support from them.

The idea is you start with random weights, then you give it the first training sample and the correct answer (this is supervised learning, remember), calculate the error, and then use that to go back and tweak each of the weights, so that there is a bit less error.[2] Then you take the second training sample and repeat. Working your way through every piece of training data is called an *epoch*. You specify the number of epochs[3] you want the algorithm to perform.

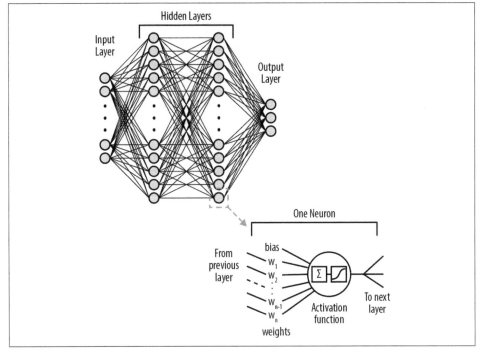

Figure 8-1. Network, layers, neurons

If you've used or studied other deep learning libraries you may have met mini batches. A mini batch of, say, size 32 means it will process 32 training samples, then go back and update the weights in one batch. H2O does not use mini batches, which means it works exactly as just described: the weights get updated after every single sample. However, when run across a multinode cluster, each node in the cluster works independently for one *iteration*, and at the end of each iteration the network

---

2 This process is called backpropagation, but H2O takes care of the whole process for us. Explanations of the sums involved are easy to find with your favorite search engine, e.g., *https://en.wikipedia.org/wiki/Backpropagation*.

3 Fractional epochs are allowed. For instance, requesting 10.5 epochs means all training data samples are processed 10 times, but the first half of the training data is also processed an eleventh time.

weights are averaged with those on every other node. One iteration can be larger or smaller than an epoch; the parameters that control this are discussed later in this chapter.

Numbers Versus Categories

Everything is a number in a neural net, and they are happiest when all your predictor variables are numeric. For instance, when we try it on the MNIST digit recognition problem there will be one input neuron per pixel, and the value will be the intensity of that pixel. However, when you have a categorical input, each possible value of that category will become one input neuron; one of that set of input neurons will be set to 1 and all the others will be set to 0. This is called one-hot encoding.

Let's say you have a gender field, and the possible values are "Male," "Female," "Unknown." You also have an age field, which is a number. This means we will have four[4] input neurons:

- Male?
- Female?
- Gender-unknown?
- Age

For a 21-year-old man, the inputs would be:

- Male = 1
- Female = 0
- Gender-unknown = 0
- Age = 21

For a 55-year-old, who didn't answer the gender question, the inputs would be:

- Male = 0
- Female = 0
- Gender-unknown = 1
- Age = 55

---

4 Possibly five: each categorical input also gets an extra input neuron for NAs and missing data. It depends if gender-unknown was encoded as NA, or as the literal string "Unknown." And possibly three: if you set use_all_factor_levels=false (it is true by default) then one of the categories can be implied by setting all of the others to zero, so one of the input neurons can be dropped.

Luckily the H2O implementation takes care of all this for you: give it a data set with a mix of numeric, integer, and enum variables, and it will do whatever data manipulation has to be done.

Numbers or Categories? (Ordered Factors)

By the way, what if your data had age as a categorical input? For example:

- under 18
- 18 to 24
- 25 to 39
- 40 to 59
- 60+

In R terminology, this is an example of an ordered factor: "under 18" is less than "18 to 24" is less than "25 to 39" is less than "40 to 59" is less than "60+". Should this be five input neurons to your network, or should you convert it to a single numeric input?

Tricky. In this case I'd leave it as five categories, because it is not obvious how to convert it to a number ([1, 18, 25, 40, 60]? [18, 25, 40, 60, 120]?). And, also, because the intent behind that data wasn't to know their *age*, it was a proxy for their *lifestyle*. However, if the age field was made up of 20 categories, each a nice, clean, five-year range, I'd be much more tempted to convert it to a single value.

Network Layers

The main two things you need to concern yourself with, when using h2o.deeplearn ing(), are the number of epochs (how long you are willing to spend training) and the shape of the network (the number of layers, and the number of neurons in each of those layers). The more layers and neurons you have, the longer it will take to train (and the slower it will be to use), so you want as few as you can get away with. While theoretically[5] one hidden layer is enough to represent all your data, whether involving nonlinear relationships or not, in practice it won't be. Anyway, most people wouldn't consider it *deep* learning if you only had one hidden layer!

---

5 Search for the universal approximation theorem.

Some hints for choosing the number of layers and neurons:

- For nonlinear problems, start with two layers and see how it does.
- The more nonlinear your problem, the more layers you need. If you feel it is just not *getting it*, try adding another layer. Or more epochs. Or more training data. But if you are up to five layers, a sixth is probably not going to help (and you are looking at a lot of training time).
- The more neurons in a layer, the more clearly it will be able to understand the data. If you feel it has the general idea, but is a bit fuzzy, try adding more neurons. Or more epochs. Or more training data.
- The more data inputs you have, the more neurons you are likely to need in the first hidden layer. Maybe.
- The more output neurons you have, the more neurons you are likely to need in the final hidden layer. Maybe.
- The more layers you have, the more likely you are to benefit from a dropout function (described in "Activation Functions" on page 193).

 You'll be able to see if more epochs is going to help or not by looking at the scoring history plot (on Flow, or plot it yourself with data from `h2o.scoreHistory(m)` in R, or `m.scoring_history()` in Python). If the line wobbles erratically, and the overall trend is sideways, not down, then more epochs is unlikely to help; try one of the other ideas. If it is merely getting rather flat, you have entered the realm of diminishing returns but, if you don't mind waiting, then more epochs might give a small improvement.

The time spent training a deep learning model is primarily decided by the number of training samples times the number of epochs. Which is a shame, as more of both is better, though with diminishing returns. But how long you *need* to spend training (to reach the same point of diminishing returns) is related to the number of weights in your model: the more you have, the more there is to learn. The number of weights between two layers is simply the product of the number of neurons in those two layers. Don't forget to count the input layer and the output layer.

Consider a 100x100 network, with 2 numeric inputs and 1 output. It has `(2 * 100) + (100 * 100) + (100 * 1) = 10,300` weights. If you add a third layer, also with 100 neurons, it goes to `(2 * 100) + (100 * 100) + (100 * 100) + (100 * 1) = 20,300` weights. It (hopefully) will understand your problem better, but might need more time to settle down and converge.

Now consider that 100x100 network, but with 10 numeric inputs, and classifying into 3 states. The number of weights is now `(10 * 100) + (100 * 100) + (100 * 3) = 11,300`. That is, there are 800 more between the input layer and the first hidden layer, and 200 more between the second hidden layer and the output layer, but the total is still dominated by the weights between the two hidden layers.

Now take the same-sized network, but this time with 5 numeric inputs and 5 enum inputs: gender (2 levels), favorite color (10 levels), Myers–Briggs personality type (16 levels), astrology sign (12 levels), and Chinese horoscope sign (12 levels). Yep, we're making the world's best online dating site. Now how many weights? Remember the earlier discussion: each enum *level* becomes an input neuron (plus an extra input neuron in each category to handle missing or unseen values). We now have 5 + 3 + 11 + 17 + 13 + 13 = 62 input neurons, so our total number of weights is `(62 * 100) + (100 * 100) + (100 * 3) = 16,500`. We still only have 10 input columns in our data, but suddenly we have 50% more weights.

Why should you care? The more weights, the slower training will be. And because if you naively use a factor with 50,000 levels (e.g., zip code), and 1000 neurons in your first hidden layer, you might have 50 million more weights than you were expecting.[6]

Activation Functions

If you remember the diagram of the neuron (Figure 8-1), near the start of this chapter, you know it has lots of (weighted) inputs coming in, and one output going out. The inputs are summed, and then it is the *activation function* that decides the value of the output.

H2O supports three activation functions:

Rectifier
> The most common activation function, and the default. It outputs the sum of its weighted inputs, but clips all negative values to zero. See the upper line in Figure 8-2. This implies that it will be generating quite a few zeros (zeros are good for training deeper networks), but also means that positive values are unbounded.

---

6 As an aside, an interesting approach using H2O and an extra data set to reduce the dimensions of large factors such as zip code is shown in this H2O World video by Madeleine Udell (*https://www.youtube.com/watch?v=zwvzGuS82MA*) (specifically from about 19:00 to 25:00).

Tanh

Short for hyperbolic tangent.[7] This takes an input range of negative infinity to positive infinity and converts that to an output range of −1 to +1. But it varies most rapidly when the sum of the inputs is close to zero. See the lower line in Figure 8-2.

Maxout

This simply outputs the highest (the max) of the inputs, meaning the weighted inputs are used directly, not summed.

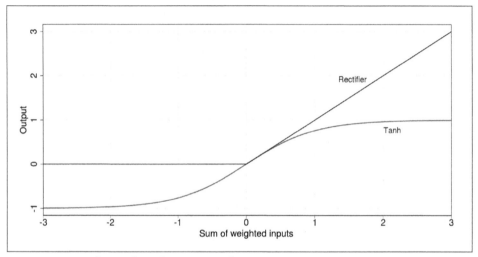

Figure 8-2. Rectifier and Tanh activation functions

You can find claims of "the best" for each of these activation functions, but it does really seem to depend on your data, so wherever possible use a grid search to try all three options. However, Rectifier is generally quicker, so if in doubt go with that. And if you get complaints about numeric instability with Rectifier or Maxout, switch to Tanh.

H2O supports the preceding three activation functions, but there are six possible values for the `activation` parameter. This is because each of the above has a "With-Dropout" variant, which allows using `hidden_dropout_ratios` to control the rate at which outputs are randomly set to zero, as a regularization technique (to avoid overfitting and give a more robust model).

---

7 Not to be confused with hyperbole and going off at a tangent, the mainstay of modern politics.

Parameters

Of all the H2O algorithms, deep learning has the most parameters. You could spend the rest of your life trying to tune them all. Some were introduced in Chapter 4; a lot of the advanced ones have been moved to an appendix at the end of this chapter. From what is left most have been divided into either scoring-related or regularization-related. But the first one that you will often be setting is to describe how many hidden layers there will be and how big each should be:

hidden

Hidden layer sizes. The default is 200,200, meaning there will be two hidden layers, with 200 neurons in each layer. If you give 60,40,20 then you will have three hidden layers, with 60 in the first, 40 in the second, and 20 in the third.

The next parameter sets the mode of operation, deciding if you want an auto-encoder or a supervised network. Auto-encoding with deep learning is covered in "Deep Learning Auto-Encoder" on page 229 in Chapter 9:

autoencoder

Defaults to false (meaning to do supervised learning). Set this to true if auto-encoding. Usually you should set activation to Tanh at the same time.

Deep Learning Regularization

The idea of regularization was introduced in "Sampling, Generalizing" on page 108. For deep learning, there are two main things you can try:

- Drop connections when connecting one layer to the next.
- Regularization.

The activation function is here, as the choice decides what other parameters you can use:

activation

This parameter has six possible values, because it is doing two things. First you can choose between three activation functions (introduced in "Activation Functions" on page 193). Then you choose whether to use dropout or not. In other words, if you want to use hidden_dropout_ratios you must specify one of "TanhWithDropout," "RectifierWithDropout," or "MaxoutWithDropout." The choice of activation cannot be changed when using checkpointing, and also you can't have a grid with some models using hidden ratios, some not. So, in those cases, I recommend you always use one of the "WithDropout" activation functions, and set hidden_dropout_ratios to 0.0 when you don't want any dropout.

hidden_dropout_ratios

You specify one ratio per hidden layer. The default of 0.5 means for each training row that is processed through the network, there is a 50% chance a neuron will pass its value on to the next hidden layer, and a 50% chance it will pass on zero. It is ignored if not using an activation function that supports dropout. Hard to choose intuitively, so it is best experimented with in a grid. Try a higher dropout rate in networks with a higher number of layers.

input_dropout_ratio

This ratio says what percentage of the input neurons to feed into the first hidden layer. Unlike `hidden_dropout_ratios` it can be used with any `activation` setting. The default is 0.0 (meaning no input dropout). If it is 0.5 then it means for each row in the training data, there is a 50% chance of each feature being used. Rephrasing, it sets half your columns to zero. A different half on each training sample, and on each epoch. This can work well if there is a lot of noise in your data, though 0.5 is quite high. It is a good one to use in a grid, perhaps initially with a wide range, e.g., 0.0, 0.1, 0.2, 0.3, 0.4, and 0.5.

l1

L1 regularization. Also known as lasso regularization. Defaults to 0, and typical values to try are 0.0001 or smaller.

l2

L2 regularization. Also known as ridge regularization. Defaults to 0, and typical values to try are 0.0001 or smaller.

max_w2

An upper limit for the (squared) sum of the incoming weights to a neuron. The default is to have no limit. This is a very direct way to stop weights from growing too big.

Deep Learning Scoring

There are a large number of parameters to control the frequency of scoring. They allow you to control the conflict, or balance, between a few concepts:

- You need accurate scores (to judge models, to know when to early-stop).
- Time spent scoring is time not spent training.
- Regular scoring means finer-grained choice for returning the best model.
- Cluster considerations.
- Training data size.

The following sidebar walks through how they work together in a realistic example. You may want to keep referring back to it as you read the parameter descriptions.

Deep Learning Scoring Example

I will assume a 3-node cluster, and I will assume 120,000 training rows, with 40,000 on each node. Early stopping defaults to stopping after five scoring rounds with no improvement.

Each node starts training on its 40,000 rows, from random weights, and effectively each is building its own deep learning model based only on the 40,000 rows. After every single row the weights/biases are updated,[8] but there is no network communication yet.

It does this for one iteration, the length of which is controlled by `train_sam ples_per_iteration`. If you left that as the default of –2 it will be decided based on other factors (such as `target_ratio_comm_to_comp`), but typically it will be a fraction of an epoch for large data sets, and could be dozens of epochs for small data sets. A higher value for `score_interval` or a lower value for `score_duty_cycle` can also mean an iteration takes longer.

At the end of the iteration, each node will stop and share its weights/biases with every other node. They get averaged (so that each node now has identical weights). Then each node will score on 3333 of its 40,000 samples (because `score_training_samples` defaults to 10,000), and then score on *all* the validation data (because `score_valida tion_samples` defaults to zero).

Now a new entry is made in the scoring history of the model. If it is the best model so far, a snapshot of the model is saved. And then each node starts training again, still on just its own 40,000 rows. At the end of the second iteration, the weights/biases are shared and averaged again.

It will consider early stopping for the first time after 10 iterations. It will make an average of the scoring metric for rounds 1 to 5, and the average of the scoring metric for rounds 6 to 10. If the second number is equal to or lower than the first number, it stops. Otherwise it does another iteration (and will compare the average of rounds 2 to 6 against 7 to 11).

If `train_samples_per_iteration` was 0, each node would do 40,000 samples per iteration. If –1, each node would do exactly 120,000 samples per iteration. If I set it to 240,000 (twice the size of my training data), each node would do 80,000 samples per iteration, and scoring would be every 2 epochs. But, be cautious about setting this higher than say 100,000 (whatever the training data size), as you want your nodes to share their weights with each other fairly frequently. Leaving `train_sam ples_per_iteration` as –2 is usually best when using multiple nodes.

---

8 Due to Hogwild!, a lock-free multithreaded stochastic gradient descent algorithm.

train_samples_per_iteration

This controls how many training rows (samples) to use per iteration; an iteration can be thought of as when the model is scored. It is an integer, and normally you will use one of the following three special values. –2 is the default, and lets H2O decide. 0 and –1 mean the same thing when on a single node: score every epoch. See "Deep Learning Scoring Example" on page 197 for how they differ when using multiple nodes.

score_interval

The minimum time between scoring models, in seconds. The default is 5. If `stop ping_rounds` is also 5, meaning there will be a minimum of 10 scoring rounds, then you know the model will build for at least 50 seconds. By the way, if other parameters (e.g., low `score_duty_cycle`, high `train_samples_per_iteration`) mean that scoring rounds are already, say, 30 seconds apart, then changing this from 5 to, e.g., 15 or 20, will have no effect.

score_duty_cycle

How much time to spend scoring, versus training. The range is 0.0 to 1.0, where lower values mean more training, while higher values mean more scoring. The default is 0.1 (10% of the time spend on scoring, 90% on training). If you set it to 0.01 then typically it will be 10 times longer between scoring events which, for instance, might mean you see a scoring history entry every 50 epochs instead of every 5 epochs.

target_ratio_comm_to_comp

Target ratio of communication overhead to computation. The default is 0.05, spending 5% on communication between nodes, and 95% of time on training each node. This only matters for multinode clusters, and also it is only used when `train_samples_per_iteration = -2`. Lowering it will either mean the scoring rounds are further apart (implying fewer of them), or have no effect at all.

replicate_training_data

Defaults to true. If true then it will replicate the entire training data set on every node in your cluster. For small data sets this can result in faster training.

shuffle_training_data

Defaults to false. If true then training data is randomly sorted. This is recommended if you have set `balance_classes` (see "Data Weighting" on page 106 in Chapter 4), for instance.

score_validation_samples

How many of the validation data set rows to use when scoring. The default of 0 means to use them all. If your validation data is large, or you are scoring more frequently, you might want to choose a lower number to speed up scoring (at the expense of accuracy); personally I would instead try to score less frequently.

When using cross-validation, the fold that is not used as training data is treated as the validation data, and this setting also applies to that too.

score_training_samples

Like `score_validation_samples`, but for when scoring on the training data instead of a validation test set. The default is 10,000, to make sure that very large data sets do not make scoring really slow. If scoring frequently, you might want to make this even lower. When using cross-validation, this is only used when making the final model.

score_validation_sampling

Only used when `score_validation_samples` has been changed from the default of 0. Defaults to "Uniform," but can also be "Stratified" (which might give better results if doing a classification and the target class is unbalanced).

 If you feel that scoring is happening more frequently than you need, lowering `score_duty_cycle` or increasing `score_interval` is often best. Explicitly setting `train_samples_per_iteration` would also do the job. If you feel early stopping is triggering too early, you could also do any of those, but in that case the best fix is often to simply increase `stopping_rounds`. For example, using `checkpoint` to restart a model, with `stopping_rounds` doubled, works well.

Building Energy Efficiency: Default Deep Learning

You know by now that this is a regression problem, unless you have jumped straight here, in which case you can learn about it at "Data Set: Building Energy Efficiency" on page 54. Run either Example 3-1 or Example 3-2 from the earlier chapter, which sets up H2O, loads the data, and defines train, test, x, and y. We are using 10-fold cross-validation, instead of a validation set. (See "Cross-Validation (aka k-folds)" on page 104 for a reminder.) The cross-validation means it has 11 times the work to do (10 folds, plus making the final model), which is sometimes a problem as deep learning is already quite slow. But this data set is small enough for it to be manageable:

```
m <- h2o.deeplearning(x, y, train, nfolds = 10, model_id = "DL_defaults")
```

In Python use:

```
m = h2o.estimators.H2ODeepLearningEstimator(model_id="DL_defaults")
m.train(x, y, train, nfolds=10)
```

That took just over 10 seconds to run, with all 8 cores fully used. It gave an average MSE of 8.15 across the 10 folds (with a standard deviation of 1.40), but a lower 6.60 on the test data.[9]

As in previous chapters, Figure 8-3 shows the predictions on the test data. The black circles are the correct answers, the 13 up arrows indicate where it was over 8% too high, and the 34 down arrows indicate where it was over 8% too low. (The small squares are where it was within 8%.)

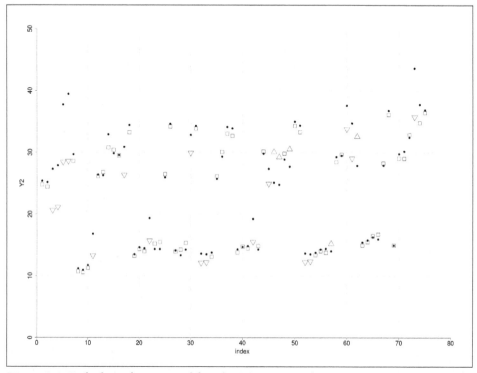

Figure 8-3. Default performance of deep learning on test data

Notice that, out of the box, this was a worse result than either of random forest or GBM, and only just slightly better than GLM. The results of all models on this data set will be compared in "Building Energy Results" on page 259 in the final chapter.

---

9 With quite a bit of variance. On another run I get MSEs 20% higher on all of train, valid, and test data, meaning the model is worse. This is simply because 10 epochs is too few, as we'll see as soon as we start tuning.

Building Energy Efficiency: Tuned Deep Learning

Deep breath. There is so much we can do here. So many parameters, so little time. There is time pressure for another reason: typically the deep learning models take more CPU time than the other algorithms we've looked at. That means we want to keep our grid searches as focused as possible. (See "Grid Search" on page 122, back in Chapter 5, if grids are new to you.)

As usual, the first thing I want to do is use early stopping (see "Early Stopping" on page 99) so that I can give each model lots of epochs, and not have to worry about it. For the first few grids, however, I will be more severe than I was with the other supervised learning algorithms: for deep learning, if it hasn't improved at least 0.5% over the last three scoring rounds, it stops. My hope is that this severity affects all models in the grid equally.[10] Here are the parameters:

```
stopping_metric = "MSE",
stopping_tolerance = 0.005,
stopping_rounds = 3,
epochs = 1000,
train_samples_per_iteration = 0,
score_interval = 3,
```

 The default stopping metric, for a regression problem, is "deviance," which is short for "mean residual deviance," which is identical to MSE when the distribution is gaussian (which is another default). I decided to specify it explicitly, in case other distributions get tried.

You will see I have also set train_samples_per_iteration to be 0, which means it will score after every epoch (which in this case means after every 600 to 625 training samples). And score_interval has been slightly reduced to 3 seconds, from the default of 5 seconds. This means that early stopping should react more quickly. In particular, because the data set is so small, I was finding the default settings meant it was doing so few scoring events that it kept reaching maximum epochs.

---

10 We could test that theory by repeating the grids with stopping_rounds set to 4, then 5, and see if the relative ordering of the best models stays the same.

To see the effect of simply adding more epochs, how about we give the previous settings a go, with everything else still set to default? I did, and the results[11] were so good, I had to run it again to see if it had somehow just got lucky. So, here is a comparison of the default model, with those two models that used 20 times more epochs:

	Default	Early#1	Early#2
Train-MSE	5.587	0.223	0.092
CV-MSE	17.510	4.854	4.908
Test-MSE	7.089	0.580	0.437
Epochs	11.519	194.000	192.000

The model is way better on all three data sets. The cross-validation models ranged from using 117 to 327 epochs. The standard deviation on the 10 cross-validation model scores was around 0.60. You may be asking why the "CV-MSE" row is so high; see the sidebar at the end of this section ("The CV Metric Mystery" on page 206).

 If you look at a plot of the scoring history, you might be surprised to see very few entries: no nice curve, just one or two straight lines. This is because of using the combination of cross-validation and early stopping: it can see how many epochs were needed in the cross-validation models, so it uses that many, and switches early stopping off. If you look at any of the 10 cross-validation models you will see more of a curve in the scoring history.

So, from that good start, how much further can we take it? The first thing to experiment with is the network layout: how many layers, and how many neurons in each. I know the problem is nonlinear, so I feel I need two hidden layers, but I don't see it as so complicated that it will need more than three layers. We have only 18 input neurons[12] so I'm going to try first hidden layer sizes of 54, 162, and 324 (18 times 3, 9, and 18, respectively).[13] I then tried halving (except 54), doubling (except 324), or keeping the second layer the same size. And where I tried a third layer, I kept it the same size as the second layer. That gave 14 combinations. To speed things up a bit, I dropped from nfolds = 10 to nfolds = 6.

---

11 I know we are not supposed to test on the test data set until the end, but the knowledge gained here is not being used to tune: the best model will still be chosen based on the results from cross-validation.

12 Eight parameters, but X6 and X8 are enums with 4 and 6 levels, respectively, plus the spare input neuron for unseen values. 6 + (4 + 1) + (6 + 1) = 18.

13 In some earlier experiments I also tried just 18 neurons in the first layer. They were better than you might expect, but still inferior to the bigger models.

If I lost you with all those combinations, refer to the next table, where the results are shown (ordered by cross-validation results):

	hidden	train.mse	xval.mse	sd	epochs	time
1	324,324,324	0.347	4.368	0.494	177	23.4
2	54,54	0.087	4.712	0.556	982	5.2
3	162,162	0.059	4.744	0.446	525	10.4
4	324,162	0.096	4.788	0.503	236	7.0
5	324,162,162	0.162	4.946	0.479	171	9.9
6	162,81,81	0.270	4.978	0.457	418	8.0
7	54,108,108	0.022	5.005	0.581	518	7.4
8	162,324,324	0.135	5.026	0.322	158	17.5
9	162,162,162	0.152	5.065	0.629	243	10.0
10	162,81	0.035	5.077	0.649	623	7.9
11	162,324	0.087	5.147	0.520	244	9.3
12	54,108	0.015	5.242	0.573	836	6.3
13	324,324	0.131	5.456	0.627	205	8.4
14	54,54,54	0.049	5.983	1.173	720	6.5

Not much to conclude from all that, is there! I actually ran it again and, unhelpfully, everything shuffled around. From these results I feel no strong need to give it more neurons or more layers. However, more epochs might bear fruit, as even with quite strict early stopping a few of the models are hitting the ceiling.

The next thing we want to consider is the best value for activation, and if dropout and/or regularization helps. There are two types of dropout: between the input neurons and the first hidden layer (input_dropout_ratio), and then leaving each of the hidden layers (hidden_dropout_ratios). There are only 8 input columns (18 input neurons) so high values of input_dropout_ratio can be expected to do badly.

When experimenting with both hidden and hidden_drop_ratios in the same grid, you must use a constant number of layers. If you want to compare, say, some 2-layer networks with 3-layer networks in the same grid, run h2o.grid twice, with the same grid ID each time: once for 2-layer, then again for the 3-layer ones. That is what I will do here.

We will use the following hyper-parameters for the grid:

- If 3 layers then just 324,162,162; if 2 layers try both 54,54 and 162,162
- RectifierWithDropout, TanhWithDropout, or MaxoutWithDropout
- Hidden dropout ratios of 0 (no dropout), 0.1 (a little dropout each time), 0.2 (drop 20%), and 0.5 (drop 50%—this is the default)
- Input dropout ratios of 0 (no dropout) or 0.1 (10% of inputs ignored)
- L1 regularization of 0 (none) or 0.00001 (1e-05)

- L2 regularization of 0 (none), 0.00001 (1e-05), or 0.0001 (1e-04)

If you have already read Chapter 7, you might remember L1 and L2 regularization. L1 regularization, in neural nets, causes the neurons to use fewer of their inputs (the most significant ones, hopefully!); this might make them more resistant to noise (not an issue in this data set, so the expectation is that L1 regularization will not help— that is why I only try one value). L2 regularization reminds me of Tall Poppy Syndrome (*http://bit.ly/2fnADqL*), because the biggest weights get knocked down, and the smaller weights survive unscathed. It encourages the network to use all its inputs a bit, and not just use a few of them. L1 and L2 seem in conflict, yet one-third of the models in this grid will try both together. We could use two grids to avoid this, but how about we just try it and see what happens?

That was a lot of combinations, so I set the grid search to use `strategy` = "Random Discrete" with `max_models` = 50 (for each of 2 layer and 3 layer). It took rather a long time.[14]

The results were quite clear: the best models used no dropout at all. The top 3 (and 9 of the top 12) were all zeros for the hidden layer dropout. The top 6 (and again 9 of the top 12) were zero for the input dropout. The models with `hidden_drop out_ratios=0.5` were definitely the worst performers.

The choice of activation function seemed quite minor. For two hidden layers, Tanh or Maxout, and no hidden dropout. For three hidden layers, Rectifier or Maxout, and either no dropout, or a little. Rectifier is notably quicker than Tanh or Maxout.

For L2 regularization, half the top models use 0.00001, half use 0. So it seems to nei-ther help nor hinder. For L1, it is again about 50-50 between 0 and 0.00001; however 0.0001 seems to make results worse.

At this stage I am quite happy with this, and don't feel the need to try other parame-ters. I'm going to take our best model, and run it again, with `nfolds=10`, and less severe early stopping, and allow it up to 2000 epochs, then use that on the test data:

```
m <- h2o.deeplearning(
  x, y, train,
  nfolds = 10,
  model_id = "DL_best",

  activation = "Tanh",
  l2 = 0.00001,   #1e-05
  hidden = c(162,162),

  stopping_metric = "MSE",
```

---

14 I ran this grid on a 2-node cluster on Amazon EC2, totalling 72 cores, and it averaged 40 seconds per 2-layer model, and 120 seconds per 3-layer model.

```
stopping_tolerance = 0.0005,
stopping_rounds = 5,
epochs = 2000,
train_samples_per_iteration = 0,
score_interval = 3
)
```

This model ended up using "only" 479 epochs. On the training data it managed an MSE of 0.148, both the best we've seen in this book. "Best on training data" can be another way to say "most overfitted," but that is not the case here, as it also gives excellent results on the test set; here it is shown next to those we got earlier:

	Default	Early#1	Early#2	Best
Train-MSE	5.587	0.223	0.092	0.148
CV-MSE	17.510	4.854	4.908	4.619
Test-MSE	7.089	0.580	0.437	0.434
Epochs	11.519	194.000	192.000	196.000

Yes, our Best model is best, but only just: all the benefit came from giving more epochs. In fact I've made this model four times now, and the test-MSE has been 0.425, 0.434, 0.581, and 0.605. Out of the 143 samples, just three are more than 8% too low, and none were too high. Figure 8-4 shows just the first 75 samples, and has just one down triangle.

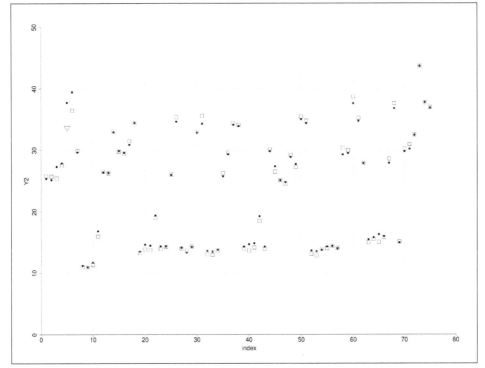

Figure 8-4. Tuned performance of deep learning on test data

The model took 3 to 4 minutes to train (including making the 10-fold cross-validation). While it is the best performer, it is also the most CPU-intensive.

The CV Metric Mystery

Earlier I promised I'd take a look at why the cross-validation results are so different. These numbers are from a run when the MSE on the test set was 0.425 (slightly better than shown elsewhere).

Here are the MSEs for the 10 cross-validation models:

```
3.486  5.882  4.903  4.172  5.186
5.232  4.087  3.328  6.048  4.285
```

The mean is 4.661, and the standard deviation is 0.63.

Under the model information I see another, slightly different, MSE metric: 4.724274. It is described as "10-fold cross-validation on training data (Metrics computed for combined holdout predictions."

But just above that I see "MSE: 0.128," which is even better than the 0.425 on the test data set. This is the model that was made based on all the training data, and that score is the score when evaluated on all the training data.

This might be a good time to remind you that the cross-validation metrics are *solely* about scoring your models;[15] they don't do anything else. They are just thrown away, and the actual model that is returned is trained on *100%* of your training data.

This data set is quite unusual in that there is no noise, no repeats: it contains exactly one sample of each building type. Of the 768 rows (in the full data), 143 (20%) are test, 562 (80% x 90%) are (constantly changing) training data, and 63 (80% x 10%) are (constantly changing) validation data. What I think is going on is that 562 is not quite enough to be representative, but when it is given the whole 625 (the full 80%) training rows, it crosses a threshold and is able to make a jump in understanding, and apply these new generalizations to the unseen test data.

Deep learning was the only algorithm that behaved this way: in all the others I saw mean cross-validation MSEs about the same as the MSE on test data.

---

15 Well, sometimes it influences things such as automatically choosing the best numbers for early stopping.

MNIST: Default Deep Learning

This is a pattern-recognition problem (see "Data Set: Handwritten Digits" on page 64, if you are not familiar with it), and so I have high hopes that deep learning is going to give the best results on it. It is a multinomial classification, trying to decide which of the digits 0 to 9 a set of 784 pixels represents.

First run either Example 3-3 or Example 3-4 from the earlier chapter, which sets up H2O, loads the data, and has defined train, valid, test, x, and y (no cross-validation this time because we instead have a validation data set). Then run either Example 8-1 or Example 8-2.

Example 8-1. Default deep learning on MNIST (Python)

```
m = h2o.estimators.H2ODeepLearningEstimator(model_id="DL_defaults")
m.train(x, y, train, validation_frame=valid)
```

Example 8-2. Default deep learning on MNIST (in R)

```
m <- h2o.deeplearning(x, y, train,
  model_id = "DL_defaults", validation_frame = valid)
```

It took just over three minutes, maxing out all eight cores on my machine. It first tells me it has dropped 67 constant columns (they were the pixels we identified as being zero in all samples when we first looked at the data). So there will be 717 input neurons, rather than 784.

Doing summary(m) (m.summary() in Python) gives details of each layer, followed by metrics such as MSE, then the cross-validation table for each of train and valid. There is a random element, so the exact numbers will be different on each run, but they will be similar. The standout feature of the result, for me, is summarized by Figure 8-5, a screenshot from the Flow interface.[16]

There is quite a lot to discuss here, but the big thing is the gap between the blue (lower) line, which is performance on the training data, and the orange (upper) line, which is performance on the validation set.

Those charts are interesting in other ways:

- They wobble about, so don't give up at the first uptick.

---

16 Though you could equally well have made this in R or Python; the data is all there in the m model object that H2O returns.

- For the validation line, logloss and MSE are quite distinctly different (not so much for the training line).
- That uptick/downtick at the end. What is that all about?

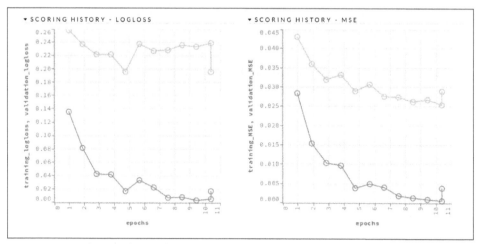

Figure 8-5. Logloss and MSE for train and valid data

What it is all about is that the `overwrite_with_best_model` parameter is true. It is using logloss to judge, and according to logloss the best model was just before epoch 5, so at the end of training it went back and used that model. That explains the downtick in the top line in the logloss chart; the uptick in the lower line is because *on our training data* it didn't think that was the best model. In the MSE chart, both jumped up at the end. This difference comes down to logloss and MSE disagreeing about the best model. (See "Classification Metrics" on page 93 for a reminder about the available metrics for multinomial classifications.)

Let's quickly run `h2o.performance(m, test)` to get performance on the test set. So, we have an error rate of 0.55% (train) versus 3.32%/3.04% (valid/test), and MSE of 0.005 versus 0.028/0.027. That ghastly demon, overfitting, has decided to show up and spoil the party. When tuning we will, therefore, want to be very aware of this.

In the model summary, it told me the "Metrics reported on temporary training frame with 9960 samples" for the training data, rather than all 50,000 samples. It was doing this for speed. It gave an error rate of 0.45% and MSE of 0.0039.

If you want to see the results on all 50,000 samples, the command is `h2o.performance(m,newdata=train)`. It was the numbers from that command that I quoted above; they are slightly worse, but close enough to make no real difference.

By the way, just as with the other models on default parameters that we have looked at in this book, the top 10 hit ratios chart shows it was still having trouble getting a few of them right even on its eighth or ninth guess.

 You might notice the validation and test results were very close. I did a test on a large (40) and realistic (each taking at least 15 minutes to build) set of tuned models on this data set, and I got 0.97 correlation on the error rate with validation and test results (0.98 for MSE and logloss). This is very good: it means we can tune for improvements in the validation set, safe in the knowledge that those improvements will carry over to our unseen test data. In absolute terms the difference in errors on 10,000 test cases ranged from +18 (model got 18 more right on the validation set) to –19 (model get 19 more correct on the test set), on the better models. The gap was a bit bigger on the weakest half a dozen models (up to –30). That means the stronger the model is, the more reliably validation data metrics indicate performance on test data.

MNIST: Tuned Deep Learning

We are going to be using the enhanced data, so use `"load.mnist_enhanced.R"` or `"load.mnist_enhanced.py"` (see "Helping the Models" on page 69 for more on what was added). First question: what difference did enhanced data make on the default settings, still sticking with the default of just 10 epochs? I tried two more runs on the "raw" MNIST data, and got (validation data set) errors of 417 and 390. (It was 332 on our run in the previous section. This high variance is common when not using enough epochs.) On the enhanced data I got 317 and 313 errors (and 292 with a later run), so over a 20% improvement.[17] The reduction in training set errors was even greater. Summary: deep learning finds it much easier to overfit our enhanced data, but the benefits on unseen data are also significant.

The next thing to try is to use more epochs, and therefore we want to set early stopping to keep computation under control:

```
stopping_metric = "misclassification",
stopping_tolerance = 0.01,
stopping_rounds = 3,
epochs = 500,
classification_stop = -1,
```

---

17 If you're curious, on the test data I get an even lower 273 errors.

These settings say it will only stop if there has been less than a 1% improvement, in misclassification,[18] over a sliding window of three scoring rounds. Oh, and if it just keeps on getting better and better, pull the plug after 500 epochs. That is strict: we'll let it train a bit more once we narrow the best parameters down. `classifica tion_stop` is zero by default, meaning it stops learning once it perfectly classifies the whole of the *training* data. But the model will keep improving its *validation* score even once this happens, so we want it off. Consider always switching it off (setting it to –1) when using early stopping.

Let's jump straight in, with enhanced data and the early stopping, and see how it does.

I did two runs and they hit the early stopping after 40 and 46 epochs. Both sucked all the marrow out of the training data—in fact the first run got a perfect score when evaluated on the training set. Validation errors were 268 and 272, respectively (out of 10,000). This compares to 317 and 313 when only given 10 epochs, so we've got another 17% improvement.

The next thing to think about is how many hidden layers, and how many neurons in each? And what other parameters are going to be important?

The challenge we are setting for this deep learning model is to look at groups of those pixels and form concepts that can be used to decide which digit it is likely to be. Because each layer is fully connected to every neuron in the previous level, as long as you have enough neurons in a hidden layer, it can learn lots of concepts in parallel. However, more layers is also going to help, so it can build more and more advanced concepts on top of lower-level ones.

There is an article on deep learning performance (*http://bit.ly/2f8K4a5*) by Arno Candel[19] where he has tuned many parameters on the MNIST data set. Much of that article's emphasis is on tuning for speed, and most experiments are on just 0.1 epochs (representative for testing speed-ups, not representative for evaluating quality), but I will shamelessly steal what I can. His very best model used 1024,1024,2048 neurons. Think back to that idea of building advanced concepts on lower-level ones, in the previous paragraph—does the final layer need more neurons to handle those advanced concepts, perhaps?

---

18 Meaning, we want to see improvement in the digit recognition, not just in the MSE or logloss.

19 Chief Architect at H2O.ai, and the main author of the deep learning code.

One practical reason to favor increasing neurons between layers, rather than decreasing, is that we have 898 input neurons, and only 10 output neurons. The number of input neurons gets multiplied by the number of neurons in the first hidden layer. So a 10,20,30 model needs 10,080 weights, but a 30,20,10 model needs 27,840 weights. Fewer weights means quicker training times.

As for other parameters, I already see overfitting on the training data, so I want to tackle that. There are both more training samples, and more columns, than in the building energy data set we previously looked at. So I will experiment with all of the following in my first grid:

l1

L1 regularization. Might help make the model more resistant to noise. Trying 0 (no regularization) and 1e-5 (a little).

input_dropout_ratio

Drop some of the input neurons. 0.1 means it will randomly set to zero 10% of the pixels. A different random set of pixels on each sample. The grid will compare 10% with 20%.

hidden_dropout_ratios

Trying 0%, 10%, and 50%. If 10% then it means at each neuron, for each training sample, there is a 10% chance it will pass on zero to the next layer instead of its actual value.

max_w2

I chose to only use this for the 4-layer networks, and experiment at comparing the default value of infinity (given as `Inf` in R, and `float("inf")` in Python), with a value of 20 (arbitrarily chosen).

In this section, I am going to stick with an activation function of Rectifier (With-Dropout). The aforementioned article concluded it was better than Maxout, and perhaps slightly better than Tanh, while being notably quicker than Tanh.

You may remember from a previous section that we cannot experiment with hid den_dropout_ratios in a grid unless we fix the number of layers of hidden neurons. But I want this first grid to experiment with 2-, 3-, and 4-layer neural networks. So the grid had to be made in three steps (as long as the same grid ID is chosen, H2O will combine the results for you). In the first step I compared these 2-hidden-layer models. The number in brackets is how many weights.

- 200 x 200 (221,600)
- 512 x 512 (727,040)

- 1024 x 1024 (1,978,368)

In the second step I tried one 3-layer model and, later on, added another one:

- 400 x 800 x 800 (1,327,200)
- 1024 x 1024 x 2048 (4,085,760)

And in the third step I tried two 4-layer models:

- 200 x 200 x 200 x 200 (301,600)
- 300 x 400 x 500 x 600 (895,400)

The final hyper-parameter I added was seed. This was solely for telling the difference between different runs, not for reproducibility: with H2O's implementation of deep learning you cannot expect the same model even if you try again with the same seed.

Naturally, with so many combinations of hyper-parameters, I set it to do "Random-Discrete." By the way, if you are still following along on a notebook, you are not going to get many models built: this is more a "go away for the weekend" grid, than a "go and get a cup of tea" grid.

So, what did we learn? The clearest thing: l1=0.00001 is way better than 0; all the top 13 models used L1 regularization. Everything else is a bit fuzzier. max_w2 seems to have no effect, and input_dropout_ratio of 0.1 versus 0.2 seems to make little difference (the best model, and four of the top- ive, use 0.2, though).

hidden_dropout_ratios is a bit more confusing. The best model used 0.1 for its 4 layers. We can say that 0.0 is poor: in one direct comparison, 0.5 had 124 validation errors (out of 10,000) while hidden_dropout_ratios=0.0 had 150. But the only direct comparison I got between 0.1 and 0.5 was that 0.5 was better by just 3 (an error rate per 10,000 of 167 versus 170).

So, what about hidden neurons? Table 8-1 shows the best 10 models, with their validation errors (per 10,000), and also the logloss on the validation data set. The right two columns show the relative time[20] it took to build the model, and the number of epochs; the asterisk marks those that hit the limit, and didn't early-stop.

Table 8-1. Best 10 models from first grid

Hidden	Errors	Logloss	Time	Epochs
300,400,500,600	121	0.0701	796	210
1024,1024	124	0.0602	2079	410

---

[20] Seconds, but on a 3-node, 108-core cluster I set up for this test.

Hidden	Errors	Logloss	Time	Epochs
1024,1024,2048	126	0.0720	3382	459
400,800,800	127	0.0673	1266	501*
1024,1024	134	0.0655	1660	200
400,800,800	137	0.0646	1419	272
512,512	137	0.0634	943	476
1024,1024	150	0.0671	2249	240
300,400,500,600	161	0.0699	1037	501*
300,400,500,600	167	0.0820	1099	501*

Well, no clear conclusion about which is best! Another way to view this table is that all of these hidden layer alternatives have about the same potential to learn. However, the 4-layer model has the best score (even if it also has the two worst scores), telling me it has the capacity to learn well on this data, so I will go with that.

The final model is shown next, and this code shows how I am giving it a less strict early-stopping criteria (not just lowering the tolerance, but increasing stopping rounds—important if it is going to wobble noisily on its way to improving) and up to 2000 epochs:

```
DLt <- h2o.deeplearning(x, y, train, validation_frame = valid,
  model_id = "DL_tuned", seed = seed,
  hidden = c(300,400,500,600),
  activation = "RectifierWithDropout",
  l1 = 0.00001,
  input_dropout_ratio = 0.2,
  hidden_dropout_ratios = c(0.1, 0.1, 0.1, 0.1),

  classification_stop = -1,
  stopping_metric = "misclassification",
  stopping_tolerance = 0.001,
  stopping_rounds = 8,
  epochs = 2000
  )
)
```

Giving a "best" model from a grid some less strict early-stopping criteria is a great time to use checkpoints (see "Checkpoints" on page 102); in this case that would have given me a 796-epoch head-start, and guaranteed a model with at least the score it got in the grid.

It took approximately two hours to build on my machine,[21] and ended up with a validation score of 130 (not as good as in the grid—see the tip for what I should have done), and on the test data it had 138 errors: easily the best of the models we have built in this book. It used 642 epochs in the end, though the model it returned was actually from epoch 275 (at 26 minutes), so it spent a lot of time bouncing around after that. The results of all four learning algorithms will be compared in "MNIST Results" on page 261 in the final chapter of this book. There is also a section in that chapter on how to improve the result further.

Football: Default Deep Learning

This data set, predicting football results based on a mix of recent performance and betting odds (see "Data Set: Football Scores" on page 71 in Chapter 3), has a lot of noise, so a bit like the MNIST data set we can perhaps expect dealing with overfitting to be our main challenge? But it is also a different kind of noise: in the MNIST data all the clues were there, and a human could expect to score over 99.5%. With the football result prediction, the human experts only reach an accuracy of 0.634.[22] That is, the clues are *not* all there.

If you are following along on your own machine, run either Example 3-6 or Example 3-7 from the earlier chapter, but make sure you load the *csv* files with the missing data removed/patched,[23] i.e., *football.train2.csv*, *football.valid2.csv*, and *football.test2.csv*. Deep learning would otherwise be handicapped by missing data. Running those listings will set up H2O, load the data, and define train, valid, test, x, xNoOdds, and y. Because valid is defined, cross-validation will not be used with this data set.

As in other chapters we are making two versions of the model, and then using compareModels() (see Example 5-1 in Chapter 5; it is also found in *football_helper.R* in the online code) to get some metrics on them. We are trying to predict if each match will be "home-win" or "draw-or-away-win." We try it two ways:

- Pre-match team strength estimates + pre-match bookmaker odds
- Just the pre-match team strength estimates

---

21 Estimated, based on taking 43 minutes on a 2-node, 72-core cluster.

22 This was the result, in "Football: Default GLM" on page 183, of using a linear model based on the average bookmaker odds of a win as the only input.

23 See "Missing Data" on page 237 in Chapter 9 for how they were made, and also why h2o.deeplearning()'s default of mean imputation is undesirable.

It is a binomial classification so we are focusing on the AUC and accuracy scores:

```
m1 <- h2o.deeplearning(x, y, train,
  model_id = "DL_defaults_Odds",
  validation_frame = valid, seed = seed)

m2 <- h2o.deeplearning(xNoOdds, y, train,
  model_id = "DL_defaults_NoOdds",
  validation_frame = valid, seed = seed)
```

The AUC scores are summarized here:

	Odds	NoOdds
train	0.647	0.607
valid	0.672	0.630
test	0.645	0.606

And the accuracy results:

	HomeWin	HW-NoOdds
train	0.612	0.586
valid	0.648	0.617
test	0.624	0.601

You can see the results are not great, but not bad. We do not seem to have any over-fitting; instead what this seems to show is the validation data set is a bit easier to make predictions on. Remember that this was time-series data, so the three data sets are consecutive in time, not randomly sampled. It may be that the particular seasons we use for valid and test were more predictable, e.g., fewer upsets, more matches following the form book. And vice versa: sometimes what smells like overfitting can just be that the test data set has more noise.

"Football Data" on page 263 in the final chapter will compare the results of all models.

Football: Tuned Deep Learning

The first thing is to allow more epochs, but to keep that under control by using early stopping. As you have already seen in this chapter, this can be the biggest improvement we will get, so let's first try that and nothing else. I will try this for both models. Here is the code for the second model; pay attention to the last four lines:

```
m2es <- h2o.deeplearning(xNoOdds, y, train,
  model_id = "DL_ES_NoOdds",
  validation_frame = valid, seed = seed,
  replicate_training_data = TRUE,

  stopping_metric = "AUC",
  stopping_tolerance = 0.01,
  stopping_rounds = 3,
  epochs = 1000
  )
```

That is saying it can have 1000 epochs (100 times more effort than the default model), but if it goes three scoring rounds with less than a 1% improvement in the AUC metric, then stop.

 I've also set `replicate_training_data` to true; because our data set it fairly small, this will speed things up if you run on a multi-node cluster, and won't have any effect if not.

Running with more epochs, on each model, gave these results (AUC):

	Odds	NoOdds
train	0.622	0.584
valid	0.632	0.605
test	0.601	0.577

And these accuracy numbers:

	Odds	NoOdds
train	0.593	0.571
valid	0.637	0.611
test	0.588	0.589

In the case of m2es it ran for about 15 times as long as the default, and did 832 epochs instead of 10. So why are the results so disappointing? The scoring history chart (again, for m2es) can answer that; see Figure 8-6 (a screenshot from the Flow interface).

As it got better at learning the training data (bottom line), it got worse at the validation data (the top line). At the end it chose the best model on the validation set, which was the first one it scored. Incidentally, over in the training data results the AUC had reached 0.9844 by epoch 331; at that point the AUC on the validation set was 0.5589, much worse than the 0.6323 it returned.

I will come back to tackling those diverging training/validation results, but next let's consider the number of hidden layers, and the number of neurons. All of the previous default models used two hidden layers, with 200 neurons in each. I will experiment with just one of our models: I've chosen the second model (predicting a home win, but without the help of the betting odds). At the end we will apply it to the data with the betting odds, and hope the best hidden layer choice applies equally well to that.

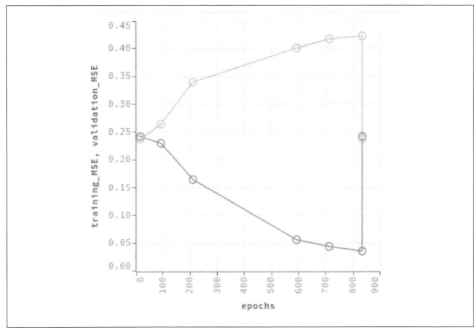

Figure 8-6. Scoring history (validation on top, training below, lower is better)

I have three questions:

- Are three layers better than two?
- Are more neurons needed in the first layer?
- Are more neurons needed in the final layer?

To answer those three questions, the three topologies I will try are 200x200x200, 400x200, and 200x400, respectively. The first one adds 40,000 weights (200x200). We have N inputs, so the second one adds 200*N weights. And we have two outputs[24] so the third one adds just 200*2 weights.

---

24 You might have expected just one output? Binomial classifications have two outputs, one for the likelihood of it being true, and one for the likelihood of it being false. They get used together for the final model output.

But, I want to consider dropouts at this point too. No, not those nerdy losers who drop out of school to start massively successful companies. If you'd been paying attention you'd know I mean these two parameters:

- `hidden_dropout_ratios`
- `input_dropout_ratio`

Rather than use a grid, I will try 0.3 for `input_dropout_ratio` (throw 30% of the inputs away each time) and 0.5,0.3 for `hidden_dropout_ratios` (drop 50% of the outputs from the first hidden layer, then drop 30% of each subsequent layer).

I will go with RectifierWithDropout for the activation function. On a hunch. Why not Tanh? Because it gives similar results to Rectifier but is slower. Why not Maxout? Because I don't think summing inputs will be so useful here. But mainly because I don't think the type of activation function will matter too much, and I want to focus my CPU cycles elsewhere. If you experiment and discover one of the others is better, let me know.

Though I am using dropouts, I will use L1 and L2 regularization too. I'll try 0.0005 (5e-4) for each. And set `balance_classes` to true. And I'm going to set `shuf fle_training_data` to true, too, because the documentation tells me to do that when I set `balance_classes`.

To get a baseline measurement, so the network topologies can be fairly evaluated, I first try all those new parameters with the default of two hidden layers, with 200 neurons in each.

Example 8-3 is what that looks like. Later versions will just change the `hidden` line:

Example 8-3. Deep learning first tuned model

```
m2_200x200 <- h2o.deeplearning(xNoOdds, "HomeWin", train,
  model_id = "DL_200x200",
  validation_frame = valid, seed = seed,

  replicate_training_data = TRUE,
  balance_classes = TRUE,
  shuffle_training_data = TRUE,

  hidden = c(200,200),

  activation = "RectifierWithDropout",
  hidden_dropout_ratios = c(0.5, 0.3),
  input_dropout_ratio = 0.3,
  l1 = 0.0005,
  l2 = 0.0005,
```

```
stopping_metric = "AUC",
stopping_tolerance = 0.01,
stopping_rounds = 3,
epochs = 1000
)
```

Here are the results, compared with the default m2 model, and the version that was just given more epochs. First AUC:

```
      Defaults MoreEpochs Drop+Reg
train   0.607     0.584    0.594
valid   0.630     0.605    0.630
test    0.606     0.577    0.604
```

Then accuracy:

```
      Defaults MoreEpochs Drop+Reg
train   0.586     0.571    0.568
valid   0.617     0.611    0.619
test    0.601     0.589    0.609
```

So dropping out is not just good for socially awkward geniuses. Figure 8-7 is the MSE chart, over time, for the model doing dropout and regularization. You might miss this if you are looking at it in black-and-white, but the validation result is the lower (better) line!

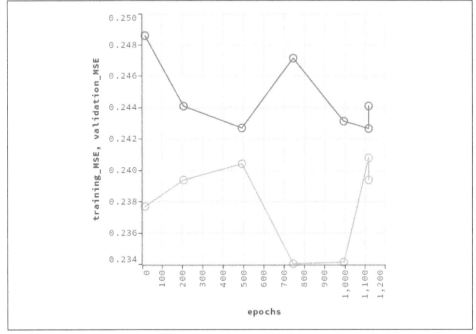

Figure 8-7. Scoring history with dropout (training on top, validation below!)

It chose the "best" model at the end, so why didn't it choose one of those at around 750 or 1000 epochs? Because this is the MSE chart, but the decision of best was made using AUC. And the best result according to AUC was at 203 epochs. If you ever find one of these scoring charts confusing, go and look at the more detailed scoring history.

Next I used those results to make the models with the different topologies previously described. After taking a first look, I decided to also try two hidden layers with 400 neurons in each.

Here is the comparison table for AUC:

	200x200	200x200x200	200x400	400x200	400x400
train	0.594	0.597	0.591	0.598	0.595
valid	0.630	0.631	0.633	0.629	0.630

And then for accuracy:

	200x200	200x200x200	200x400	400x200	400x400
train	0.568	0.571	0.563	0.570	0.565
valid	0.619	0.621	0.618	0.615	0.618

So more input neurons in the first layer didn't help. And it didn't really help in the second layer either. But a third layer does seem to have helped, if only slightly. (Though, without running more experiments I cannot say for sure if this isn't just random variation we are seeing.)

Well, if three is good, then four must be even better? AUC then accuracy:

	200x200	200x200x200	200x200x200x200
train	0.594	0.597	0.5
valid	0.630	0.631	0.5

	200x200	200x200x200	200x200x200x200
train	0.568	0.571	0.501
valid	0.619	0.621	0.421

Oh. That's a "no" then. Those are some really bad results. It looks like there is just too much noise in the data set to be able to train a 4-layer network.

To make my final model I will go with 200x200x200, but relax the early-stopping criteria, so it can have up to 2000 epochs (up from 1000 epochs), unless it fails to improve by 0.1% over 4 scoring rounds (was: 1% over 3 scoring rounds). This model will be tried on the test data to predict home wins, and I will make versions both with and without the odds data.

Here are those new early-stopping criteria; the rest of the code is identical to the version shown previously:

```
stopping_metric = "AUC",
stopping_tolerance = 0.001,
stopping_rounds = 4,
epochs = 2000
```

Here are the final results for our two models. First the AUCs:

```
      HomeWin HW-NoOdds
train  0.635    0.596
valid  0.678    0.632
test   0.648    0.616
```

Next, the accuracy values:

```
      HomeWin HW-NoOdds
train  0.595    0.567
valid  0.649    0.618
test   0.617    0.606
```

How have we done? Well, extra epochs improved the train and validation scores, but our reference AUCs were 0.675 for the validation data set, and 0.650 for the test data. One above, one below. And on accuracy, the targets were 0.650 and 0.634, so we've done poorly there. A reminder that "Football Data" on page 263 in the last chapter of this book compares all the algorithms on this data set.

Summary

Tuning deep learning can feel more like art than science, and with so many parameters it can always leave you feeling like you missed something important.

The superior performance on the MNIST data was what we expected. The poor performance on the football data was a bit unexpected: it tells me that with difficult, noisy, data sets deep learning can fail to outperform the other algorithms, and take longer doing it. The building energy results were the most interesting. It needed both the full training data (not just the 90% that cross-validation gave it), *and* the extra epochs from switching to early stopping, to get a big jump in comprehension—one that none of the algorithms managed. Similarly, "Deep Learning Auto-Encoder" on page 229 (in the next chapter) shows a trend between increasing the number of hidden neurons and MSE but, again, it really only appeared when given enough epochs.

So, I'm still wondering if I missed something important on the football data.

The remainder of this chapter gives a list of all the other parameters that might be that "something important." Or you can jump ahead to the next chapter, to see what H2O offers for unsupervised learning.

Appendix: More Deep Learning Parameters

My main criterion for putting a parameter here, rather than at the top of the chapter, was that I didn't use it in this book:

missing_values_handling

Handling of missing values. If "Skip" then rows with missing values are ignored. If "MeanImputation," which is the default, then missing values are assigned the mean value of that column.

use_all_factor_levels

This is true by default, meaning there is one input neuron for every level for each enum (categorical, factor) variable. If you set it to false then the first level in each enum is dropped. This can be done with no loss in accuracy (and a small speed-up in training speed, due to one less neuron). However, if you have set `vari able_importances` to true, then you should keep `use_all_factor_levels` as true.

max_categorical_features

The maximum number of categorical features, enforced via hashing (Experimental). The default is to have no limit.

single_node_mode

The default is false. If true, then it will run on a single node of your cluster. I find cluster scaling to be quite efficient for deep learning, so it is hard to imagine a need for it that is not better served by tweaking `target_ratio_comm_to_comp`.

fast_mode

Enable fast mode (minor approximation in backpropagation). It defaults to true.

force_load_balance

Force extra load balancing to increase training speed. Defaults to true.

standardize

Defaults to true, meaning the data will automatically be normalized. If false then you need to scale the data as part of your data preparation.

sparse

Defaults to false. Set it to true if your data has lots of zero values, to make it more efficient.

sparsity_beta

Sparsity regularization (Experimental). The default is 0.0.

You can specify the initial state of the neural network; you might do this if you had previously trained the neural net. (In fact, if you just wanted to load a previously

---

trained network, and not train it any more, set these parameters, and also set epochs to zero.)

initial_biases

A list of H2OFrame IDs to initialize the bias vectors of this model with.

initial_weights

A list of H2OFrame IDs to initialize the weight matrices of this model with.

But normally you will let the weights be initialized randomly. The following two parameters allow you control over that:

initial_weight_distribution

This defaults to "UniformAdaptive," but the alternatives are "Uniform" and "Normal." (UniformAdaptive is an optimized initialization that considers the size of the network.)

initial_weight_scale

This is a double. If `initial_weight_distribution` is "Uniform," then this is the range. For example, if you give 0.5, then the initial weights will be randomly between –0.5 and +0.5. If `initial_weight_distribution` is "Normal" then this is the standard deviation for weights. That is, the same 0.5 would have 68% of weights between –0.5 and +0.5, but 16% would be above +0.5, and 16% would be below –0.5. The default value is 1.0.

The remaining parameters have to do with the learning rate. I find the H2O default behavior to be intelligent enough that I would rather spend my tuning time on other things. Then there is the fear of not knowing if I've made things worse! If you want to learn more about these, many neural net video and book courses cover them:

rate

Learning rate. Higher will be less stable, while lower means it will take longer (more epochs) to converge. The default is 0.005.

rate_annealing

Learning rate annealing: rate / (1 + rate_annealing * samples). Default is 1e–6.

rate_decay

Learning rate decay factor between layers (N-th layer: rate*alpha^(N-1)). Default is 1, meaning it is not used by default.

adaptive_rate

Adaptive learning. Defaults to true.

epsilon

Adaptive learning rate smoothing factor (to avoid divisions by zero and allow progress). The default is 1e–8.

rho

Adaptive learning rate time decay factor. Defaults to 0.99.

momentum_ramp

Number of training samples for which momentum increases. The default is 1e–6 (one million training samples).

momentum_stable

Final momentum after the ramp is over. The default is 0.0.

momentum_start

Initial momentum at the beginning of training. The default is 0.0.

nesterov_accelerated_gradient

Use Nesterov accelerated gradient. It is a boolean and defaults to true; there is not usually a good reason to try false.

CHAPTER 9

Unsupervised Learning

Take a look at Figure 9-1, and tell me what you see.

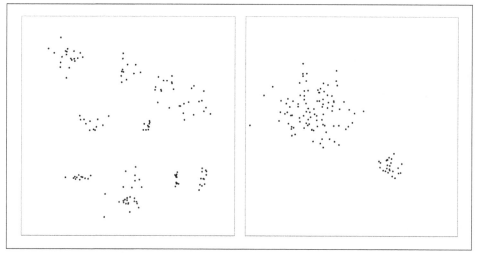

Figure 9-1. Two scatterplots

It doesn't matter what the x- and y-axes are in those two plots; imagine each plot represents a scientific domain. For the chart on the left you likely identified about 10 different concepts, so that domain is likely to have about 10 specialist words; some are blurring into each other, so maybe 9, maybe 11 or 12? But the domain on the right has two concepts, and is only going to have two specialist words. Or they might be describing weather conditions over a year. The chart on the left might be describing a place with lots of distinct weather patterns, so the weather becomes a talking point, and lots of weather phrases enter the vocabulary ("Is it chucking it down outside?" "No, just a light drizzle"). The chart on the right might represent the climate of

Southern California, where only two weather phrases are needed ("lovely and sunny," and "slightly cloudy").

The point is, you didn't need to know the subject or the "correct answer" to be able to do something useful with the data you were given, and this is a core strength of human intelligence. In machine learning, it is called unsupervised learning, and this chapter will look at some of the functionality H2O has for it.

This automatic organization of the data can be thought as a form of data compression. If you have 5000 input columns, that are quite sparse and contain lots of duplication, you might use the techniques in this chapter to reduce them to a more manageable, and information-dense, 12 columns; then you can use one of the supervised learning techniques on those 12 columns.

K-Means Clustering

The idea behind k-means is to divide your data up into k groups (you have to specify k) such that each data item is closer to the center of its cluster than to the center of any other cluster. It is doing what I asked you to do in those scatterplots earlier.

For this section I am going to use a Natural Language Processing (NLP) example. But as space is limited, and I want to keep this chapter focused, I am going to take the tf-idf (more on that in a moment) data that someone else has made, and direct you to their article and GitHub site; see the following sidebar.

NLP Data Preparation

I got this data by running *cluster_analysis.ipynb*, found at *http://bit.ly/2gaYcEm* and described very well in Brandon Rose's article (*http://bit.ly/2g9P1QX*). He took a list of the best 100 movies (*http://imdb.to/2g4Wxht*), then fetched their story descriptions from the IMDB site, and did a lot of processing in Python, using NLTK (*http://www.nltk.org*).

He went on to do some analysis and make some charts, but I stopped before the k-means clustering section, just after the `terms = tfidf_vectorizer.get_fea ture_names()` line. `terms` is a list of words, or short phrases, found in one or more synopses. `tfidf_matrix` holds the data I want; it is a sparse matrix with 100 rows and 563 columns. The columns are the terms, the rows are the movies. The values are what is called Term Frequency–Inverse Document Frequency (*http://bit.ly/2fDQSRb*), or tf-idf. They range from 0.0 to 1.0, and a high value means that word in that document[1] is important or signficant. A zero means the term is not in the synopsis; most values are zero.

---

1 Each movie synopsis counts as a document; the *corpus* is the set of all 100 movie synopses.

To export the data for use in H2O I used the following commands—first turn that sparse matrix into a pandas data frame, then export it as a *csv* file:

```
d = pd.DataFrame(
  tfidf_matrix.todense(),
  index=titles,
  columns=terms
  )
d.to_csv("tfidf.csv")
```

H2O currently has very little native NLP support, but this shows how easy it is to integrate with NLTK, or your preferred library. Note that I could have used `tfidf = h2o.H2OFrame(d)` to load it directly into H2O (or `h2oContext.asH2OFrame()` from Sparkling Water, if this was big data on a Spark cluster). But making a *csv* file means I will still have it tomorrow when I come up with a new idea. (I also manually shortened some movie titles, purely for book formatting reasons, which was also very easy because I had saved the *csv* file.)

The *csv* file has 564 columns: the first one is the name of the movie, the other 563 are the terms that were extracted. I want to use those 563 values to divide the movies up into 5 clusters; if we get lucky the set of movies in each cluster will be similar to each other. Example 9-1 shows how to do that in R. Most of it should be familiar by now; `tapply` is an R function to group the values in one column (movie names) by another column (each movie's k-means group), then apply the given function (print) to each group.

Example 9-1. k-means example, in R

```
library(h2o)
h2o.init(nthreads = -1)

tfidf <- h2o.importFile("./datasets/movie.tfidf.csv")

m <- h2o.kmeans(tfidf, x = 2:564, k = 5,
  standardize = FALSE, init = "PlusPlus")

p <- h2o.predict(m, tfidf)

tapply(as.vector(tfidf[,1]), as.vector(p$predict), print)
```

Example 9-2 is how to do that in Python; see the inline comments.

Example 9-2. k-means example, in Python

```python
import h2o
h2o.init()

tfidf = h2o.import_file("./datasets/movie.tfidf.csv")

from h2o.estimators.kmeans import H2OKMeansEstimator
m = H2OKMeansEstimator(k=5, standardize=False, init="PlusPlus")
m.train(x=range(1,564), training_frame=tfidf)

#Get the group that each movie is in
p = m.predict(tfidf)

#Join that to our movie names, then download it
d = tfidf[0].cbind(p).as_data_frame()
d.columns = ["movie","group"]

#Iterate through and print each group
for ix, g in d.groupby("group"):
    print "---",ix,"---"
    print ', '.join(g["movie"])
```

I set a couple of optional parameters. First `init="PlusPlus"`,[2] which I felt gave better results than the default of "Furthest," or the other alternative, "Random." (You can also specify your own initialization values.) I also set `standardize` to false, because the data is already nicely between 0.0 and 1.0. The `m` object tells you quite a lot of information, including how many items are in each cluster, but if you want to find out which item is in which cluster you have to ask it to predict them!

It runs quickly, a matter of seconds. Here is the first of the five groups:[3]

Schindler's List	One Flew Over Cuckoo Nest	Gone with the Wind
The Wizard of Oz	Lawrence of Arabia	Forrest Gump
E.T. the Extra-Terrestrial	LOTR: Return of the King	Gladiator
Saving Private Ryan	Raiders of the Lost Ark	Streetcar Named Desire
Best Years of Our Lives	My Fair Lady	Ben-Hur
Doctor Zhivago	Platoon	The Pianist
The Exorcist	The Deer Hunter	All Quiet on Western Front
Mr. Smith Goes Washington	Terms of Endearment	The Grapes of Wrath
Shane	The Green Mile	Close Encounters 3rd Kind
The Graduate	Stagecoach	A Clockwork Orange
Wuthering Heights		

---

2 See *https://en.wikipedia.org/wiki/K-means%2B%2B* for a description of this initialization algorithm.

3 They will change each time you run it, unless you set a seed (123 used here).

Here is the second group:

```
Raging Bull             Citizen Kane              Singin' in the Rain
12 Angry Men            Amadeus                   Gandhi
Rocky                   To Kill a Mockingbird     Braveheart
Dances with Wolves      City Lights               Good Will Hunting
Network
```

And the third group:

```
It's a Wonderful Life   Philadelphia Story        American in Paris
Patton                  The King's Speech         A Place in the Sun
Out of Africa           Tootsie                   Giant
Nashville               Yankee Doodle Dandy
```

The fourth group has both *Godfather* movies in it; most of the Westerns seem to be in here too:

```
The Godfather               The Shawshank Redemption  Casablanca
Titanic                     The Godfather: Part II    Psycho
Sunset Blvd.                Vertigo                   On the Waterfront
West Side Story             The Silence of the Lambs  Chinatown
Some Like It Hot            Unforgiven                Good, Bad and Ugly
Butch Cassidy & Sundance    Treasure of Sierra Madre  The Apartment
High Noon                   Goodfellas                The French Connection
It Happened One Night       Midnight Cowboy           Rain Man
Annie Hall                  Fargo                     American Graffiti
Pulp Fiction                The Maltese Falcon        Taxi Driver
Double Indemnity            Rebel Without Cause       Rear Window
The Third Man               North by Northwest
```

And the fifth has some scary ones like *Jaws* and *The Sound of Music*:

```
The Sound of Music          Star Wars                 2001: A Space Odyssey
Bridge on the River Kwai    Dr. Strangelove           Apocalypse Now
From Here to Eternity       Jaws                      The African Queen
Mutiny on the Bounty
```

I'm sure you can see how this can form the basis of a "People who enjoyed *Saving Private Ryan* also enjoyed *Platoon*" movie recommendation system, but the fact that the five groups change so much from run to run makes me cautious. It might just be that the input data needs more work.[4]

Deep Learning Auto-Encoder

We previously had a whole chapter (Chapter 8) on using `h2o.deeplearning()` for supervised learning, but now we will look at it for unsupervised learning. You switch

---

4 The combination of stopwords and stemming seemed to give some strange terms. Doing some proper grammatical parsing would improve results, though, would also give a huge increase in computation time. But all that is outside the scope of this book.

it into this mode by setting `autoencoder` to true. The other difference is to *not* set the y argument (i.e., the field you want to learn, in supervised learning).

It is a bit of a trick: it still does supervised learning, but it copies your input layer to be the output layer (aka "the answer"). In other words, it tries to learn the inputs. That might sound a bit pointless, but what is happening is that the hidden layers are being forced to summarize the data, to compress it. All the tuning knowledge we learned in the earlier chapter can be applied.

As an example of its use, I am going to take the same NLP data set that was used in "K-Means Clustering" on page 226, where we have 100 movies, and 563 terms, and see if we can reduce those 563 dimensions to just *two* dimensions. That is quite an ask, but I have chosen two because then I can plot the results.

The nice thing about this data set is there are only 100 rows, so the experiments can be quite quick. Example 9-3 is *almost* the simplest possible auto-encoder: there will be 563 input neurons, going down to just two neurons in a single hidden layer, then going to 563 output neurons. It will train for the default 10 epochs.

Example 9-3. Minimal auto-encoder example, in R

```
m <- h2o.deeplearning(
  2:564, training_frame = tfidf,
  hidden = c(2), autoencoder = T, activation = "Tanh"
  )
f <- h2o.deepfeatures(m, tfidf, layer = 1)
```

I said *almost*: I've added `activation = "Tanh"` instead of using the default Rectifier. You *can* use the default Rectifier, but:

- It gives poor results: x or y will be zero for many of them, giving a clustering along the bottom and left.
- In more complex auto-encoders you will get complaints of numerical instability.

So, with auto-encoders I recommend always using Tanh.[5]

The code in Python (Example 9-4) is quite similar, though note that layers (and column indices) count from zero, whereas in R they counted from one.

Example 9-4. Minimal auto-encoder example, in Python

```
m = h2o.estimators.deeplearning.H2OAutoEncoderEstimator(
  hidden=[2],
```

---

5 Maxout is not supported for auto-encoding.

```
    activation="Tanh"
    )
m.train(x=range(1,564), training_frame=tfidf)
f = m.deepfeatures(tfidf, layer=0)
```

Despite the simplicity, it gives acceptable results, with an MSE of 0.035. Figure 9-2 shows the movies plotted by the value of the two reduced dimensions.

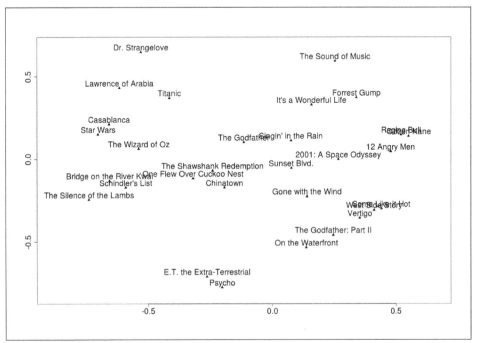

Figure 9-2. Movies in two dimensions, made by the simplest auto-encoder.

 In this series of plots only the first 30 movies are plotted each time, to stop them looking too cluttered. You will see overlapping names. These are not printing errors! It is where the algorithm has not managed to separate those two movies in the meager two dimensions it has been given.

By the way, I am plotting the first 30 with R code like this:

```
d <- as.matrix(f[1:30,])
labels <- as.vector(tfidf[1:30, 1])
plot(d, pch = 17)  #Triangle
text(d, labels, pos = 3) #pos=3 means above
```

Next I made 19 models, where I experimented with the amount of reduction: between 2 and 20 dimensions. For each model, hidden was set to 128,64,nodes,

64,128, where nodes ranged from 2 to 20. So 563 input nodes linked to the first hidden layer with 128 nodes, then to 64 nodes in the second hidden layer, then the 2+ nodes of interest are the third hidden layer, then back up to 64, then up to 128 in the fifth and final hidden layer, and then finally out to 563 output nodes. I first tried this with 5 epochs (the upper line in Figure 9-3), and then again with 400 epochs (the mostly lower line).

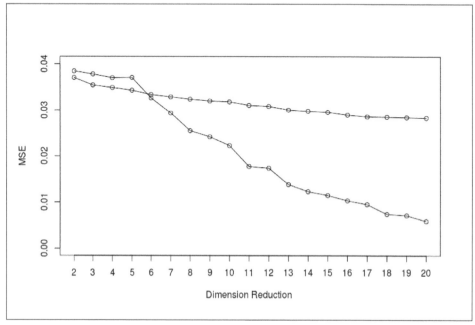

Figure 9-3. Model quality (lower is better) by number of dimensions

The more dimensions in the middle hidden layer the easier it is to learn, but the steeper angle of the lower curve means it needs plenty of epochs to take advantage of this. It is curious that the first four values did *worse* with more epochs.

Stacked Auto-Encoder

A neural net model can be built up in stages, which is a useful technique, even with supervised learning, when you find you want more layers but learning is too slow or just not working.

 Terminology alert: You might also see *stacking* models used to mean ensembles (described in Chapter 10). But with auto-encoding neural networks it means learning one layer at a time.

Staying with the movie NLP data set:

```
m1 = h2o.estimators.deeplearning.H2OAutoEncoderEstimator(
  hidden = [128,64,11,64,128], activation = "Tanh", epochs = 400
  )
m1.train(x = range(1,564), training_frame = tfidf)
f1 = m1.deepfeatures(tfidf, layer = 2)

m2 = h2o.estimators.deeplearning.H2OAutoEncoderEstimator(
  hidden = [2], activation = "Tanh", epochs = 400
  )
m2.train(x = range(0,11), training_frame = f1)
f2 = m2.deepfeatures(f1, layer = 0)
```

What is happening is that a model m1 with 5 hidden layers, and 11 neurons in the middle layer, is trained on the raw data, tfidf.[6] Then that third hidden layer is extracted into f1. f1 is a transformation of tfidf, still with 100 rows, but now only 11 columns. m2 then uses f1 as its input, and it builds a much simpler model, reducing 11 input nodes to 2 hidden nodes then back out to 11 output nodes. At the end the results are put in f2. f2 has 2 columns, but still has 100 rows, one for each movie.

I can't objectively say if Figure 9-4 looks any better: this is unsupervised learning, after all! But the key point here is that f1 could have been used as the training frame into any algorithm, whether another auto-encoder, as here, or a supervised learning algorithm such as random forest.[7]

A common example you might see is to auto-encode the MNIST data set, into two columns, which you then plot to show the digits (normally color-coded). If you have got it right you should see each digit clustering together nicely. It is also interesting to see the different clustering you get when using PCA (see "Principal Component Analysis" on page 234) to reduce the same data to two dimensions.

You might then train on just those two columns. Or add them to the data, just like the enhanced data that was added before (see "Helping the Models" on page 69).

---

6 Stacked auto-encoders usually model a single layer at a time; I wanted to show here that you don't have to do it that way.

7 If you go back to Brandon Rose's article, and code, you will see the genre of each movie is available. Could that be used for supervised learning?

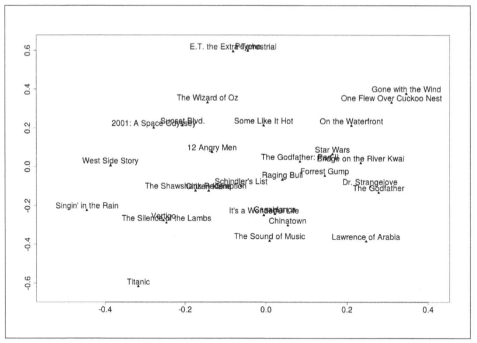

Figure 9-4. Movies in two dimensions, made by a stacked auto-encoder

Principal Component Analysis

Principal component analysis is normally called PCA, though the H2O API and R call it prcomp. It is another way to reduce the dimensionality of numeric data. Wikipedia (*https://en.wikipedia.org/wiki/Principal_component_analysis*) tells me "PCA can be done by eigenvalue decomposition of a data covariance matrix or singular value decomposition of a data matrix." Fortunately I don't need to know my eigenvalue from my eigenvector to be able to use it.

I am going to call PCA with k = 2, meaning I just want to get the first two principal components. The first one will be the x-axis in my plot, and accounts for as much variability in the data as it can. The second one, which will become my y-axis, gets as much of the remaining variability as it can, while being orthogonal to the first principal component. So, with PCA each additional dimension brings along less information. This is in contrast to using an auto-encoder to reduce dimensions—there the dimensions are all equal citizens. (See Figure 11-4 in Chapter 11 for a visual example of the difference.)

The data, and application, is the same as shown in "Deep Learning Auto-Encoder" on page 229: take the tf-idf scores for 563 terms used to describe 100 movies, then reduce the 563 dimensions to just two, so that they can be plotted.

Here is the complete code, in R:

```
library(h2o)
h2o.init(nthreads = -1)

tfidf <- h2o.importFile("./datasets/movie.tfidf.csv")
m <- h2o.prcomp(tfidf, 2:564, k = 2)
p <- h2o.predict(m, tfidf)
```

After running that code p will have 2 columns and 100 rows, and plotted it looks like Figure 9-5 (again, just the top 30 movies, to avoid it getting overly messy).

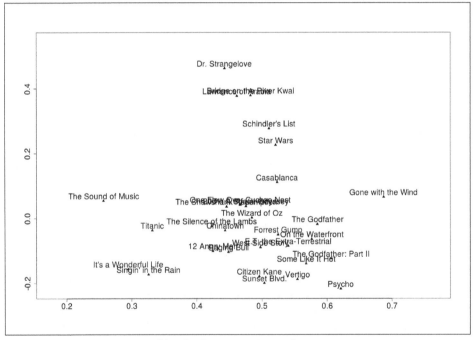

Figure 9-5. Movies organized by the first two principal components

Despite a few more overlaps, it looks just as plausible as any of the other plots of this data: the two *Godfather* movies are quite close, as are *The Wizard of Oz* and *Silence of the Lambs*.

GLRM

GLRM stands for Generalized Low Rank Model, and it's another algorithm for reducing the number of columns, while maintaining as much information as possible.[8] The additional thing that GLRM brings is being able to cope with nonnumeric data and missing data.

GLRM is also being suggested as a lossy compression algorithm (to reduce storage requirements), and, related to that, as a way to fill in missing values. I will look at that at the end of this chapter. But here I am going to run it on the same NLP movie data as I did with auto-encoder and PCA:

```
library(h2o)
h2o.init(nthreads = -1)

tfidf <- h2o.importFile("./datasets/movie.tfidf.csv")

m <- h2o.glrm(tfidf, cols = 2:564, k = 2)
X <- h2o.getFrame(m@model$representation_name)
# Y <- m@model$archetypes
```

GLRM works by taking the 563 column by 100 row data, and creating two smaller matrices: X, which is 2 columns by 100 rows, and Y, which is 563 columns by 2 rows. That is, 56,300 cells have been reduced to 200 + 1126 = 1326 cells. Y is commented out here, as it not being used in this example. To restore your original data (also not needed here) you would do X * Y. You can do this with h2o.proj_archetypes(m, tfidf) or h2o.predict(m, tfidf) or h2o.reconstruct(m, tfidf).[9]

As in the previous sections we can plot the contents of X, and attach movie names (Figure 9-6).

 GLRM contains a number of options, including transform. The default is "NONE," but if you change this default then you should also set reverse_transform to be true when calling h2o.proj_archetypes. For example, h2o.proj_archetypes(m, tfidf, reverse_transform = TRUE).

---

8 It builds on top of k-means: in fact if you look on Flow you will see that for every GLRM model a k-means model has also been built.

9 Yes, it is strange you need the original data tfidf, when the point of X and Y was that they can replace it, and so free up storage. Also strange that there appears to be three functions to do the same thing.

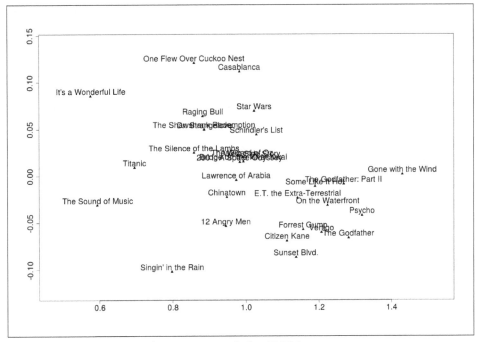

Figure 9-6. Movies in two dimensions, made by GLRM

Missing Data

The building energy and MNIST data sets came to us perfectly formed: no missing data at all. The same cannot be said for the football data. It was hard enough just to get it all into a single file, but at the point we left it (at the end of Chapter 3) there were quite a lot of NAs (the early years had no stats, and the set of bookmakers that we get odds from changes year to year). If we run GLM or deep learning on it, with missing data handling set to "Skip," then any row that has an NA in *any* column will get ignored completely.

The missing fields in our train, valid, and test data sets are different. You can see number of missing values by looking at the data on Flow, for instance, but to investigate this issue more deeply, I loaded the data into H2O (see Example 3-6 from Chapter 3) to set up `train`, `test`, `valid`, `x`, `y`, and so on, then I ran the following lines to download all the data into the R client:

```
d <- as.data.frame(train)
dv <- as.data.frame(valid)
dt <- as.data.frame(test)
```

R has a nice couple of idioms to help. First, to find out how many rows we have with no NAs in any column, use sum(complete.cases(d)). 15,648 in training, 1,984 in the validation data set, and only 310 in the training data. mean(complete.cases(d)) gets that as a percentage: 38%, 97%, and 15%. That is a lot of data we could potentially be throwing away, especially in the test data set.

Second, to see what percentage of each column is a missing value, use col Means(is.na(d)). Here is a sample:

Div	Date	HomeTeam	AwayTeam	FTHG	FTAG
0.000	0.000	0.000	0.000	0.000	0.000
HTR	HS	AS	HST	AST	HF
0.262	0.350	0.350	0.350	0.350	0.350
HY	AY	HR	AR	B365H	B365D
0.350	0.350	0.350	0.350	0.450	0.450
...	...	...	...	...	...
BbAvH	BbMxD	BbAvD	BbMxA	BbAvA	BbOU
0.600	0.600	0.600	0.600	0.600	0.600
BbAv<2.5	BbAH	BbAHh	BbMxAHH	BbAvAHH	BbMxAHA
0.600	0.600	0.600	0.600	0.600	0.600
HST1	AST1	HF1	AF1	HC1	AC1
0.000	0.000	0.000	0.000	0.000	0.000
AR1	res1H	res1A	res5H	res5A	res20H
0.000	0.000	0.000	0.000	0.000	0.000

In the training set, all the columns starting "Bb" are 60% missing. The other betting odds columns vary from 35% to 55% missing. 34% of rows have no match stats (number of corners, etc.), and 26% don't have the half-time result.

The validation data is completely different: dv[!complete.cases(dv),'Date'] tells me that there were 45 matches affected in mid-August, and that 3 more matches were affected in April, i.e., just 2.3%, and just betting odd columns. The test data is different again: 85% of columns SJH, SJD, SJA are missing.

The test data is the easiest to fix: if we remove the SJH, SJD, and SJA columns, we end up with 2032 complete cases. So it jumps from 15% complete to 99.8% complete! The way to remove columns in H2O is by doing a copy, specifying the columns we want to *keep*.[10] Look at this code, but don't run it just yet:

```
test <- test[!(colnames(test) %in% c('SJH', 'SJD', 'SJA'))]
```

Naturally, if you remove some columns from the test data set, you need to remove those same columns from the training and validation data sets. But we need to think what to do about *all* the missing data. There have been entire books written about

---

10 Remember to then do dt <- as.data.frame(test) to get the data again, if you plan on any more client-side analysis with it.

missing data, entire conferences on the subject, so brace yourself, because I'm about to reduce it to two techniques:

- Throw It Out
- Make It Up

You just saw an example of *Throw It Out*, when we got rid of the entire SJH/SJD/SJA columns. The "Skip" behavior of GLM and deep learning, which ignores data rows with any NA, is another example.

The very simplest approach to *Make It Up* is to set it to zero. I did that, kind of inadvertently, when adding the previous-match stats (see "The Other Third" on page 82). Figure 9-7 shows the histogram of HS (home shots in each match) on the left, with HS1 (shots by the home side in their previous match), on the right. Have I done a bad thing here? Maybe. But before you shun me, ostracize me, shut me out of your life forever, we should consider the alternatives.

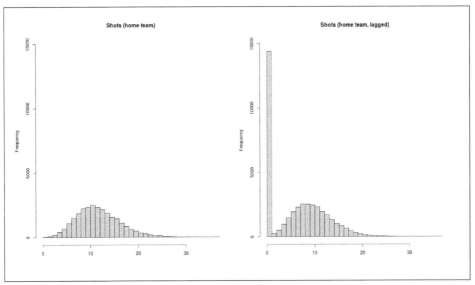

Figure 9-7. Comparison of HS and HS1 distribution (with zero)

One step up the sophisticated scale is to take the mean of the column and replace all missing values with that. And GLM and deep learning will do this for you, for all NAs, if you specify `missing_values_handling = "MeanImputation"`. There is also the `h2o.impute()` function, which offers not just mean, but also median and mode options. (*Imputation* is what statisticians call making things up.) Surely that is going to be better than using a zero? Figure 9-8 is what mean imputation looks like for that same HS1 field.

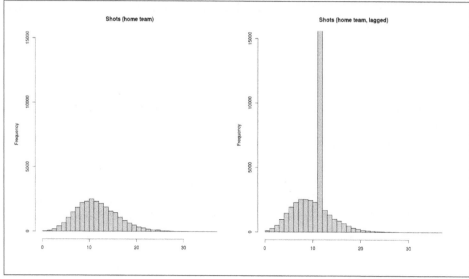

Figure 9-8. Comparison of HS and HS1 distribution (with mean imputation)

I'd argue that in some situations this is just as bad. What I mean is that for algorithms like GLM, which will use HS1 as a numeric field in mathematical equations, yes, the second way is better. But for tree algorithms, that cut the numbers up into ranges, the second way has disguised the difference between a genuine 12 and a "shrug, no idea what actually happened." Using a zero is better for the tree algorithms, as zero was a rare value.

Both approaches, zero or mean, are poor.[11] The ideal would be something that kept the shape of the histogram. One way that might work, with HS1, is to guess that if a team scored zero goals they likely made fewer shots than a team that scored one goal, while a team that scored two goals likely made more shots, and so on. A quick check shows a 0.23 correlation between home-side goals and home-side shots, and a 0.37 correlation between home-side goals and home-side shots on target (the "HST" field).

With up to 60% values missing, it is the betting odds columns that are causing the most anguish. New bookmaker sources get added, bookmakers go broke, or merge, and generally it all gets horribly messy. But, every cloud has a silver lining, and the Ag layer here is that all those bookmaker odds are highly correlated. "Estimating HS1 based on goals scored" is a level of making stuff up that gives even a politician pause, but if the odds of a home win from our other bookmakers range from 1.35 to 1.39,

---

11 I should've used a blank value instead of zero; then H2O would have loaded them as missing values, and they would not have appeared in the histogram at all. But, stay with me, it will all work out for the best.

for a certain match, we are going to be fairly safe going with 1.37 for any missing bookmaker values.[12]

GLRM

Unhappy with both "Skip" and "MeanImputation" options, I first tried the GLRM algorithm to fill in the data. My first try was a very naive `h2o.glrm(train, k = 9)`. It took so long I had to abort it, and found out that it was trying to work with 3830 columns! Each unique date, and each unique team name, had become a column. So I tried again, using just x, the list of column names we can validly use to learn a model from.

Objective is the measure of error in GLRM, and the default 50 iterations gave an objective of 2.76 million, and completed in 12.4 seconds; by increasing to 200 iterations it reduced the objective 839K, and increased the run time to 45 seconds. Here is the code to make the model, and then to make a version of `train` with no missing values:

```
m <- h2o.glrm(train, cols = x,
  k = 9, max_iterations = 200
  )
train2 <- h2o.reconstruct(m, train)
```

`train2` just contains the x columns, and the column names are all different, so it would take some data hacking to merge these in to replace just the missing values in `train`. But the real problem with `train2` is the values are outside the range of values in the original data. For instance, betting odds *always* have to be above 1.0. But some of the restored betting odds values were not just below 1.0 but were even negative. Other fields had a range of –1.0 to +1.0, but were being given values outside that range.

I made a number of attempts to use GLRM's various parameters, or to try just using the odds columns, or different values for k, or more iterations, but couldn't get past this fundamental flaw.

Lose the R!

I got much better results when I switched from using GLRM to using GLM. The idea is, for any given column, make a linear model to predict it based on the value in all the other columns. There are 39 columns that have at least one missing value, so this requires making 39 linear models.

---

12 That isn't mean imputation. Mean imputation is the mean over the whole column. This is the average of selected fields over a *row*.

As a first step, I decided to drop all data prior to the 2000/2001 season. It only consisted of the final result, no match stats, no betting odds, so very little to impute off of. That was done with this code, which creates a new data frame on the H2O cluster, and also gives it a friendly name:

```
train2000 <- h2o.assign(train[14237:nrow(train),], "train2000")
```

The following R loop shows how the fields storing betting odds were filled in. Because these columns are so highly correlated, I just trained each line model from the other odds columns and nothing else. That is what the setdiff(oddFields, y) statement is doing:

```
dNew <- as.data.frame(train2000)
colnames(dNew) <- colnames(train2000)

lapply(oddFields, function(y){
  missingCount = sum(is.na(dNew[,y]))
  if(missingCount == 0)return(NULL)

  m <- h2o.glm(setdiff(oddFields, y), y,
    train2000, model_id = paste0("GLM_",y),
    lambda_search = TRUE
    )
  res <- h2o.predict(m, train2000[is.na(train2000[,y]),])
  v <- as.vector(res)

  dNew <- get('dNew', envir = .GlobalEnv)
  dNew[is.na(dNew[,y]),y] <- as.vector(res)
  assign('dNew', dNew, envir=.GlobalEnv)
  })
train2000x <- as.h2o(dNew, destination_frame = "train2000x")
```

The first couple of lines prepare a client-side data frame to store the imputed data in, and the last three lines in the loop are some R hackery to insert results, replacing just the missing values.[13]

The final line uploads the filled-in data to the H2O cluster, which is essential so we can reference it in the next block of code, which will fill in gaps in the other fields. It allows using the imputed odds data as a field to learn from when filling in the stats fields. Other than that, the following loop works just like the previous one:

```
mostFields <- setdiff(colnames(train), c("Date", "HomeTeam", "AwayTeam") )
lapply(statFields, function(y){
  missingCount <- sum(is.na(dNew[,y]))
  if(missingCount == 0)return(NULL)

  m <- h2o.glm(setdiff(mostFields, y), y,
```

---

13 I was able to do all these columns in one go because it would fit in memory. If you are dealing with Bigger Data, this might have to be done one column at a time.

```
    train2000x, model_id = paste0("GLM_",y),
    lambda_search = TRUE
    )
  res <- h2o.predict(m, train2000x[is.na(train2000x[,y]),])
  v <- as.vector(res)

  dNew <- get('dNew', envir = .GlobalEnv)
  dNew[is.na(dNew[,y]),y] <- as.vector(res)
  assign('dNew', dNew, envir=.GlobalEnv)
  })
train2000x <- as.h2o(dNew, destination_frame = "train2000x")
```

To get higher-quality results, `valid2000x` was made by merging the new training data with the current validation data:

```
trainValid <- h2o.rbind(train2000x,valid)
```

The two loops were the same. And the test data was filled in in just the same way, using the merger of three data sets:

```
trainValidTest <- h2o.rbind(train2000x, valid2000x, test)
```

Why not just merge `train`, `valid`, and `test` at the start, and run the loops once, instead of three times? Because that would be infecting the training data with knowledge of the future. When dealing with time-series data you need to keep thinking what data was available at what point in time, and remember that the test data represents unseen data that your model will be used on in production.

The final step was to export those data frames to *csv* files:

```
path = "/path/to/datasets/"
h2o.exportFile(train2000x, paste0(path",football.train2.csv"))
h2o.exportFile(valid2000x, paste0(path",football.valid2.csv"))
h2o.exportFile(test2000x, paste0(path",football.test2.csv"))
```

Unlike importing data, relative paths are not allowed by `exportFile()`, so a full path must be given.

I used GLM almost out-of-the-box, the only customization being to specify lambda search (and even that was not needed). Of course, it didn't need to be GLM, and I imagine any of random forest, GBM, or deep learning would have done the job just as well, if not better.

But GLM was good enough, and is quick, and stays quick when scaled across clusters.

To close this section, the comparison of HS and HS1 in *football.train2.csv* is shown in Figure 9-9. The distributions look almost exactly the same!

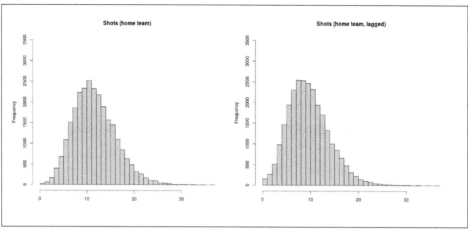

Figure 9-9. The final imputed HS1 data

See I told you it would all work out in the end. (Smug grin.) Where did all the zeros go, do I hear you cry? It turns out that practically all of them were in the pre-2000 data. So, that huge imbalance went away when I truncated away the first 14,237 rows. I know, it feels like cheating. But, all's well that ends well!

Missing Data Strategy

GLM worked well, so let's use it everywhere? Unfortunately there is no single best approach for dealing with missing data. To illustrate[14] this, let's have a think about what the choices mean for missing data in a birthday column:

Zero
> Everyone gets set to January 1st.

Mean
> Everyone gets set to June 30th.

GLM, etc.
> Everyone gets an arbitrary birthday, as there are no useful predictors.

Skip
> Ignore everyone who hasn't told us their birthday.

---

14 The bad choices here are very obvious. They won't always be.

Remove Column
    No one's birthday is used.

If marketing wants to send out birthday cards to customers, Skip is what you want, the others are all very stupid. If you want to build a model from this data, Remove Column is likely best. Those are not the only choices. Leaving birthday-unknown as just another categorical level would work (though this would most likely slow the model down for no advantage compared to Remove Column). A marketing campaign to ask customers their birthday is good. And maybe another database can contain useful predictors, such as noticing the number of friend posts on a person's Facebook feed is much higher on one day of the year.

Never deal with missing data on your response variable; instead, simply remove those rows. This happens automatically with the H2O supervised algorithms.

 When imputing data, *always* keep the original (on disk, in a data warehouse; where doesn't matter). Never "fix" the data by writing over the original. Someone may come up with a better approach in the future. Government regulation might enforce a different one. And today's predictor variable may be tomorrow's response variable.

Summary

This chapter showed how to use H2O with Natural Language Processing, but was mainly about dealing with data when the correct answer is either unavailable or does not exist. Sometimes this is a means to an end, for instance when creating better or additional training data for a supervised learning algorithm, and sometimes it is the end in itself, such as clustering or filling in missing values.

This chapter also took a detailed look at dealing with missing data, and you should now know when to specify the `missing_values_handling` parameter, when you need to do something as part of the data preparation stage, and when you don't need to do anything. We also saw how H2O can be of use at any stage in your pipeline, not just to build the big model at the end.

We have now looked at four supervised learning algorithms, and a variety of unsupervised ones. The next chapter will take a quick look at everything in H2O that has not already been dealt with.

CHAPTER 10

Everything Else

There is lots still to say: enough to fill another book! This chapter will introduce quite a few topics, without going into too much detail, but pointing you toward where you can find out more.

This chapter starts with a look at where to get the latest documentation, and how to Use The Source, Luke! Then we look at how to upgrade H2O, and how to install it from source. Which leads on to how to set up clusters, which leads on to Spark and Sparkling Water. Finally, a look at other algorithms: naive bayes and ensembles.

Staying on Top of and Poking into Things

H2O is well-documented, so *http://docs.h2o.ai* should be your first port of call. The latest user guide is at *http://docs.h2o.ai/h2o/latest-stable/h2o-docs/index.html*.

If you want to see if, say, any new parameters have been added to GBM, you could go to the REST API Reference (*http://bit.ly/2g6l5Hg*), then find GBMParametersV3 (*http://bit.ly/2grKqyH*). Alternatively, regularly check Changes.md (*http://bit.ly/2g6qqhK*) over on the GitHub site!

If you wanted to see how GBM is implemented in Java you would start at the Java-docs (*http://bit.ly/2g3rEZc*), find "hex.tree.gbm," then "GBM." The corresponding code will be over on Github (*http://bit.ly/2grIfv9*).

Random forest is called DRF in the REST endpoints, and hex.tree.drf (*http://bit.ly/2fNoOZl*) in the Java source; everything else is fairly much named how you would expect.

Installing the Latest Version

Installing from packages, as shown back in the first chapter ("Install H2O with R (CRAN)" on page 3 and "Install H2O with Python (pip)" on page 5) is going to be good enough for most people. However, installing the latest stable version (or even the latest bleeding-edge version) is not that much harder.

Unfortunately the latest versions do not have nice aliases, like "stable" and "nightly," so I cannot just give you some instructions to copy and paste; it changes with each release. Instead, go to the H2O download page (*http://www.h2o.ai/download/*), click the link for the latest stable release of H2O, and follow the instructions for either R or Python there.

Instead, go to the H2O R download page (*http://www.h2o.ai/download/h2o/r*) or the H2O Python download page (*http://www.h2o.ai/download/h2o/python*) and follow the instructions given there.

Building from Source

Some people are hopeless control freaks, but not you—you have a genuine reason to need to compile everything from source. How to build H2O from source (*https://github.com/h2oai/h2o-3#Building*) are the instructions you are looking for. There are a couple of dependencies beyond what you need to just install and run H2O, but it is not too bad. There are subsections for various platforms (including Hadoop).

Running from the Command Line

Throughout the book we have let our R or Python client start H2O for us. This is the easiest way, and also makes sure the versions are compatible.

But if the client finds H2O is already running, it will happily connect to that running instance. Starting H2O separately like this has some advantages. The main one is stability. When you close your client it closes H2O for you, too. If you only ever have one client, and you never need H2O running when that client is closed, that is just what you want; if not, it will cause problems!

The following example shows how to start H2O with 3GB of memory, on the local IP address and default port:

```
java -Xmx3g -jar /path/to/h2o.jar
```

The other reasons for using the command line usually have to do with starting clusters on a remote server. You can get help on all the current command-line options with:

```
java -jar /path/to/h2o.jar --help
```

The H2O you start must still be the same version as the version of the client you have installed.

If you need to pass authentication details to S3 or HDFS, you can specify "core-site.xml" like this:

```
java -jar h2o.jar -hdfs_config core-site.xml
```

See the documentation on what should go inside that XML file (*http://bit.ly/2goq6xt*).

I mentioned in "Privacy" on page 3 that H2O calls Google Analytics to record which versions are being used. If you need to opt out, the command-line argument -ga_opt_out is an alternative to creating the *.h2o_no_collect* file in your home directory:

```
java -Xmx3g -jar /path/to/h2o.jar -ga_opt_out
```

Clusters

H2O data structures, and its algorithms, have been built with clusters in mind, rather than as an afterthought. Even so, there are a few restrictions with H2O clusters:

- Each H2O node on the cluster must be the same size. So if the smallest machine in your cluster has 3GB free, every node must be given 3GB, even if some of them have 64GB.[1]
- Machines cannot be added once the cluster starts up.
- If any machine dies, the whole cluster must be rebuilt.[2] No high availability support.
- Each node must be running the same version of *h2o.jar*. (And if you are planning to control the cluster from, say, an R client, then that also must be running the same API version as your *h2o.jar*.)
- Nodes should be physically close, to minimize network latency.

For more than one of those reasons, you should favor a few big nodes over lots of small nodes. And for models that take many hours to create, use regular checkpoints

---

1 You *could* try running 20 3GB nodes on your 64GB machine, but chances are you'd be better off just running a single 64GB node, and not bothering with the little 3GB machine.

2 And the whole cluster becomes unusable if a single node gets removed: you cannot even export data or models from the rest of the cluster.

(see "Checkpoints" on page 102 in Chapter 4) and model-saving (see "Model Files" on page 51 in Chapter 2).

An H2O cluster can be created in one of two ways:

Flatfile
> A simple textfile giving the IP address and port of each node in the cluster. You must prepare this file identically on each machine. You specify it when starting *h2o.jar* with `-flatfile myfile.txt`.

Auto-discovery
> If you specify `-network 192.168.1.0/24` when starting *h2o.jar*, then it will hunt through that subnet to find all nodes and join them together in a cluster. This is slower than the flatfile, but saves you having to create that file and upload it to every node beforehand.

You can also give your cluster a name, and specify this name when starting on each node. I recommend you do this (and name your flatfile with the same name). It becomes essential if you want to run two or more clusters on the same subnet.

You have a few minutes to get all the nodes started before the first one will complain and shut down. However, as soon as a client (R, Python, Flow) connects to any node in the cluster, the cluster will lock down, and no further nodes can be added.

To connect to your cluster, just use `h2o.init()` giving the IP address of any node. There is no master node; they are all equal peers. *However*, the first node listed in the cluster status (get it from Flow, `h2o.clusterStatus()` in R, or `h2o.cluster_status()` in Python) sometimes has special status when it comes to importing or exporting data or models. And sometimes it is the node your client is connected to. I recommend you connect to the *first node* when you plan to be using the local filesystem for import or export, to avoid any confusion.[3] For importing data, the data has to be visible by all nodes in the cluster, which generally means you will need to have a copy on each node, in exactly the same place. I find it easier to be using S3 or HDFS. Alternatively, run your R or Python client on the node that has the data, and use upload file instead of import file.

EC2

Setting up an H2O cluster on Amazon EC2 machines is nice and easy because of a set of pre-made scripts (*https://github.com/h2oai/h2o-3/tree/master/ec2*). Those scripts have a Python/boto dependency, but this is solely for running the AWS commands. So if you already have scripts to set up AWS servers in some other language, it is

---

3 This behavior is in flux at the time of writing.

quite possible to learn what you need from these scripts and then integrate it into the code you already have.

You will find the Flow UI listening on port 54321 of each machine in your cluster. Extract the global DNS name from either the script output, or from the EC2 Management Console. A nice touch is that each machine in the cluster will also come with RStudio installed; you will find it on port 8787.

Those scripts implement the following steps:

1. Start a set of EC2 instances, recording their IP addresses.
2. Once they are all running, get that information, and *h2o.jar*, on each node.
3. Start *h2o.jar* on each node.

SSH is used for steps 2 and 3.

The script default is to have no security group. Instead, I recommend that you create a security group[4] called "for_h2o" that allows inbound connections on TCP ports 22, 8787, 54321, and 54322, and UDP ports 54321 and 54322.[5] Then find the "security-GroupName" line in *h2o-cluster-launch-instances.py* and set it to read:

```
securityGroupName = 'for_h2o'
```

Other Cloud Providers

There are no ready-made scripts for Azure, Google, Rackspace, Digital Ocean, and the other cloud providers. But there is no reason H2O cannot run there. Assuming you are familiar with scripting their APIs, you should be able to borrow and adapt the EC2 scripts quite easily.

Hadoop

Running H2O on Hadoop is like the normal setup, but you should fetch and install a version for your specific Hadoop setup by going to the H2O download page (*http:// www.h2o.ai/download/*), choosing the latest stable release, then clicking on the "Install on Hadoop" tab, and following the instructions there. Then instead of java h2o.jar, you will do hadoop jar h2odriver.jar. (There are additional parameters: view the previous URL to get the latest ones.) After that you can use Flow, or connect to H2O using your R or Python client, just as with the local version. Data can be loaded from HDFS as we've already seen in earlier chapters.

---

4 It needs to be created in each region you want to use those scripts.

5 If you will never use RStudio on the cluster you can drop 8787; similarly, if you will use RStudio or other R/ Python clients only running on the cluster, you do not need to open the 54321/54322 ports.

Spark / Sparkling Water

In some ways Spark and H2O are competing products: they are both about analyzing Big Data, in-memory. However, each has its strengths,[6] and "Sparkling Water" is a way to get them to work together closely so you can get the best of each world. There are versions for Spark 2.0, 1.6, 1.5, 1.4, and 1.3.

Sparkling Water is run as a regular Spark application. You run the H2O functions using Scala.[7] Once the data is inside an H2O data frame, it can be shared with Spark functions, without involving a memory copy (using the `asRDD()` or `asDataFrame()` functions).

To learn more about Sparkling Water, the best resources are the booklet, which can be found at *http://docs.h2o.ai* or directly at *http://bit.ly/2g2zfJg*, and then the directory of examples on GitHub (*http://bit.ly/2f8xgEb*).

Naive Bayes

There is another supervised machine-learning algorithm, naive bayes. I didn't look at it in the main section of the book, as it is a bit more limited, with binomial and multinomial classifications only, and not so many parameters, and well, basically, there wasn't enough space to include *everything*.

Naive bayes is often associated with NLP (Natural Language Processing) applications, such as spam recognition or sentiment analysis. But, to get you started, Example 10-1 is the iris example from the first chapter ("Our First Learning" on page 7), done with naive bayes instead of deep learning.

Example 10-1. Naive bayes on the Iris data set, in R

```
library(h2o)
h2o.init(nthreads = -1)

datasets <- "https://raw.githubusercontent.com/DarrenCook/h2o/bk/datasets/"
data <- h2o.importFile(paste0(datasets",iris_wheader.csv"))
y <- "class"
x <- setdiff(names(data), y)
parts <- h2o.splitFrame(data, 0.8)
train <- parts[[1]]
test <- parts[[2]]
```

---

6 H2O is considered to be considerably faster than the algorithms in MLLib, though the latter offers a lot more algorithms. Spark is currently better at the data preparation and data munging steps than H2O.

7 From the documentation site you can also find links to PySparkling and RSparkling, which are Python and R interfaces to Sparkling Water.

```
m <- h2o.naiveBayes(x, y, train)
p <- h2o.predict(m, test)
```

That manages the same 28 out of 30 score I got in the first chapter, so naive bayes is certainly not an algorithm just for NLP applications. Your next stop should be the API documentation (it is supported from R, Python, and also Flow).

Ensembles

Imagine you are putting together a team of three for a quiz night. Further, imagine that you are a god when it comes to Python, are rather good at math and physics, think sports are for losers, and don't even own a TV, preferring to play online video games. For some of you that will require a lot of imagination, I'm sure. One option, what with you being so clever, is to just enter the quiz night solo. Alternatively, you could invite Bob (an R guy, but on the plus side he is better at statistics and League of Legends than you) and Betsy (she studied chemistry, but she is not so bad as she uses Python and you like the same video games) to be in your team, the Brainy Boffins. Or should you invite your brother-in-law, Viv, who is a lawyer and always watching the TV news and shouting at politicians to clean up their act; and old school friend, Valerie, who knows everything about hockey, football, and half a dozen other sports, and can also tell you who performed at the Super Bowl halftime show, every year, for the past 20 years? Valerie can be very boring.

I hope you chose wisely. This is the basic idea behind ensemble algorithms: a group of algorithms, conferring over their final answer, is better than a single algorithm, because it can balance out the weaknesses and oversights. And the greater the differences between the algorithms, the better.

Having decided to use an ensemble you have three main decisions to make:

- Whether to use a library, or roll your own
- What member models
- How to combine their results

Taking them in order: H2O has an ensemble package (*http://bit.ly/2fVjtPK*); it doesn't come with H2O, so you need to install it separately. It only supports R currently.

You could make your member models by training the best model for each algorithm. An alternative approach is to run a random grid search over a wide range of parameters, and choose the best few models that have a good diversity of model parameters. For example, if your top-two deep learning algorithms had different network layouts, one with (200,200) hidden layers, and the other with (50,40,40,40), then they are likely to be useful ensemble members, as they will be seeing the world in different ways.

To combine results, you could take a page out of random forest's book: use averaging for regression, and use the most common result for categorization. Or you could use any supervised learner introduced in this book, to take take the output of each member model, and decide the ensemble's output.

Stacking: h2o.ensemble

I mentioned H2O's ensemble package, h2o.ensemble(). At the time of writing it only supports regression and binomial classification, so I'm going to show a quick example applied to the building energy data set, which was a regression problem. It can be used in one of two ways:

h2o.ensemble()
> You specify wrapper functions for each element of the ensemble. It then builds those models, then trains a metalearner to combine their results.

h2o.stack()
> You pre-build the constituent models, and pass them in as a list. It trains a metalearner to combine their results.

So, use h2o.stack() if you already have the models, and h2o.ensemble() if you don't. I personally find specifying the wrapper functions as much work as just making the model myself, so for that reason I will show h2o.stack(). But you need to prepare the models in a certain way:

- All models must have been built with cross-validation
- All the same value for nfolds
- fold_assignment = "Modulo"
- keep_cross_validation_predictions = TRUE

If you use h2o.ensemble() these details are taken care of for you:

```
library(h2oEnsemble)

source("load.building_energy.R")

RFd <- h2o.randomForest(x, y, train, model_id="RF_defaults", nfolds=10,
  fold_assignment = "Modulo", keep_cross_validation_predictions = T)
GBMd <- h2o.gbm(x, y, train, model_id="GBM_defaults", nfolds=10,
  fold_assignment = "Modulo", keep_cross_validation_predictions = T)
GLMd <- h2o.glm(x, y, train, model_id="GLM_defaults", nfolds=10,
  fold_assignment = "Modulo", keep_cross_validation_predictions = T)
DLd <- h2o.deeplearning(x, y, train, model_id="DL_defaults", nfolds=10,
```

```
    fold_assignment = "Modulo", keep_cross_validation_predictions = T)

  models <- c(RFd, GBMd, GLMd, DLd)
```

The preceding listing prepares the models (default settings, except for the cross-validation settings required for the ensemble), and puts them in a list object:

```
  m_stack <- h2o.stack(models, response_frame = train[,y])
  h2o.ensemble_performance(m_stack, test)
```

This code then calls h2o.stack giving that list, and requires you specify a one-column H2O frame with the correct answer; this is different to the other H2O algorithms, which take train and y as two separate parameters.[8] I then call h2o.ensemble_performance() to evaluate how it does on the test data. It will output how each individual model did, and then how the ensemble did. The results look like the following:

```
  Base learner performance, sorted by specified metric:
        learner      MSE
  3 GLM_defaults 9.013281
  4  DL_defaults 7.651445
  1  RF_defaults 3.626491
  2 GBM_defaults 2.547896

  H2O Ensemble Performance on <newdata>:
  Family: gaussian

  Ensemble performance (MSE): 2.55156175744006
```

Oh. The ensemble did slightly worse than just the best model by itself. If I use an ensemble of just the best model, and models of close strength[9] (i.e., the random forest and the GBM) I instead get a slight improvement:

```
  Base learner performance, sorted by specified metric:
        learner      MSE
  1  RF_defaults 3.626491
  2 GBM_defaults 2.547896

  H2O Ensemble Performance on <newdata>:
  Family: gaussian

  Ensemble performance (MSE): 2.51780794131118
```

---

8 I left the metalearner parameters as the default, so it will use h2o.glm to decide how to combine the four models. This could have been any of the other H2O supervised learning algorithms.

9 To avoid biasing the results, we need to decide to do this before evaluating on test data, so base it on the evaluation on the results on train.

You might want to go ahead and use this on the tuned models... but, because the deep learning model (with an MSE of 0.388) is so much stronger than any of the other models, it works best as a team of one.

Categorical Ensembles

For categorization models, I use a different approach, taking advantage of the fact that H2O doesn't just return a prediction, it returns a confidence in each category being the correct answer. You may remember back, way back, in the first chapter of this book, that we looked at those confidence numbers; here it is again as a reminder:

```
predict          Iris-setosa   Iris-versicolor  Iris-virginica
-----------      -----------   ---------------  --------------
Iris-setosa      0.999016      0.0009839        1.90283e-19
Iris-setosa      0.998988      0.0010118        1.40209e-20
...
Iris-virginica   1.5678e-08    0.3198963        0.680104
Iris-versicolor  2.3895e-08    0.9863869        0.013613
```

It was 99.9% sure about those two setosa, 98% sure about the versicolor, but only 68% sure about the virginica. What you tend to see, with a good model, is that almost all the answers it felt confident about were correct, but that most of the wrong answers had lower confidence. How do ensembles comes into this? Think back to our quiz team, on a four-choice question: Viv is fairly sure (he says 60% sure) the answer is benzene, while you are guessing and think 40% benzene and 20% each of the other answers, but Valerie tells you she is *certain* that $C_6H_{12}O_6$ is glucose, because she has just finished reading a book on diabetes. You go with Valerie's confidence... and win the contest.

That idea can be wrapped up in just a few lines of code:

```
predictTeam <- function(models, data){
probabilities <- sapply(models, function(m){
  p <- h2o.predict(m, data)
  as.matrix(p[,setdiff(colnames(p), "predict")])
  }, simplify = "array")
apply(probabilities, 1, function(m) which.max(apply(m, 1, sum)) )
}
```

It works by getting each model's predictions, grabbing the probabilities as a three-dimensional array, then working through that array to choose the answer that has the highest average confidence across all models.[10] It returns the index of the category it thinks is best. You will see it in action in the next chapter, and for more details, and more code, see my blog post (*http://bit.ly/2g3pGIq*) on the subject.

---

10 Implemented with sum, rather than mean, as they are equivalent inside a which.max().

Summary

Well, that was a whirlwind tour of some things I didn't have space in the book to go into in more detail. The next chapter, the final one in this book, will bring together all the results of the supervised learning experiments on each of the three data sets, and also give some ideas for what to do when they are not good enough.

CHAPTER 11

Epilogue: Didn't They All Do Well!

This book compared three data sets on the four supervised machine-learning algorithms that H2O offers:

- Random Forest (Chapter 5)
- GBM (Chapter 6)
- GLM (Chapter 7)
- Deep Learning (Chapter 8)

In each case I first tried them on the default settings, the minimal set of parameters: H2O API commands that will comfortably fit on one line. That was then followed by trying to tune some of the many parameters that H2O offers, choosing the best model (based on performance on either cross-validation or a validation data set), and evaluating that on the unseen test data. Because the results are scattered throughout the book, I want to quickly bring them together here, and see what insights are to be found. As a bonus section, I show some ideas for improving results by methods other than just parameter tuning.

By the way, in the online code you will find *epilogue.*.R* files that contain the code to make each of the default and tuned models, as well as some code to compare them. (You will also find timing information, and dput() output of the results, in the comments.)

Building Energy Results

This was a regression problem, and MSE was the key metric. A chart was also made for each model, using triangles to represent results that were 8% above or below the correct answer.

This data set was sensitive to how it got split. In other words, some test data splits, and some cross-validation folds, are harder to predict than others. So to fairly compare algorithms, the use of a random seed when splitting the data is important; the results in Figure 11-1 are all based on the exact same 143 unseen test samples.

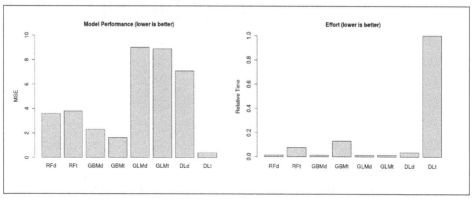

Figure 11-1. Comparison of all default and tuned models (building energy)

Model	Time/sᵃ	MSE	V.Low	V.High
RF, default	1.3	3.596	13	14
RF, tuned	7.3	3.802	17	8
GBM, default	1.3	2.318	7	7
GBM, tuned	12.4	1.640	4	2
GLM, default	1.3	9.013	27	33
GLM, tuned	1.3	8.904	26	27
DL, default	3.5	7.096	34	13
DL, tuned	93.9	0.425	3	0

ᵃ Timings were done on a single node, 36 cores.

RF tuning: ntrees from 50 to 200; max_depth from 20 to 40; sample_rate from 0.632 to 0.9, mtries from 2 to 4; col_sample_rate_per_tree from 1.0 to 0.9, score_tree_interval set to 10. But the choice of random seed has as much effect as anything.

GBM tuning: ntrees from 50 to 1000 (with early stopping of 4 rounds of zero improvement; score_tree_interval of 5), min_rows from 10 to 1 (though I am not convinced), sample_rate from 1 to 0.9, col_sample_rate from 1 to 0.9, learn_rate from 0.1 to 0.01, seed of 373.

GLM tuning: Change family to tweedie, with tweedie_variance_power of 1.55, tweedie_link_power of 0, lambda search on, alpha of 0.33, and max_iterations of 100.

DL tuning: Almost the entire benefit came from the switch to early stopping, which effectively meant an increase from 10 epochs to just under 200 epochs. Other tweaks were activation of Tanh, L2 regularization of 0.00001, and two hidden layers each with 162 nodes (instead of the default 200 nodes).

Deep learning was the clear winner, though only when given enough resources. GBM beat random forest, which in turn beat GLM. Only GBM and deep learning made any worthwhile improvement when tuned.

Ideas for further work: Can deep learning be tuned further? Would Rectifier (instead of Tanh) give the same results, but train more quickly? Would an ensemble of deep learning and GBM give even better results? Also, it would be interesting to use the methodology in the paper the data came from: use cross-validation on the *whole* data set, and repeat 100 times to get a mean and standard deviation.

MNIST Results

This was a 10-way classification problem, and the key metric was the error rate: how many it misclassified out of the 10,000 test samples. This is a very well-studied problem, and everyone uses the same test data set, so there is bound to be lots of (inadvertent or otherwise) tuning on that supposedly unseen data. However, I tried to stay honest and choose the final model, each time, based on results on the *validation* data set. Figure 11-2 compares the error rates on the test set of each model, and also how long each model took to build.

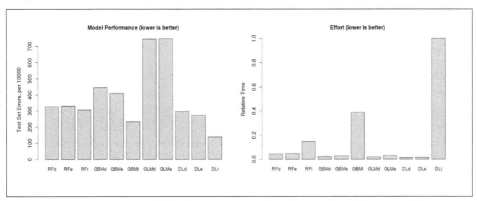

Figure 11-2. Comparison of all default, enhanced, and tuned models (MNIST)

	Time/s[a]	Errors-Test	MSE-Test	Errors-Valid	MSE-Valid
RFd	117	327	0.065	372	0.069
RFe	126	331	0.061	347	0.064
RFt	385	306	0.05	317	0.052
GBMd	61	445	0.048	481	0.051

	Time/s[a]	Errors-Test	MSE-Test	Errors-Valid	MSE-Valid
GBMe	75	410	0.041	428	0.044
GBMt	1026	233	0.019	214	0.018
GLMd	55	746	0.068	782	0.073
GLMe	87	745	0.069	796	0.074
DLd	34	304	0.027	332	0.028
DLe	42	273	0.024	292	0.026
DLt	2636	138	0.012	130	0.012

[a] These times are on 72 cores, organized as 2 nodes of 36 cores each. However, the tree algorithms didn't use the second node very effectively.

For the models, XXd means default settings, XXe means default settings but with enhanced data, and XXt means the final tuned model.

RF tuning: `min_rows` from 1 to 2, `mtries` from 28 (sqrt of columns) to 56 (but didn't really matter), `sample_rate` from 0.632 to 0.9, `col_sample_rate_per_tree` from 1.0 to 0.9, `max_depth` from 20 to 40, `ntrees` from 50 to 500 (and early stopping of 0.01% improvement over 3 scoring rounds, with `score_tree_interval` of 3).

GBM tuning: Almost all the benefit came from moving from 50 to about 300 trees (it was given 400 trees, combined with early stopping of 0.1% improvement over 3 scoring rounds, with `score_tree_interval` of 10). But the other tweaks were: `sample_rate` from 1.0 to 0.95, `col_sample_rate` from 1.0 to 0.8, `col_sample_rate_per_tree` from 1.0 to 0.8, `learn_rate` from 0.1 to 0.01.

GLM tuning: Every tuning tried, even just putting lambda search on, failed. So the tuned model is identical to the base model.

DL tuning: Deep learning got a 20% improvement from switching to enhanced, then another 17% improvement by giving it 40–50 epochs instead of the default of 10. The best model used 4 layers, with 300,400,500,600 neurons, activation function of RectifierWithDropout, L1 regularization of 0.00001, `input_dropout_ratio` of 0.2, and `hidden_dropout_ratios` of 0.1, and it was given 2000 epochs and early stopping (0.1% improvement over 8 scoring rounds required, measured on misclassification, `classification_stop` off).

The relatively simplistic data engineering only helped with GBM and deep learning. However, the comparison was only done while still on default settings and the point of the enhanced data was to give the algorithms more opportunities to learn. Often more trees/epochs are needed for additional columns (or rows) to bear fruit. As an aside, most models got a worse score on the validation data set compared to the test set. So the validation data set maybe contained more hard-to-read samples?

The tuned deep learning model was the clear winner, though it also used the most effort. Tuned GBM was second, and took the second most effort. However, the third and fourth best models were the deep learning models that only had 10 epochs, and they were much quicker.

Ideas for further work: See "How Low Can You Go?" on page 265 for some further experiments, and their results.

Football Data

This was a binomial classification problem: will it be a win for the home side or not (implying a draw or a win for the away side)? Our key metric was accuracy (using, for threshold, the average of the optimal threshold on training and validation data). There were two models considered: using the help of expert opinion in the form of betting odds, and then not using them.

There was also a GLM made to predict HomeWin using just "BbAvH," which is the average bookmaker odds of a win for the home team. This was used as the benchmark. There was another benchmark I could have used, the simplest possible model for a binomial problem, which is to always guess the biggest class.[1] In this case it means always guessing "no-win," and it gives an accuracy of 0.573 on the test data. In Figure 11-3 I have used that as the baseline of the chart. You can clearly see that *all* models did better than that, even those built without the help of the betting odds.

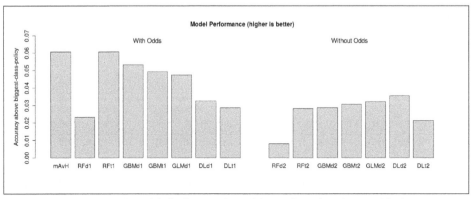

Figure 11-3. Comparison of default/tuned models, with and without odds data

---

1 See table in "Setup and Load (Again)" on page 86.

This next table compares the results for the first model (using all columns):

Model	Time/s[a]	Valid	Test
Biggest-class		0.579	0.573
Benchmark	1.4	0.650	0.634
RFd1	19.7	0.632	0.596
RFt1	78.2	0.649	0.634
GBMd1	10.5	0.644	0.626
GBMt1	27.0	0.649	0.622
GLMd1	1.3	0.650	0.620
DLd1	6.6	0.649	0.606
DLt1	46.7	0.652	0.602

[a] These times are on 72 cores, organized as two nodes of 36 cores each. However, the tree algorithms didn't use the second node very effectively.

And then for the second model, without the benefit of the bookmaker odds:

Model	Time/s	Valid	Test
Biggest-class		0.579	0.573
RFd2	14.5	0.602	0.581
RFt2	54.9	0.613	0.601
GBMd2	7.4	0.607	0.602
GBMt2	33.7	0.608	0.604
GLMd2	1.3	0.615	0.605
DLd2	5.5	0.610	0.609
DLt2	54.3	0.620	0.594

RF tuning: `sample_rate` of 0.35 instead of default of 0.632, `min_rows` increased from 1 to 60, `mtries` of 5 instead of 7. Trees were increased from 50 to 500, with early stopping criteria of 0% improvement (of AUC) over 4 scoring rounds.

GBM tuning: Learn rate reduced from 0.1 to 0.01, `balanced_classes` set to true, `col_sample_rate` 1.0 to 0.9, `col_sample_rate_per_tree` 1.0 to 0.9 and `sample_rate` 1.0 to 0.8, `min_rows` increased from 10 to 40, `max_depth` of 12 (instead of default of 5). It was given 400 trees and early stopping (4 scorings rounds with no improvement on the misclassification metric, with `score_tree_interval` set to 10).

GLM tuning: None of the ideas tried got anything better than the default model. And both were worse than just building a GLM on a single column I chose.

DL tuning: All the tuning was done on the no-odds model; notice how it made the with-odds version worse. Overfitting! Anyway, three hidden layers, each with 200 neurons, `balance_classes` was set to true, `activation = "RectifierWithDropout"`, `hidden_dropout_ratios = c(0.5, 0.3, 0.3)`, `input_dropout_ratio = 0.3`, `l1 = 0.0005`, `l2 = 0.0005`, and 2000 epochs with early stopping set to require at least a 0.1% improvement (on the AUC metric) over 4 scoring rounds.

Two conclusions, one positive, one not. The positive is that all the models did better than simply guessing the biggest class. On the other hand all models were disappointing: they should have at least been able to replicate the result that a GLM could get on just a single input. Only random forest managed that (it was also the most responsive to tuning).

Ideas for further work: These results surprised me, so there is some fertile study here to understand why more sophisticated models did worse. Making ensembles of the models should improve results, especially if random variation is a big part of the problem. There is also loads of potential for gathering additional data sets. Weather? Manager changes? Signings? Injuries? And maybe a per-division, or even per-team, model could work better?

How Low Can You Go?

With most of this book written, I decided to go back to the MNIST problem, and see how low I could go if I got rid of some artificial constraints:

- Throughout this book I've been following the rule of choosing one best model for each algorithm. But here I will also try ensembles of models.
- I've tried to keep things relatively small, so you should be able to run everything on a reasonably powered notebook. But here I'm going straight to a cluster of machines on EC2.
- In Chapter 3 I didn't do much pre-processing (to stay on-topic); but here there is going to be quite a lot of manipulating the data before giving it to H2O.

I am going to keep this as a high-level overview, not showing code, and instead pointing you to some blog posts of mine if you want more details.

The More the Merrier

More training data rows are better. If you have enough data your machine-learning algorithm can be (relatively) dumb and it will still outperform the competition. But it has to be new data: just doing 20 exact copies of the 50,000 MNIST rows is of very little use.[2]

---

2 In the case of deep learning it would be the same as increasing epochs by a factor of 20.

And not just new data—the ideal is training data that is going to be similar to the ones in the test data that we got wrong. We want more *scruffy* handwriting samples. There are a few ways to get that. If we had money to throw at the problem, one idea is to hire some doctors (or any group of people notorious for unreadable handwriting) and ask them to spend an hour writing out digits. Scan them in, rescale each to 28x28 pixels, and do any other pre-processing that was done on the original MNIST data. Another way to find the most difficult samples is introduced in a moment. But I simply looked at ones in the validation data set[3] that it got wrong, and observed they were often fatter, often had some extra lines, and were often quite distorted.

I used R's imager library (*https://github.com/dahtah/imager*). As described in this long blog post (*http://bit.ly/2g0BNqM*), this was not as simple as simply throwing a few rotations in: extra actions were needed, such as resizing, and re-sharpening (image processing tends to make the images more blurred), and re-histogram-ing (making sure the image had about the same shades of gray).

I prepared nine effects, each with a random element:

- rotate
- warp (make it "scruffier")
- shift (move it 1 pixel up, down, left, or right)
- bold (make it fatter)
- dilate (make it fatter)
- erode (make it thinner)
- erodedilate (one or the other)
- scratches (add lines)
- blotches (remove blobs)

I then defined "all" and "all2," which combined most of them.

In the end I made 20 new versions of each of train and valid data: 10 of a specific effect, 10 of either "all" or "all2." I gzipped the *csv* files and uploaded them to S3. It took just under 3 hours to generate all the files on a fast, 36-core, Amazon EC2 instance. However I didn't make the effort to parallelize the R code, so most of the time those 36 cores were going to waste.

A funny thing happens when I train models on this generated data: the training data error is higher than the validation or test set error! For example, I might get 1.5% error on the training data, but 1% on both validation and test. This is sometimes a

---

3 Remember, I am not allowed to look at the test data when making tuning decisions.

sign you have overfitted (not the case here, as it happens on all models, however sophisticated), or that you have a bug.

 Always consider the possibility of bugs. A few months ago, I wasted two weeks trying to tune models (financial data) and couldn't understand why I kept getting near-random results, however many epochs I threw at it, and however many clever ideas I tried. It turned out to be a lag bug: my predictor variable and my response variables were for different time periods. Another time I was testing to see how many epochs were needed to perfectly (over-)fit some training data, but more epochs gave a *worse* score. Turned out I was accidentally training on the validation test set.

However, here it is a sign that the training data is not representative. That is, I deliberately generated data that is on average harder than the original data and that generated data now makes up 95% of the training data. And some of it will be impossibly hard: a "3" might have got so distorted that it looks like a 1, or a scratch has turned it into a 9.

Ideally I'd like an infinite supply of training data that is perfectly representative of the real-world data the model will be used on. But, if I had to choose, I'd prefer it to be slightly harder, than slightly easier.

Still Desperate for More

Why did I generate new data from my 10,000 validation samples too? To give myself more options. I desperately wanted to use the validation data—the increase from 50,000 to 60,000 training samples would give me 20% more training data, and that means a much greater chance that my model gets to see some awkward digits that are currently tripping it up. I did a few experiments with no validation data set, i.e., using all 60,000 samples for training. But it was like working blind—I had no reliable way to tell when the model was good and when it was overfitting.[4] I also needed a validation data set when I wanted to rank models for use in an ensemble (more on that in a moment).

So, I did a compromise. I kept the first 1000 validation samples (and threw away the first 1000 samples in each of the data files generated from validation data), and added the other 9000 samples both from the original validation data and the 20 generated files. The code to do this filtering was Example 2-1, shown near the end of Chapter 2. This extra 189,000 rows took me to a total of 1,239,000 training rows.

---

4 Cross-validation? Yes, that might also have worked, but would have increased the model-making time by so much more.

Using just 1000 validation samples worked fairly well. It still correlated fairly well with the test data. That was my hope: it was why I arbitrarily cut at row number 1000, rather than stealing away, say, the most interesting 9000 for training, and keeping the easiest 1000 for validation.

But 1000 did turn out to be a bit small. The problem was, I was aiming for an error rate of 0.5%, which means just five errors. It is hard to compare models with 6 out of 1000 with those that got 7 or 8 errors out of the 1000, and know it has generalized better, rather than just getting lucky on one sample. But 60 errors out of 10,000, compared to 70 or 80, is less likely to just be due to luck.

Filtering for Hardness

In any real-world training data there are going to be samples that your model finds easier to learn, and those it finds harder to learn. Of course, it is staring us in the eyes with the MNIST data: the easy samples are the nice neat ones, that look just like the mean images we made (Figure 3-5) before. The hard ones look like Bart Simpson drawing with his right hand.[5] While skateboarding.

I know the Lisa Simpsons of the world are going to be deeply offended, but all we really need to see are the handwriting samples of the most Bart-like people. Oh, with one important detail: the mean of their handwriting samples must match the mean of the whole population.

Here is how to get the hardest 1000 of the 50,000 MNIST training samples:

1. Make a relatively simple model, on all 50,000 training samples. For example, `m <- h2o.deeplearning(x, y, train, valid)`.
2. Run `p <- h2o.predict(m, train)`.
3. Get the prediction probabilities, and the maximum probability.
4. Sort them, and choose the lowest 1000.

Point 3 is the key one: if our model is 99.9% confident of an answer it must be finding it easier than one where it was only 80% confident. Whether it is right or wrong does not matter: only how easy or difficult the model finds it. Well, except being wrong is also very important to know. So I replaced the actual prediction probability with 0.1 when the model got it wrong, to be sure they were included.

---

5 That is, his wrong hand. Bart, like a disproportionate number of cartoon characters, is left-handed. I'll leave you to work out why.

I still needed all 50,000 samples, so what have I gained by doing this? Well, I could speed up learning subsequent models by just using those 1000. Or I could weight them (see "Data Weighting" on page 106 back in Chapter 4) so the model spends more effort learning them. Or when generating data I could use just these hard samples as the starting points. (I didn't, but I suspect it would mean I could get the same results with something like 200,000 generated samples, instead of 1.2 million generated samples.)

Auto-Encoder

In "Deep Learning Auto-Encoder" on page 229 a deep learning auto-encoder was used as a way to reduce a data set to just two dimensions, so that it could be visualized. But another way auto-encoders can be used is to work around the difficulty with training many-layered neural networks: learn them one or two layers at a time, as an unsupervised auto-encoder, then add one or two supervised layers at the end.

You may remember from that discussion how Figure 9-3 showed that you get a lower MSE the more dimensions you give it (as long as you also give it enough epochs). The MNIST data is larger and I didn't have time to do a rigorous experiment to find the best values. Instead I tried a few small experiments, mostly inconclusive, then decided to get a variety of input data by building three auto-encoders:

AE200
Large, with 200 hidden units. A single layer. Quite high dropout/L2.

AE32
Small: 32 hidden units. Lower dropout/L2.

AE128
Two layers. The first layer is almost the same size as the input (768 hidden nodes), but with relatively high dropout and high L2, then the second layer is 128, but no dropout. It is built in two stages.

Please see my blog post (*http://bit.ly/2gnk9S4*) for more details, and code.

This gave me 360 features, and I used them *instead of* the 784 raw pixels. I still kept the 113 enhanced features that were introduced in "Helping the Models" on page 69.

This proved quite effective, bringing the results of the individual models from the 120 to 140 range down to the 80 to 110 range, and into the 70s (0.7% error) when used in an ensemble (see "Ensembles" on page 272). Though this was also done in conjunction with starting to use generated data, so it is hard to know how much each contributed.

Convolute and Shrink

The best performing models on the MNIST data set are based on convolutional neural networks (*http://bit.ly/2g31tn4*) (CNNs). H2O does not offer them,[6] and they can get very computationally intensive. The idea is that you match, e.g., 5x5 patterns, as sliding tiles, all over your image. This is alternated with a shrink layer, where the maximum pixel value is chosen from each (nonoverlapping) 2x2 block. This gives, say, a 12x12 output *per pattern*. You might then repeat with a 3x3 pattern, and another round of 2x2 shrinkage. Most of this is inspired by the human visual system, and Internet searches will find plenty of papers explaining the idea in more detail, and variations people have tried.

Are you thinking this sounds a bit like the 113 extended fields I added? Kind of, but they are crude in comparison, and don't use patterns: they were the mean of each pixel group.

I decided to try what I call "Poor Man's Convolution," somewhere between a real CNN and those extended fields. I generated twelve 5x5 patterns (more on that in a moment), then did a 2x2 max shrinking pass, giving me twelve 12x12 outputs. That is 1728 columns that I could then feed to H2O's supervised deep learning. (I also used the auto-encoder-generated columns, and I still kept the 113 extended fields, but I dropped the raw pixels. Including the answer column, my training data frame now had 2202 columns.)

But how could I train the 5x5 patterns? Well, I took a look at some academic papers for what their patterns looked like, and they reminded me of the outputs I had seen applying auto-encoders and PCA to images. So I made six 5x5 patterns by using a one-layer auto-encoder with six hidden nodes, and I made another six 5x5 patterns by taking the first six principal components returned by h2o.prcomp(). For training data I took the 1000 hardest training samples, and extracted all 5x5 overlapping windows, which gave 576,000 training samples. See Figure 11-4 for what the 12 patterns look like (top row), and how they modify an MNIST digit. The six columns on the left are the patterns from the auto-encoder. The six on the right are from PCA; the increasing amounts of noise with each additional PCA dimension is striking.

My training set of 1,239,000 rows and 2202 columns was 17GB when compressed in H2O's memory, and I used four "c4.8xlarge" instances on EC2 to work with this: together they gave a cluster of 144 cores and about 180GB memory.

---

6 The DeepWater project, in development as I write, will add support for them, as well as GPU support.

Here are the four deep learning models I built (each taking one to two hours on that cluster), and their individual scores:

Model ID	Valid Error	Hidden Nodes	Dropout	L1,L2	Test Score
DLt2	4	400,500,600,700	0.1	1e-5,0	73
DLt1	6	300,400,500,600	0.1	1e-5,0	57
DLx1	8	800,800,800	0.3	1e-4,1e-4	58
DLb1	12	1024,2048	0.1	1e-5,0	93

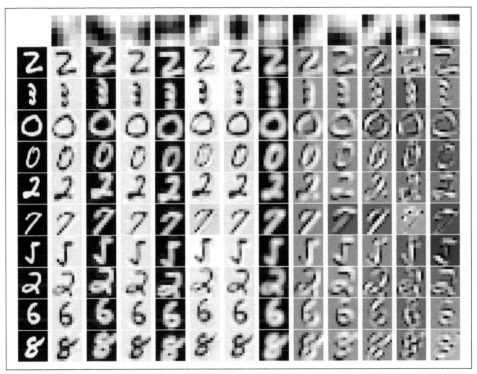

Figure 11-4. 12x12px convoluted-and-shrunk images (first six columns are from an auto-encoder, second six are from a PCA)

This did indeed give the best scores yet (described in a moment), and this approach is much quicker to train than a normal CNN, so I will consider using it again. But it didn't give results as good as the best convolutional networks do on the MNIST data.

Ensembles

In "Categorical Ensembles" on page 256 (in Chapter 10) I described an ensemble technique to average the prediction probabilities of multiple models. When using ensembles you want models that are as distinct from each other as possible, which presents us with a problem because, once the models were tuned, the deep learning model was considerably better than the other algorithms. On the bright side, deep learning has a lot of knobs to fiddle with, so by varying the number and size of the hidden layers, the dropout ratios, etc., you can engineer in a bit of variability.

What I found was that an ensemble of relatively weak models got more of a boost than when the models got stronger. One of my early experiments had eight models (two different deep learning configurations, and our best random forest model[7]) with these scores:

	Test Error	Hidden Nodes
DLt1	144	300,400,500,600
DLt2	140	300,400,500,600
DLb1	120	1024,1024
DLb2	143	1024,1024
RFt1	302	Tuned random forest
DLt1_TV	130	300,400,500,600
DLt2_TV	127	300,400,500,600
RFt1_TV	284	Tuned random forest

The scores range from 120 (1.2%) to 302 (3.02%), but when using all eight in an ensemble it got a score of 105. That is almost 70 better than the mean error of those eight models, and 15 better than the best one. Just the six deep learning models got 107: adding in the much weaker random forests was worth (a net improvement of) two more answers.

However, when I tried an ensemble of the best three deep learning models, the ones from the poor man's CNN experiment, their ensemble scored a disappointing 56—only one better than the best model. The problem, I feel, is that by pushing to get the best performance out of each model, I have lost a lot of the variability between them.

---

7 There was no generated data being used at this point. The *TV* suffix indicates it used all 60,000 samples for training, with no validation data set, using the same number of epochs or trees as DLt1/RFt1 had.

That Was as Low as I Go...

I hope this bonus section was educational. That score of 56 (a 0.56% error rate), from the ensemble, was the best score I had at the point I ran out of time. My expectation beforehand was that the usefulness order would be:

1. Much more training data
2. Ensemble
3. Poor man's convolution
4. Bigger models
5. Auto-encoder instead of pixels

I've not done enough experiments to say for sure, but my gut feeling is that the actual usefulness was:

1. Much more training data
2. Auto-encoder instead of pixels
3. Poor man's convolution
4. Ensemble (but more useful with weaker models)
5. Bigger models

Summary

Deep learning came out on top on both the first data set (a regression on a small data set), and the second (a 10-way classification on a larger data set), but on the third (a binomial classification on data with a large random element) it was a simple GLM, followed by random forest, that fared best.

One common theme was that tweaking parameters quickly reached a point of diminishing returns: the models are generally very good with default settings. Especially when combined with giving more trees/epochs and then using early stopping.

As the bonus section showed, your energy can usually be better spent on data engineering and gathering more data, than on fine-tuning parameters.

Good and bad results apart, I hope this book has given you a good feel for when each algorithm might shine, and for how to go about evaluating and improving your models, as well as for how the design and features in H2O make these experiments just about as easy as they could possibly be.

Index

Z

zero

as indicator of missing data, 60

no data vs., 84

About the Author

Darren Cook has over 20 years of experience as a software developer, data analyst, and technical director, working on everything from financial trading systems to NLP, data visualization tools, and PR websites for some of the world's largest brands. He is skilled in a wide range of computer languages, including R, C++, PHP, JavaScript, and Python. He works at QQ Trend, a financial data analysis and data products company.

Colophon

The animal on the cover of *Practical Machine Learning with H2O* is a crayfish, a small lobster-like crustacean found in freshwater habitats throughout the world. Alternate names include crawfish, crawdads, and mudbugs, depending on the region.

There are over 500 species of crayfish, over half of which occur in North America. There is great variation in size, shape, and color across species. Crayfish are typically 3 to 4 inches in North America, while certain species in Australia grow to be a staggering 15 inches and can weigh as much as 8 pounds.

Like crabs and other crustaceans, crayfish shed their hard outer shells periodically, eating them to recoup calcium. They are nocturnal creatures, possessing keen eyesight as well as the ability to move their eyes in different directions at once.

Crayfish have eight pairs of legs, four of which are used for walking. The other legs are used for swimming backward, a maneuver that allows the crayfish to dart quickly through the water. Lost limbs can be regenerated, a capability that comes in handy during the competitive (and often aggressive) mating season.

Crayfish are opportunistic omnivores who consume almost anything, including plants, clams, snails, insects, and dead organic matter. Their own predators include fish (they are widely regarded as a tackle box staple), otters, birds, and humans. More than 100 million pounds of crawfish are produced each year in Louisiana, where it was adopted as the state's official crustacean in 1983.

Many of the animals on O'Reilly covers are endangered; all of them are important to the world. To learn more about how you can help, go to *animals.oreilly.com*.

The cover image is from *Treasury of Animal Illustrations* by Dover. The cover fonts are URW Typewriter and Guardian Sans. The text font is Adobe Minion Pro; the heading font is Adobe Myriad Condensed; and the code font is Dalton Maag's Ubuntu Mono.

Learn from experts.
Find the answers you need.

Sign up for a **10-day free trial** to get **unlimited access** to all of the content on Safari, including Learning Paths, interactive tutorials, and curated playlists that draw from thousands of ebooks and training videos on a wide range of topics, including data, design, DevOps, management, business—and much more.

Start your free trial at:
oreilly.com/safari

(No credit card required.)

Lightning Source UK Ltd.
Milton Keynes UK
UKHW020116140223
416945UK00010B/1223

9 781491 964606